Minorities in West Asia and North Africa

Series Editors
Kamran Matin
University of Sussex
Department of International Relations
Brighton, UK

Paolo Maggiolini
Catholic University of the Sacred Heart
Milan, Italy

This series seeks to provide a unique and dedicated outlet for the publication of theoretically informed, historically grounded and empirically governed research on minorities and 'minoritization' processes in the regions of West Asia and North Africa (WANA). In WANA, from Morocco to Afghanistan and from Turkey to the Sudan almost every country has substantial religious, ethnic or linguistic minorities. Their changing character and dynamic evolution notwithstanding, minorities have played key roles in social, economic, political and cultural life of WANA societies from the antiquity and been at the center of the modern history of the region. WANA's experience of modernity, processes of state formation and economic development, the problems of domestic and interstate conflict and security, and instances of state failure, civil war, and secession are all closely intertwined with the history and politics of minorities, and with how different socio-political categories related to the idea of minority have informed or underpinned historical processes unfolding in the region. WANA minorities have also played a decisive role in the rapid and crisis-ridden transformation of the geopolitics of WANA in the aftermath of the Cold War and the commencement of globalization. Past and contemporary histories, and the future shape and trajectory of WANA countries are therefore intrinsically tied to the dynamics of minorities. Intellectual, political, and practical significance of minorities in WANA therefore cannot be overstated. The overarching rationale for this series is the absence of specialized series devoted to minorities in WANA. Books on this topic are often included in area, country or theme-specific series that are not amenable to theoretically more rigorous and empirically wider and multi-dimensional approaches and therefore impose certain intellectual constraints on the books especially in terms of geographical scope, theoretical depth, and disciplinary orientation. This series addresses this problem by providing a dedicated space for books on minorities in WANA. It encourages inter- and multi-disciplinary approaches to minorities in WANA with a view to promote the combination of analytical rigor with empirical richness. As such the series is intended to bridge a significant gap on the subject in the academic books market, increase the visibility of research on minorities in WANA, and meets the demand of academics, students, and policy makers working on, or interested in, the region alike. The editorial team of the series will adopt a proactive and supportive approach through soliciting original and innovative works, closer engagement with the authors, providing feedback on draft monographs prior to publication, and ensuring the high quality of the output.

More information about this series at
http://www.palgrave.com/gp/series/15127

Maurizio Geri

Ethnic Minorities in Democratizing Muslim Countries

Turkey and Indonesia

palgrave
macmillan

Maurizio Geri
ACT-NATO
Norfolk, VA, USA

Minorities in West Asia and North Africa
ISBN 978-3-319-75573-1   ISBN 978-3-319-75574-8 (eBook)
https://doi.org/10.1007/978-3-319-75574-8

Library of Congress Control Number: 2018936613

© The Editor(s) (if applicable) and The Author(s) 2018
This work is subject to copyright. All rights are solely and exclusively licensed by the Publisher, whether the whole or part of the material is concerned, specifically the rights of translation, reprinting, reuse of illustrations, recitation, broadcasting, reproduction on microfilms or in any other physical way, and transmission or information storage and retrieval, electronic adaptation, computer software, or by similar or dissimilar methodology now known or hereafter developed.
The use of general descriptive names, registered names, trademarks, service marks, etc. in this publication does not imply, even in the absence of a specific statement, that such names are exempt from the relevant protective laws and regulations and therefore free for general use.
The publisher, the authors, and the editors are safe to assume that the advice and information in this book are believed to be true and accurate at the date of publication. Neither the publisher nor the authors or the editors give a warranty, express or implied, with respect to the material contained herein or for any errors or omissions that may have been made. The publisher remains neutral with regard to jurisdictional claims in published maps and institutional affiliations.

Cover image © Hes Mundt / Alamy Stock Photo
Cover design by Laura de Grasse

Printed on acid-free paper

This Palgrave Macmillan imprint is published by the registered company Springer International Publishing AG part of Springer Nature.
The registered company address is: Gewerbestrasse 11, 6330 Cham, Switzerland

Preface

Almost half century ago, Samuel Huntington[1] explained how state capacity is fundamental to guarantee order in societies in transition. Francis Fukuyama[2] revived this concept, arguing that a strong and effective state is fundamental for the stability of democratizing countries. But strong institutions are not enough to make democracy and political order compatible: institutions also need to be inclusive, to foster participation and respect freedom of all parts of society, including ethnic minorities.

This can be seen today in many fledgling democracies, but also in more mature and stable ones. From Myanmar to the Philippines, from Hungary to Poland, we see how newly or less newly democratized states are passing from a process of re-authoritarianization, as some scholars call it,[3] in which populism erodes the liberal democratic values and structures of a country. One of the first things to indicate such a trend in a country is the repression of minorities, who are often targeted as scapegoats. The exclusion and repression of old or new minorities (like immigrants in the European case) causes those democracies to start down the path of regression in their polity and society towards a more authoritarian system.

---

[1] Samuel P Huntington, *Political order in changing societies* (New Haven: Yale University Press, 1968).

[2] Francis Fukuyama, *Political order and political decay* (New York: Farrar, Straus and Giroux, 2014).

[3] Andrea Kendall-Taylor and Erica Frantz, "How Democracies Fall Apart. Why Populism Is a Pathway to Autocracy", Foreign Affairs, December 6, 2016, accessed September 30, 2017, https://www.foreignaffairs.com/articles/2016-12-05/how-democracies-fall-apart.

This book aims to concentrate on democratizing Muslim majority states, for several reasons. First is that so-called Arab exceptionalism, and the recent democratic failure or success of the Arab Spring countries, depends on a fundamental domestic variable: the exclusion or inclusion of ethnic, religious or political minorities by the new regimes (as we saw for example in Egypt or Iraq with respect to Tunisia or Morocco). Second, when we talk about democracy, there is no Islamic exceptionalism because a majority of Muslim citizens actually live in democracies (mostly on the Asian continent), and several Muslim states are democracies; nevertheless, the majority of Muslim countries (mostly in the Arab World) are not democracies. Third, studies of social conflict in Muslim countries typically emphasize sectarian divisions but ignore ethnic differences. Likewise, theories of democratization in Muslim countries examine the rights of religious minorities but overlook the inclusion of ethnic minorities. Finally, by examining states with ethnic diversity but very little religious diversity, the research controls for the effect of religious conflict on minority inclusion, and so allows for future generalization and comparison to minority inclusion in democratizing states that are not Muslim.

Therefore, the main question this book aims to answer is: What factors explain the differences in how democratizing Muslim countries treat their ethnic minorities? In other words, why do democratizing Muslim majority states differ in their approaches to the incorporation of ethnic minorities? The research represents a comparative analysis of two similar cases with different outcomes: Turkey and Indonesia. The focus of the book is to analyze specifically the securitization (Buzan et al. 1998) of Kurds in Turkey and the "autonomization" (drawing from Lijphart 2004 and Kymlicka 2001) of Acehnese in Indonesia to understand what independent variables affect these different results. The cases chosen are the two democracies in the Muslim world that are most recognized by scholars. Hypotheses will be tested using four variables: the elites' power interest, following rational choice theory; international factors, following the international system and structural theories; institutions and the history of the state, following the historical-institutionalist theory; and finally the ontological security of a country, following critical theories.

Evidence analyzed in the book shows that none of these variables is necessary *and* sufficient, as none of them alone can cause the outcome of the dependent variable studied here: they are not uniquely sufficient to cause either securitization or autonomization. Nevertheless, there may be treated as prescriptive elements or policy suggestions to fledgling

Muslim-majority (and non-) democracies facing the challenge of including minorities, in particular if there is an open armed conflict with a self-determination movement of a minority. These countries should consider intervention by external mediators, a process of decentralization, and a very gradual transition of power among elites, hoping to have inclusive historical institutions that do not require excessive reform, a peaceful and secure regional situation that will not impact domestic issues with minorities, and a respectable national identity conducive to high levels of ontological security. It is not an easy situation to establish, but it is what all countries interested in fostering stable democratization processes should aim for.

Norfolk, VA, USA   Maurizio Geri

Acknowledgements

When you write a book, there are many people to thank. This book stems from the work done for my PhD dissertation, and so I want to thank first my dissertation supervisor Dr. David Earnest, who helped me not only with the research but also to improve my professional and human qualities. Also, I thank Dr. Regina Karp and everyone in the Graduate Program in International Studies at Old Dominion University, where I spent 4 years of my life starting my academic career with great faculty, supportive staff, and amazing colleagues who have always been helpful with their constant inputs. Thanks also to the many colleagues I met over these years of study in the USA and at the many international or national conferences I attended, especially those organized by the International Studies Association, the Association for the Study of the Middle East and Africa, and the Conference on World Affairs at University of Colorado Boulder. I am also grateful to the think tanks and research centers where I had the good fortune to collaborate with top-rate scholars, including at the Carter Center, the Washington Institute for Near East Policy, the Allied Command Transformation of NATO, the Center for Nonviolence and Peace Studies at the University of Rhode Island, and Nonviolence International. Finally, I thank my family, who helped me to reach this point in my life, and my mentor and best friend Shadia Marhaban.

I dedicate this book to the Kurds and the Acehnese, for a brighter future, and to all minorities around the world, the disenfranchised, the underdog, those excluded and discriminated against. Here's to you, for a future in which all humankind will find the path to social justice, human equality, and freedom.

Contents

1 Introduction   1
Theoretical Approach   8
Case Studies and Possible Hypothesis   13
Organization of the Book   16
References   18

2 Literature Review   21
Inclusion Versus Exclusion of Minorities in Democracies   21
Inclusion Versus Exclusion of Minorities in Democratization Processes   25
Strategies of Inclusion in Democracies   28
Outcomes of Theoretical Interest: Securitization and Autonomization   31
Independent Variables. Four Schools: Rationalism, Structuralism, Historical Institutionalism, and Critical Theory   41
References   52

3 Research Design   59
Research Method and Sources   59
Case Study Choice and Selection Criteria   61
Causal Mechanism to Research in the Two Case Studies   70
References   75

4 Securitization and Autonomization in Turkey and Indonesia: A Brief History and Review of the Period of Democratization	79
The Kurdish Issue in Turkey: A History of Exclusion and Securitization	79
Turkish Democracy: Recent Developments	89
Turkish Resecuritization of the Kurdish Minority	96
The Acehnese Issue in Indonesia: A History Between Autonomization and Securitization	102
Indonesian Autonomization of the Acehnese Minority	106
References	114
5 Political Elites' Power Interest and Rational Decision Making	121
Introduction	121
Theoretical Background	122
Theories Applied to Case Studies	125
Evidence for Turkey: From Autonomization to Securitization	128
Evidence for Indonesia: From Securitization to Autonomization	139
Conclusions	145
References	147
6 International Factors: Geopolitical Issues, International Community, and Diaspora	151
Introduction	151
Theoretical Background Applied to Case Studies	152
International Factors for Turkey	155
International Factors for Indonesia	166
Conclusions	174
References	176
7 Historical Institutionalism: Nationalism, Institutions and Citizenship of Ethnic Minorities	181
Introduction	181
Theories Applied to the Case Studies	183
Evidence from Turkish History	187
Evidence from Indonesian History	192
Conclusions	197
References	198

8	**Interacting Variable: Ontological Security**	201
	Introduction	201
	Ontological Security as a Concept	205
	Turkey: Ontological Insecurity and Securitization of Kurds	209
	Erdogan's Narratives Expressing Ontological Insecurity	216
	Indonesia: Ontological Security and Autonomization of Aceh	221
	Narratives of Indonesian Presidents in Democratic Transition	225
	Conclusions	229
	References	231
9	**Conclusions**	235
	Summary of Findings	235
	Some Meta Questions	239
	Rival Explanations and Next Steps	243
	References	247

Index 249

About the Author

Maurizio Geri holds a PhD in International Studies/Conflict and Cooperation from Old Dominion University in Norfolk, Virginia. He is an independent analyst on democratic issues and international security in the regions of Europe, the Middle East, Southeast Asia, and Latin America and he collaborates with NATO as strategic analyst on regional partnership, especially with WANA (West Asia and North Africa) region. Originally from Italy, where he earned his BA in Political Science and MA in Cultural Studies, he has professional experience in peacekeeping and human rights defense in Latin America and South Asia. His main research interests include democracy and democratization, collective and human security, and global affairs, as well as Islam and democracy, European Integration, the redistribution of geostrategic power toward Asia, and the politics of the Middle East. He has conducted research at various different universities and think tanks, including Old Dominion University on foreign affairs issues, at the University of Florence on European democracies and the Arab Spring, at the Carter Center on political campaigns in Latin America, at the NATO Allied Command Transformation on strategic foresight analysis for future risks, at Nonviolence International on peace and security in the Middle East, and at the University of Rhode Island on Martin Luther King's nonviolent strategy. The results of his research have also been present at many international conferences, including the annual conferences of the Association for the Study of the Middle East and Africa in Washington, DC; the annual conventions of the International Studies Association in the USA and Latin America, and the Conference on World Affairs at the University of Colorado Boulder. He has also delivered lectures at foreign universities, such as Maltepe University in Istanbul, Turkey, Syiah Kuala University in Aceh, Indonesia, and the Universidad Iberoamericana/ Centro de Investigación en Sociología Política in Guerrero, Mexico. Geri collaborates with Wikistrat and runs a blog on international affairs and democracy (www.democraticgeography.net). He lives between Florence, Italy, and Washington, DC, often traveling to Latin America and Asia for political activism or cultural travels.

CHAPTER 1

Introduction

This book examines the following question: What explains the different treatments of ethnic minorities in democratizing Muslim-majority countries?[1] The answer to this question is of crucial importance because democratic transitions, in all countries, are sustainable only if they are inclusive, and not if they transform themselves, as we saw in several failed cases, into a "tyranny of the majority."[2] Specifically, the democratic transition of the two case studies featured in this research, Turkey and Indonesia, took different paths also because of the differences in their approaches to the inclusion of ethnic minorities. Furthermore, the future security and the risk of radicalization in these, as well as other, democracies around the world are also affected by the inclusion or exclusion of ethnic minorities. Therefore, this book tries to show, even if indirectly, the consequences for

---

[1] Muslim-majority democracies are different from the so-called Muslim democracies that some scholars use; the latter imply some Muslim influence in the government. One scholar speaking about "Muslim democracies" is Cesari, who argues that Westernization and nation-building processes in Muslim states have not created liberal democracies in the Western mold but instead push the politicization of Islam by turning it into a modern national ideology. Also, Cesari, citing in particular Indonesia, Senegal, Tunisia, and Egypt, uses the term "unsecular democracy" for democracies that accept free/fair elections and some civil liberties but reject liberties seen as a threat to the national community/identity based on Islam (sexual and spiritual sphere and rights of the self). See Jocelyn Cesari, *The awakening of Muslim democracies* (New York: Cambridge University Press, 2014).

[2] Alexis de Tocqueville, *Democracy in America* (New York: Saunders and Otley, 1835).

democracy and security of the incorporation of ethnic minorities in modern democracies.

Today the threat to democracy that has fallen under the gaze of everyone is that both fledgling and mature democracies risk becoming securitized states, in a permanent state of exception, if they fail in their openness, tolerance, integration, and inclusion of old and new minorities. This is why the present study is important not only for Muslim-majority countries, which happen to have a low number of democracies, for reasons that will not be considered in this study, but for all countries wishing to increase their level of freedom and justice for all members of society.

There are 47 countries in the world where Islam is the religion of the majority of the population, but the literature on democratization generally considers just two of those countries to be democracies: Turkey and Indonesia.[3] In the past, this has caused scholars to consider the relationship between Islam and democracy a difficult and sometimes even impossible one.[4] Furthermore, the few studies that have examined this relationship have mostly adopted a religious perspective, at least until the so-called Arab Spring. Today, we have clear evidence that Islam is not a significant factor in explanations of democratization,[5] even if studies find a statistically significant negative relationship between Islam and democracy.[6] This is because Islam in and of itself, just like all other religions, cannot be considered a factor hindering democratization and, furthermore, cannot be painted with such a big brush as a monolithic set of religious and cultural values impacting the political institutions of a country from an

---

[3] See Edward Schneier, *Muslim democracy: Politics, religion and society in Indonesia, Turkey and the Islamic world* (New York: Routledge, 2016). Other scholars also consider other Muslim countries to be democracies (in particular Senegal and Mali, the latter until the coup in 2012), for example, Paul Kubicek, *Political Islam and democracy in the Muslim world*, Boulder-London: Lynne Rienner Publishers, 2015.

[4] See, among others, Samuel Huntington, *The clash of civilizations and the remaking of world order* (New York: Simon & Schuster, 1996).

[5] As Schneier, among others, definitively showed, the democratization issue of so-called Muslim democracies around the world is not the Islamic religion but variables like poverty, nation-building, civil infrastructure, and belonging to regions late to achieve independence from colonial rule, which makes it difficult to build strong nation-states or civic cultures. Edward Schneier, *Muslim democracy: Politics, religion and society in Indonesia, Turkey and the Islamic world* (New York: Routledge, 2016).

[6] See on this, among others, Charles Rowley and Nathanael Smith, "Islam's democracy paradox: Muslims claim to like democracy, so why do they have so little?" *Public Choice*, 139 (3) 2009: 273–299.

essentialist perspective. Nevertheless, the majority of Muslim countries (mostly in the Arab World) are not democracies, and international factors (including the history of colonization followed by authoritarian regimes supported by external powers) or internal factors, like economic issues, institutional problems, and weak civil society, are not enough to explain this fact.

In the literature of comparative analysis, including in the one comparing Muslim-majority democracies,[7] there is a real gap on how Muslim-majority countries democratize and how they include ethnic minorities in this process, and that is the reason for this book. Studies of social conflict or democratization in Muslim countries typically emphasize sectarian religious divisions but tend to overlook ethnic differences. To redress this deficiency, this study examines the incorporation of ethnic minorities in democratizing Muslim countries, analyzing in particular two competing modes of treatment, one of repression and one of accommodation: the "securitization"[8] of Kurds in Turkey and the "autonomization"[9] or granting of autonomy to Acehnese in Indonesia. By examining states with ethnic heterogeneity but very little religious diversity, this study controls for the effect of religious conflict on minority inclusion. This makes it possible to examine citizenship regimes independently of established religions and permits future generalization and comparison to minority inclusion in democratizing states that are not Muslim. Therefore, to further clarify, a comparison of only Muslim-majority countries with respect to democratization—an approach that scholars usually do not adopt to study democratization in majority Christian or Buddhist countries—is not based on a negative evaluation of the relationship between Islam and democracy, with an Orientalist approach looking at the limits of the religion of Islam for democratization (or even the role of Islam in democratization periods). On the contrary, the book emphasizes a comparative need for generalization and, at the same time, a need for causal analysis of an overlooked but

---

[7] Paul Kubicek, *Political Islam and democracy in the Muslim world*, Boulder-London: Lynne Rienner Publishers, 2015.

[8] Barry Buzan, Ole Waever, Jaap de Wilde, *Security: A new framework for analysis* (Boulder: Lynne Rienner Publishers, 1998).

[9] See for this concept Arend Lijphart, *Patterns of democracy. Government forms and performance in 36 countries* (New Haven: Yale University Press, 1999). Will Kymlicka, *Politics in the Vernacular: Nationalism, multiculturalism, and citizenship* (Oxford: Oxford University Press, 2002).

important element of democratization in pluralistic societies, the treatment of ethnic minorities.

The research presented here is important because it lies at the intersection of several current theoretical debates in international relations theory and comparative politics field: democratization, national security, and radicalization. This work has three indirect objectives: to prove the extent to which Muslim countries with ethnic minorities can make their democratization more efficient and sustainable, to suggest how this improvement may be carried out in a way that guarantees stability and national security for the country, and to show how this can avoid social radicalization, which is often connected to the disenfranchisement or repression of minorities.

These three goals may seem to be in conflict at first glance. Democratization requires the inclusion of previously excluded parts of society. At the same time, concerns about national security may grow for some sectors of society and lead to a type of differentiation—including juridical discrimination or repression—for the sake of social stability and harmony. For example, democratization may encourage self-determination movements but also clashes caused by new ethnic groups migrating to a country. The prevention of radicalization may require an investment in security and, again, control of some specific minority groups. Such control could have opposite effects of increasing polarization and extremism in a democratizing society. This study therefore is of fundamental importance for the future balance among democratization, security, and deradicalization because it analyzes how modern democracies may resolve the possible tensions among these three different goals while integrating minorities in an inclusive process. In this sense, the book seeks to explain why some states may succeed at this while others fail.

Regarding specifically democratization processes, it is impossible to identify the moment at which a democratizing state becomes an established democracy. Democracy is a never-ending process, with ups and downs and with different criteria for different times, and democratization can always be reversed, as we have seen throughout human history and around the world.[10] Often, transitions to democracy create procedural or

---

[10] For example, Bratton and van de Walle list four possibilities for transitions: precluded, blocked, flawed, or successful transitions. See Michael Bratton and Nicholas van de Walle, *Democratic experiments in Africa: regime transitions in comparative perspective* (Cambridge: Cambridge University Press, 1997).

"formal" democracies but not liberal, "substantive" democracies, like the case of "one party" or "dominant party" systems.

Previously, the failure or success of transition to democracy specifically in Muslim-majority countries—apart from the problem of possible foreign influences that may have an important impact on democratic transitions, particularly in the Arab world—often depended on the exclusion or inclusion of ethnic, religious, or political minorities by the new regimes. This can be considered one of the most important domestic factors of "Arab exceptionalism"[11] and one of the causes of the failure of the "Arab Spring" (with the sole exception of Tunisia) considered as the possible "fourth wave" or reactivation of the "third wave" of democratization in the world.[12] These failures have kept the countries of the Middle East as outliers on the global path to democracy. From the problems in Egypt (among which is the lack of inclusion of secular forces in the government made by the Muslim Brotherhood) and Iraq (where Sunni Muslims were suddenly excluded from the al-Maliki regime) to the successful experience of inclusive processes in Tunisia, where power is shared between secular parties and the Islamist Ennahda party, or even Morocco, a monarchy that, following the Arab Spring protests, went through several democratic reforms, including for minorities' rights, we see the extent to which strong and inclusive institutions, economies, and societies are crucial for the stability of the democratizing regimes in the region, as everywhere else in the world, as Acemoglu and Robinson among others famously argued.[13] The institutions, economies, and societies in this area have suffered from their past, in particular from the fact that the old processes of nation-state building often sidelined the self-determination right of minorities (from Armenians to Kurds, from Berbers of Maghreb to Arabs of Palestine), creating states that oppressed ethnic minorities. Therefore, dealing with past institutional, economic, and identity issues is a crucial point for the sustainability of democratization processes in the region, as well as in the other Muslim-majority countries in Africa or Asia that have moved beyond postcolonization nation-building. As we will comment later, in non-Muslim-majority countries and in so-called mature democracies, the

---

[11] Larry Diamond, "Why are there no Arab democracies?" *Journal of Democracy* 21 (1) 2010: 93–104.

[12] Samuel P Huntington, *The third wave: democratization in the late twentieth century* (Norman: University of Oklahoma Press, 1991).

[13] Daron Acemoglu and James Robinson, *Why nations fail: The origins of power, prosperity, and poverty* (London: Profile books, 2013).

problem of the inclusion of old or new ethnic minorities is crucial for the sustainability of the "never ending" democratization processes.

Regarding the national security issue, the exclusion or inclusion of minorities—in cases of separatist movements—has an evident impact on security questions, both in Muslim and non-Muslim countries. Since the end of the Cold War, intrastate conflicts have become more frequent while interstate conflicts have almost disappeared. Samuel Huntington was right in arguing that conflicts, after the end of bipolar ideologies, would follow the ethnic, cultural, and religious cleavages within states rather than those between nation-states. Nevertheless, he was wrong in the positioning of these cleavages, as they would be drawn not among states—with alliances of similar countries against one another, as he suggested—but instead would be within states, with the dissolution of multiethnic and multireligious countries and the subsequent reconstruction of cleavages and sectarianism. The exclusion—and, more specifically, the exclusively security-focused approaches to minorities and local identities, including the displacement of large sections of populations to break their possible self-determination movements—is evidently contributing to insecurity and instability in the Middle East, a region already in chaos since the implosion of the post-Ottoman order. Therefore, the inclusion of minorities, in step with the transition from a state-security-only approach, based on repression, to a more so-called human security approach, based on participation, will be important for the future of national security as well as of democratization in the region.

Finally, the inclusion of minorities could also represent one of the fundamental and lasting solutions to radicalization, in particular the current form of Salafi–Jihadist terrorism. Scholars argue that DAESH/ISIS arose first of all because of the exclusionary al-Maliki government in Iraq, and also because of the radical and exclusionary Wahhabi ideology, which was spread around the region by Saudi Arabia. Also, the foreign fighters that support DAESH often come from situations of marginalization, exclusion, and consequent radicalization—even if radicalization is a complex process based also on economic issues, identity alienation, and psychological crisis that are not directly related to exclusionary processes.[14] Exclusionary pro-

---

[14] Peter R. Neumann, "The trouble with radicalization," *International Affairs* 89, 4 (2013): 873–893. Also: James M. Dorsey, "Ethnicity, Tribalism, and Pluralism in the Middle East and North Africa: Solutions to Conflict?," *MEI Insight*, No. 135, Middle East Institute, National University of Singapore, January 5, 2016, pp. 1–12.

cesses have been supported also by the fact that collective identities of populations have shifted recently in the Middle East, with the construction and reconstruction of ethnic and religious cleavages and sectarianism that facilitated the possibility of exclusion.

Therefore, the radicalization of ideological or religious positions is a social problem that goes beyond the current Salafi terrorism. Following the Arab Spring, some political groups that came to power (such as the Muslim Brotherhood in Egypt or the *Ennahda* party in Tunisia), for example, started to radicalize their position in part also because of past political exclusion and oppression. This had negative effects on the legitimacy and sustainability of the new regimes. Even with the Acehnese of Indonesia, one of the two cases examined in this study, the current application of Sharia law has happened following a long history of suppression of local religious identity, a process that also contributed to the radicalization of new ideas and policies.

To conclude on this point, pluralism and inclusion are not sufficient paths for a sustainable democratization but nonetheless are foundational elements in every democracy, even mature democracies that must still strive to maintain their legitimacy and substantiality.[15] For this reason, this study can be useful for all states that uphold democratic values in a globalized world that is witnessing a mutation of the old forms of nation-states: the problem of the inclusion of ethnic minorities contributes to the tensions that arise between integration and security versus radicalization and instability. Today this represents one of the crucial problems that policymakers must face in their attempts to create cohesive and peaceful societies hit by economic and identity crises, even in the so-called West. To say with Dorsey: to create pluralist and inclusive states in Middle East and Europe requires "fostering inclusive national identities that are capable of accommodating ethnic, sectarian and tribal sub-identities as legitimate and fully accepted sub-identities in Middle Eastern and North African, as well as Western countries, and changing domestic policies in the West towards minorities, refugees and migrants."[16]

---

[15] Freedom House, for example, includes in its 8 points of Political Rights checklist for all democracies one important element for minorities: "Do cultural, ethnic, religious, and other minority groups have reasonable self-determination, self-government, autonomy, or participation through informal consensus in the decision-making process?"

[16] James M. Dorsey, 2016, p. 3.

Theoretical Approach

Almost all countries in the world are ethnically diverse, apart from the two Koreas, Japan, Poland, and a few other Central European nations, from which, after centuries of war, originated the concept of nation-state.[17] But while in some countries, such as those of the former Federal Republic of Yugoslavia, Rwanda, or Syria, ethnic and religious differences have been used by political elites to socially construct and reconstruct identities in order to fuel sectarian and ethnic conflicts,[18] in others, such as Canada or Indonesia, such differences have been accepted and protected by the constitution as a fundamental element of pluralism and tolerance and, thus, as the basis for future democratic developments.

The inclusion of minorities in Europe—unlike in the USA, where immigration from different communities has a longer history of integration—has been defined in two broad categories. The first is the assimilationist approach,[19] along the lines of the French model, and following the American one; this approach integrates minorities by substantially erasing their differences in an attempt to create an egalitarian society. The other is the multicultural approach,[20] based on the German and British model, but also on the approach in countries like Canada or Australia. The multicultural approach integrates minorities but permits them to maintain their identities and cultures in an attempt to create a cosmopolitan society. Today, it seems that both the assimilationist and multiculturalist approaches

---

[17] See on this Max Fixer, A revealing map of the world's most and least ethnically diverse countries, *The Washington Post*, May 16, 2013. From: https://www.washingtonpost.com/news/worldviews/wp/2013/05/16/a-revealing-map-of-the-worlds-most-and-least-ethnically-diverse-countries/.

[18] See on this James D. Fearon and David D. Laitin, "Violence and the Social Construction of Ethnic Identity," *International Organization*, Volume 54, Issue 04 (Autumn 2000): 845–877.

[19] The Chicago school formulated the concept of assimilation as incorporation into a common cultural life, as applied to American society, in the 1920s. See Robert Ezra Park and E. W. Burgess, *Introduction to the science of sociology* (Chicago: University of Chicago press, 1924). Later, in the 1960s, authors like Gordon made a distinction between acculturation and "structural assimilation" in which a minority group joins social clubs, institutions, and so forth. See Milton Myron Gordon, *Assimilation in American life: The role of race, religion, and national origins* (New York: Oxford University Press, 1964).

[20] Multiculturalism is considered to exist when a society is unitary in the public domain but encourages diversity in private or communal matters. See the seminal work of John Rex, *Ethnic minorities in the modern nation state: Working papers in the theory of multiculturalism and political integration* (New York: St. Martin's Press, 1996).

have failed to build genuine integration of migrants and autochthonous peoples in Europe: on the one hand a forcing of a common identity and on the other a classification in cultural boxes have failed to recognize diversity while at the same time providing equal citizenship.

This has been the environment where some terrorist groups have been growing, with the result of manipulating weakened minds to resort to violence, including the Jihadist attacks in Europe. Some scholars such as Stuurman speak about the specific "Islamophobic assimilationist mood"[21] after the 9/11 attacks, in France and in Europe more broadly. The repression of Muslim identity with the goal of assimilation (for example, the French ban on the headscarf in public or the prohibition of Halal food in public kitchens) contributed to Islamic radicalization. Nevertheless, we cannot say that multiculturalism, which promoted the segregation and division of cultures into "boxes," had better results in other countries because the events caused by Jihadist radicalization also happened in multicultural countries including the UK, Belgium, and the Netherlands.[22]

Therefore, in one way or another, different cultural identities must be taken into account in our modern migratory societies, which today are living through a transition from the traditional "nation-state" to a new polity that struggles to appear even if gradually it is emerging. An ideal policy would take the good parts of each system: the maintenance of cultural identities of multiculturalism, but not as sealed compartments, and equality in a society of citizens of assimilationism, but without erasing people's varied needs. In reality, on the European continent, we are looking nowadays at the embryonic development of different types of policies that could be categorized into big spheres: the "securitization" and the "autonomization" of new migrants.

These policies could be seen as being on the same continuum of the two traditional approaches: securitization as the extreme form of assimila-

---

[21] Siep Stuurman, *Citizenship and cultural differences in France and the Netherlands*. In: Richard Bellamy, Dario Castiglione, and Emilio Santoro (ed.) *Lineages of European citizenship: Rights, belonging and participation in eleven nation-states* (New York: Palgrave Macmillan, 2004): pp. 167–186.

[22] Kenan Malik, "The Failure of Multiculturalism. Community Versus Society in Europe," *Foreign Affairs*, December 8, 2015, accessed on September 30, 2017. https://www.foreignaffairs.com/articles/western-europe/failure-multiculturalism. Kenan Malik, "Terrorism has come about in assimilationist France and also in multicultural Britain. Why is that?," *The Guardian*, November 14, 2015, accessed September 30, 2017. http://www.theguardian.com/commentisfree/2015/nov/15/multiculturalism-assimilation-britain-france.

tion and autonomization as the extreme form of multiculturalism. The first approach favors constant surveillance and control of migrants (a mutation of the failed assimilationist approach). The second approach supports an extreme "autonomization" of migrants, with their attempted repatriation (like a mutation of the failed multiculturalism).

The book will explain later in detail the processes of securitization and autonomization, but here we can provide a brief explanation of the two terms. The securitization process comes from a critical theory based on a "broadening" process of security concepts, famously formulated by the Copenhagen School after the Cold War. According to this school, when a state labels some issue (including a minority) only as a "security issue," it puts it outside the political arena, justifying in this way extraordinary security, policing, and military measures to deal with it. These security policies create a "permanent state of exception" that forms power relations of exclusion, constructing the issue as a threat to national identity. This approach leads to criminalization of minority groups and often to a violent conflict with them. The theoretical reference for this approach is the work of Buzan, Waever, and de Wilde,[23] who for the first time conceptualized the theory.

"Autonomization," on the other hand, is not a theory but a term specifically coined for this research. This book defines autonomization as a process opposed to securitization, in which the minority issue that was in the past outside the political arena (being in an armed conflict or anyway in a securitization phase) moves or returns to the political arena. A key feature can be a peace process predicated on some form of autonomy or policies of autonomy toward the minority launched by the state to respond to the minority community's request for some form of self-determination. This process of incorporation of the minority—we say incorporation because the autonomous minority remains a subject of the state authority; it does not become fully independent of the nation-state—can be considered a process of inclusion because there is some sort of attempt to meet the minority's rights and needs. Therefore, by bringing the issue back into the political arena, the autonomization process provides for minority rights through the devolution of authority and limited self-governance within a region, even if the process does not provide complete sovereignty.

---

[23] Barry Buzan, Ole Waever, Jaap de Wilde, *Security: A new framework for analysis* (Boulder: Lynne Rienner Publishers, 1998).

This book does not analyze the negotiation and peace processes that may lead to the autonomization of minorities, though it will touch on them briefly in the Indonesian case. For the concept of autonomization, the first theoretical reference in political philosophy is based on specific minority rights that the state should guarantee to ensure justice for national minorities, as proposed by Canadian political philosopher Will Kymlicka.[24] The main theoretical reference in democracy studies instead comes from Dutch political scientist Arend Lijphart and his concept of "consociational democracy" based on power sharing.[25] The consociational approach may include policies of autonomy with respect to ethnic minorities, so the concept of autonomization developed here refers to Lijphart's work as the theoretical basis of such inclusion of minorities.

But why should concepts like securitization and autonomization help us to understand the treatment of minorities in democracies, either fledgling Muslim democracies or mature Western democracies? Conventional studies on the treatment of minorities usually focus on the assimilation approach versus the multiculturalist one. By contrast, very few studies have analyzed the strategies of securitization and autonomization as alternative policies regarding ethnic minorities. Nevertheless, there is evidence that these strategies are increasingly preferred policies in developing and democratizing states, particularly in Muslim regions, for dealing with minorities. Examples include the autonomization of Kurds in Iraq (with the creation of the Kurdistan region in 2005 and the request for its independence in the referendum of September 2017), the securitization of the Rohingya minority in Myanmar (today almost in a situation of genocide), the securitization of the Bangsamoro minority in the Philippines (in particular since the Duterte presidency), and in some forms of the Uzbek minority in the Kyrgyz Republic. The Moroccan and Senegal cases, two Muslim-majority countries at different stages of democratization, are also interesting examples. On the one hand, Morocco started recently with more recognition and recovery of Berber culture (for example, today Berbers can broadcast in Tamazight), policies that we could very well consider a form of autonomization of Berbers, even if they represent the majority

---

[24] Will Kymlicka, *Politics in the Vernacular: Nationalism, Multiculturalism, and Citizenship* (Oxford: Oxford University Press, 2002).

[25] Arend Lijphart, *Patterns of democracy. Government forms and performance in 36 countries* (New Haven: Yale University Press, 1999).

of the population whose language was lost due to Arabization.[26] On the other hand, Morocco is still applying some form of securitization to the Sahrawi[27] minority in the Western Sahara region, but it seems to be moving slowly toward the autonomization phase with a negotiated peace process. Senegal had a thirty-year conflict with its small Jola ethnic minority (around half a million people) in the Casamance region and today has moved on from the securitization phase to an autonomization phase, with a ceasefire and some form of decentralization since 2014.[28] Thus, as we see, there are several examples of Muslim-majority democratizing countries that must deal with ethnic minorities and struggle with their inclusion and, as a result, with the full flourishing of their democratization.

This book therefore analyzes only the two paths in the "differentialist" approach (to borrow a term from Brubaker, who uses it in reference to multicultural approaches): one more inclusive, autonomization, and one more exclusive, securitization. This does not mean that some states choose only these two strategies in the long run. The fact of the matter is, however, that states seem to go down similar paths of trying before adopting integrative approaches to minorities (either through assimilation or multiculturalism) during the phase of nation-building.[29] When the nation-building phase is passed, if the issue of minorities reappears, especially in connection with the presence of a separatist movement, the state responds first with securitization and then sometimes with policies of autonomy. This may depend on different factors that represent the four "independent variables" of this book: the benefits accruing to the ruling elites, the influence of the international arena, the type of nationalism in the country's history and institutions, and the level of ontological security of the country.

---

[26] Moroccans are of mixed Arab-Berber descent, but many Berbers, being "Arabized" as the majority of the Berbers in Maghreb, have lost their language.

[27] As with most peoples from Maghreb, the Sahrawi culture is mixed, with Berber-Tuareg characteristics, as well as Bedouin Arab and black African characteristics.

[28] Note that the Jola minority is also a religious minority that follows a syncretistic religion based on traditional African religion, with Christian and Muslim influences.

[29] Senem Aslan, *Nation-Building in Turkey and Morocco. Governing Kurdish and Berber Dissent* (New York: Cambridge University Press, 2014).

Case Studies and Possible Hypothesis

This book focuses on two emblematic cases, sometimes treated as models of non-Arab Muslim democracies: Turkey[30] and Indonesia. First, both Turkey and Indonesia showed that democratic values and commitment to Islam are not incompatible. Turkey was considered the only Muslim-majority democracy since World War II, even if its politics featured regular military influence. But since 2002 Turkey has also seen a moderate Islamist party in power without the repressive intervention of the army, making it flourish for several years on the democratic path and showing how Islam and democracy were not incompatible. Even more than Turkey, Indonesia has been deemed a successful democracy in the last two decades because of its ability to transition from a dictatorship to a democratic system while maintaining stability and prosperity, despite ethnic conflicts and religious riots. Islam in Indonesia's democratization had a different role from that in Turkey because Islamist political parties in Indonesia, with their exclusionary politics caused by their attacks on secularism, remained on the political fringes and could never win national elections. Therefore, these cases are interesting for any study of the interrelation between Islamic culture (even political culture) and democracy, as other recent books also argue.[31]

Second, Indonesia and Turkey are good subjects to study because these countries have many similarities (what in academia are called "control variables" in research), even though they seem to have taken different paths in the treatment of their ethnic minorities during the time of their democratization. As previously discussed, on the one hand, the repression and securitization of the Kurdish minority—or at least of the Kurds wishing to politically mobilize as an ethnically distinct community—with a self-determination movement continues. On the other hand, Indonesia represents an accommodation with the settlement of a similar armed conflict, which concluded with decentralization and autonomy for the Aceh region.

Third, the book focuses on the inclusion of ethnic nonreligious minorities since religious minorities might be related to theological questions that lie beyond the scope of this study. By contrast, political minorities

---

[30] For some years, and in particular following the Arab Spring, this has no longer been the case. See on this, among others, Paul Kubicek, "Debating the merits of the 'Turkish model' for democratization in the Middle East," *Alternatives: Turkish Journal of International Relations*, 11 (3) 2013: 66–80.

[31] Edward Schneier, *Muslim Democracy: Politics, Religion and Society in Indonesia, Turkey and the Islamic World* (New York: Routledge, 2016).

often have an ethnic base that makes identity an important factor; therefore, in the future, we could expand our research to include political minorities representing ethnic groups as well.

The time frame this study analyzes (apart from a historical introduction to the respective treatments of minorities) focuses on each state's democratization: for Indonesia from the end of dictatorship in 1998 to 2005 when Aceh achieved autonomy, and for Turkey since 2002, with what we might call a "new democratization," with the electoral success of a moderate Islamist party without the intervention of the military as in the past, to 2016, when Turkey suffered through another one of its military coups, which failed this time and launched a new era of repression and authoritarian rule, making the country no longer a substantive democracy. Since 2011 in particular, the regime of the Justice and Development Party (in Turkish: *Adalet ve Kalkınma Partisi*, AKP) had already started making a gradual turn toward authoritarianism and a shift toward the repression of the Kurdish minority after a few years of openness. But in 2016, the peace process in Turkey ended, which led to renewed securitized of the Kurdish minority, in an attempt to reduce them to silence or expel from the country. This study's analysis relates specifically to the policies of securitization and autonomization implemented by the Turkish government with respect to the Kurdish minority and the Indonesian government with respect to the Acehnese minority. Therefore, the book focuses on the timeframe between the initiation of democratization and the final "solution" of the minority issue, either autonomization for Aceh or final securitization for Kurds.

Indonesia seems to have passed through three periods of relations with the Acehnese: a multicultural period during nation-building after decolonization since World War II, with a pluralist and multinational constitution; a securitization period with the Acehnese minority during thirty years of war; and finally to policies of autonomy marked by the end of the conflict and the negotiation of a regional autonomy for Aceh in 2005 when the country consolidated its democracy (even though at the beginning of the democratization process, between 1998 and 2002, securitization actually increased). By contrast, after a period of general assimilation in Turkey and repression of local rebellion during nation-building since 1923, the country passed to securitization of the Kurdish minority during the insurgency of the Kurdistan Workers' Party (or PKK) in 1984, including the depopulation of Kurdish villages by the Turkish military. When Turkish democratization took an important step forward in 2002, the new ruling party, the AKP, started to grant some minority cultural rights and later even started a peace process that lasted two years between 2013 and 2015. Nevertheless, this process did not produce a phase of autonomy as occurred in Indonesia; on the contrary, Turkey once again returned to the phase of securitization, accompanied by a democratic reversal, starting in particular with the increasing power of the AKP as a result of general elections in 2015 and finally with the purges following the attempted military coup in 2016.

From a minority point of view, when the formation of the government in a new democracy continues to exclude the minority that had a history as a separatist movement, this minority continues the insurgency, as in Aceh/East Timor after 1998 or Kurdistan in Turkey after 2002. Some cases around the world show that if democratization and decentralization led to the inclusion of the minority, the insurgency would stop the fight, to the benefit of the stability of the democratization process itself. For example, in Senegal, which since 1999 has strengthened its democratic institutions after 40 years with the same party in power, the state began a peace process with the Casamance group in 2004. Today it can be considered a "test case for advanced decentralization policy," as President Sall declared in 2012.[32] This does not mean, however, that decentralization must be forced; it needs instead to flow from the minority group's initiative, as the Yemeni case shows. The Yemeni civil war stemmed from this issue, when President Hadi's concept of forced decentralization started to exclude the Shia Houthis who, destined to administer their poor mountainous region, eventually rebelled.

One possible hypothesis to explain these different outcomes refers to the four factors that will be revealed in the third chapter. For now, it is worth noting that Kurdish nationalism in Turkey, in particular following the birth of Kurdish autonomous regions in bordering countries Iraq and Syria, has threatened the national unity of a very centralized state. This threat has been directed not only at the identity and institutions of a very nationalist state and the ontological security of its "Turkishness" but also at the political power of the ruling party. Even if at the beginning of its rule the AKP modified traditional Turkish policies toward Kurds with a new accommodative approach, after a few years the strategy changed as this process did not bring the expected benefits to the ruling party. In

---

[32] See Crisis Watch Database, Senegal, *Crisis Group*, accessed on September 30, 2017. http://www.crisisgroup.org/en/publication-type/crisiswatch/crisiswatch-database. aspx?CountryIDs={7C99E8F1-62A0-41EA-9FDF-953D084593B9}.

particular, when the AKP lost the majority in the 2015 elections because the Kurdish People's Democratic Party (with liberal and leftist views, in contrast to the moderate Islamist approach of AKP) won seats in parliament for the first time. For these reasons, the struggle for political power by the elites, international factors arising from the crumbling of the Middle East order, traditional nationalistic institutions arising from the history of the state's formation, and the level of ontological security will be analyzed as the possible causes of the securitization of the Kurdish minority.

By contrast, in the Indonesian case, the Acehnese minority did not threaten the national unity and identity of Indonesia because the country was already a pluralistic nation. Likewise, Acehnese autonomy did not threaten Indonesia's ontological security because of its geography, history, and culture (since in religious societies there is a high level of trust and security, Indonesian society enjoyed a high level of ontological security). Similarly, the political power of the elites remained unchallenged by Acehnese autonomy because the Acehnese minority never had the power to shift political support to or from ruling parties. Finally, the international arena had an impact not at the geopolitical or regional level—Aceh being the region at the tip of Sumatra surrounded only by the Indian Ocean—but instead in the international community that pushed for the solution of the ethnic conflict, in particular after the 2004 Tsunami. Thus, as we can see, the relevant factors in both cases produced opposite outcomes.

Finally, we need to acknowledge that this study recognizes that the minority groups themselves shape the different processes and approaches of the state by reacting to the state's policies in different ways. However, for the purposes of this book, the conceptual focus is on the state, not on the societal-minority actors. Also, mediation processes have different approaches with different results and may impact the solution of minority conflict, but again the study does not analyze this aspect for the minority inclusion, which could represent a topic for future research.

Organization of the Book

This study is composed of nine chapters. In the next chapter, "Literature review," the literature on the political incorporation of ethnic minorities and on the independent variables studied in the research is reviewed. Starting with the definition of ethnic minority identity, the chapter proceeds to a review of the theories with respect to the inclusion versus exclusion of minorities in democratization and to the strategies of inclusion in democracies. The chapter continues with the literature review on the two outcomes of the dependent variable (the treatment of ethnic minorities): securitization and autonomization. Finally, the four factors or independent variables—the elites and power interest, rational choice theory, international factors and geopolitics, historical institutions and citizenship following historical-institutionalist theories, and, finally, ontological security following critical theory—are discussed.

Chapter 3, "Research Design," concerns the research methodology of the study, based on a comparative qualitative analysis and in particular on case study analysis. After explaining the choices of case studies and selection criteria (with the control variables of the cases) the chapter presents the causal mechanism of research in the two case studies, with the four independent variables.

Chapter 4, "Securitization and Autonomization in Turkey and Indonesia: A Brief History and Review of the Period of Democratization," presents an introduction to the history of the two case studies, analyzing the recent period of democratization of the two countries, to provide a background for the following chapters that test the four hypotheses of the study.

Chapter 5, "Political Elites' Power Interest and Rational Decision Making," analyzes the first independent variable. Following a discussion of the theoretical background, with the relevant theories applied to the case studies, the chapter presents the evidence supporting this hypothesis on the importance of political elites' power struggle for Turkey and Indonesia.

Chapter 6, "International Factors, Securitization, and Autonomization," also starts with the theoretical background as applied to the case studies and then discusses the various international factors at play in connection with Turkey and Indonesia (from geopolitical and security issues to the European Union for Turkey, and from the international community to International Non-Governmental Organizations and the Association of Southeast Asian Nations for Indonesia), presenting the evidence supporting this second hypothesis.

Chapter 7, "Nationalism, Institutions and Citizenship of Ethnic Minorities: Historical Institutionalism and Securitization," explores the history and institutions of the two countries in an effort to determine whether the institutions created at the founding of Turkey and Indonesia might account for their different treatments of ethnic minorities.

Chapter 8, "Interacting Variable: Ontological Security," refers not to rationalist-materialist-historical explanations, as the other variables, but to a critical theory variable, the ontological security of a state. Also, this chapter, like the others, applied a theoretical background to the cases and then sections based on evidence to support this last hypothesis.

Finally, Chap. 9 draws the conclusions of the study, with some proposals for future research directions.

References

Aslan, Senem. 2014. *Nation-Building in Turkey and Morocco. Governing Kurdish and Berber Dissent*. New York: Cambridge University Press.

Bratton, Michael, and Nicholas van de Walle. 1997. *Democratic Experiments in Africa. Regime Transitions in Comparative Perspective*. Cambridge: Cambridge University Press.

Buzan, Barry, Ole Waever, and Jaap de Wilde. 1998. *Security: A New Framework for Analysis*. Boulder: Lynne Rienner Publishers.

Cesari, Jocelyn. 2014. *The Awakening of Muslim Democracies*. New York: Cambridge University Press.

Crisis Watch Database, Senegal, *Crisis Group*. http://www.crisisgroup.org/en/publication-type/crisiswatch/crisiswatch-database.aspx?CountryIDs={7C99E8F1-62A0-41EA-9FDF-953D084593B9}. Accessed 30 Sept 2017.

Daron, Acemoglu, and James Robinson. 2013. *Why Nations Fail: The Origins of Power, Prosperity, and Poverty*. London: Profile Books.

De Tocqueville, Alexis. 1835. *Democracy in America*. New York: Saunders and Otley.

Diamond, Larry. 2010. Why Are there No Arab Democracies? *Journal of Democracy* 21 (1): 93–104.

Dorsey, James M. 2016. Ethnicity, Tribalism, and Pluralism in the Middle East and North Africa: Solutions to Conflict? *MEI Insight*, No. 135, Middle East Institute, National University of Singapore, January 5, 2016, pp. 1–12.

Fearon, James D., and David D. Laitin. 2000 Autumn. Violence and the Social Construction of Ethnic Identity. *International Organization* 54 (04): 845–877.

Fixer, Max. 2013. A Revealing Map of the World's Most and Least Ethnically Diverse Countries. *The Washington Post*, May 16, 2013. https://www.washingtonpost.com/news/worldviews/wp/2013/05/16/a-revealing-map-of-the-worlds-most-and-least-ethnically-diverse-countries/. Accessed 30 Sept 2017.

Gordon, Milton Myron. 1964. *Assimilation in American Life: The Role of Race, Religion, and National Origins*. New York: Oxford University Press.

Huntington, Samuel. 1991. *The Third Wave: Democratization in the Late Twentieth Century*. Norman: University of Oklahoma Press.

———. 1996. *The Clash of Civilizations and the Remaking of World Order*. New York: Simon & Schuster.

Kubicek, Paul. 2013. Debating the Merits of the 'Turkish Model' for Democratization in the Middle East. *Alternatives: Turkish Journal of International Relations* 11 (3): 66–80.

———. 2015. *Political Islam and Democracy in the Muslim World*. Boulder/London: Lynne Rienne Publishers.

Kymlicka, Will. 2002. *Politics in the Vernacular: Nationalism, Multiculturalism, and Citizenship*. Oxford: Oxford University Press.

Lijphart, Arend. 1999. *Patterns of Democracy. Government Forms and Performance in 36 Countries*. New Haven: Yale University Press.

Malik, Kenan. 2015a. The Failure of Multiculturalism. Community Versus Society in Europe. *Foreign Affairs*, December 8, 2015. https://www.foreignaffairs.com/articles/western-europe/failure-multiculturalism. Accessed 30 Sept 2017.

———. 2015b. Terrorism Has Come about in Assimilationist France and Also in Multicultural Britain. Why Is that? *The Guardian*, November 14, 2015. http://www.theguardian.com/commentisfree/2015/nov/15/multiculturalism-assimilation-britain-france. Accessed 31 Jan 2016.

Neumann, Peter R. 2013. The Trouble with Radicalization. *International Affairs* 89 (4): 873–893.

Park, Robert Ezra, and E.W. Burgess. 1924. *Introduction to the Science of Sociology*. Chicago: University of Chicago Press.

Rex, John. 1996. *Ethnic Minorities in the Modern Nation State: Working Papers in the Theory of Multiculturalism and Political Integration*. New York: St. Martin's Press.

Rowley, Charles, and Nathanael Smith. 2009. Islam's Democracy Paradox: Muslim Claim to Like Democracy, So Why Do they Have So Little? *Public Choice* 139 (3): 273–299.

Schneier, Edward. 2016. *Muslim Democracy: Politics, Religion and Society in Indonesia, Turkey and the Islamic World*. New York: Routledge.

Stuurman, Siep. 2004. *Citizenship and Cultural Differences in France and the Netherlands*. In *Lineages of European Citizenship: Rights, Belonging and Participation in Eleven Nation-states*, ed. Richard Bellamy, Dario Castiglione, and Emilio Santoro, 167–186. New York: Palgrave Macmillan.

CHAPTER 2

Literature Review

INCLUSION VERSUS EXCLUSION OF MINORITIES IN DEMOCRACIES

The inclusion of minorities has always been considered an important feature of a stable and prosperous democracy. Almost two centuries ago, Alexis de Tocqueville cautioned democracies about the risk of the "tyranny of the majority."[1] Today we can say that, even if almost all practitioners and scholars of democracy agree that there is no single path or single pattern of what makes a country more or less democratic, the way a state treats its minorities remains one of the most important criteria to measure the depth, substantiveness, and meaningfulness of a democracy.

Actually as the definition of democracy we can give a minimalist definition, of an "electoral democracy" requiring only contestation (free and fair elections) and the autonomy of the government, as Dahl argued in his famous work *Polyarchy*.[2] But an alternative, much broader and substantive, definition is the classically termed "liberal democracy," and we could also say "substantive," "meaningful," or "inclusive" democracy, moving

---

[1] Alexis de Tocqueville, *Democracy in America* (New York: Saunders and Otley, 1835).
[2] Robert A. Dahl, *Polyarchy. Participation and opposition* (New Haven: Yale University Press, 1971).

from what Habermas called the "procedural" to the "substantive" realm.[3] The so-called Community of Democracies, for example, proposes today among its criteria participation in the organization: free, fair, and periodic elections, a multiparty system, the rule of law, separation of powers, and military accountability to civilian government, as well as a respect for human rights, fundamental freedoms, and the inherent dignity of the human being.[4]

If the minimalist definition was more typical of past democratic studies, today's scholarship on democracy is expanding its definition. More recently, Dahl himself, for example, argued that a democracy requires several political institutions: elected officials; free, fair, and frequent elections; freedom of expression; alternative sources of information; associational autonomy; and inclusive citizenship.[5]

One of the most important scholars on democracy, Charles Tilly,[6] takes the debate between minimalist and substantive definitions of democracy and divides the definitions of democracy into four main approaches: constitutional, substantive, procedural, and process-oriented approaches. For the first one, which looks at formal rules of democracy (for example, presidential or parliamentary systems), the problem is that "large discrepancies between announced principles and daily practices often make constitutions misleading."[7] The substantive approach concentrates on what governments do, not how they are structured, and so if they are more or less inclusive too. However, problems with this approach are the question of what value to assign to the different outcomes and that concentrating only

[3] Michel Rosenfeld, Andrew Arato (ed.), *Habermas on law and democracy: Critical exchanges* (Berkeley: University of California Press, 1998).
[4] The Community of Democracies is an international organization, established in 2000 to bring together governments, civil society, and the private sector in the pursuit of a common goal: supporting democratic rule and strengthening democratic norms and institutions around the world. Participating states pledge to uphold the democratic values expressed in the core principles of the Warsaw Declaration, including "The right of persons belonging to minorities or disadvantaged groups to equal protection of the law, and the freedom to enjoy their own culture, to profess and practice their own religion, and use their own language." From: "The Warsaw Declaration," Community of Democracies, accessed on September 30, 2017. https://www.community-democracies.org/Visioning-Democracy/To-be-a-Democracy-The-Warsaw-Declaration.
[5] Robert A. Dahl, "What political institutions does large-scale democracy require?" *Political Science Quarterly*, 120, 2 (Summer, 2005): 187–197.
[6] Charles Tilly, *Democracy* (New York: Cambridge University Press, 2007).
[7] Tilly, *Democracy*, p. 7.

on the substance of how a government does well *for* the people may neglect the issue of guaranteeing a government *of* and *by* the people. Procedural approaches concentrate on democratic forms, similar to the constitutional ones, and have the opposite problem to the substantive approaches: how to guarantee that the government is *for* the people, with freedoms and equalities. Finally, process-oriented approaches start from individual autonomy and progress to processes that guarantee control over our own individual lives. The problem with concentrating on processes is that it tends to overlook substance without devoting attention to functioning governments.

Therefore, a mix of procedures and substance seems best, taking into account, however, that democratization is a never-ending process of adjustment and renewal, as we can see also in the developed world of so-called mature democracies. For this reason, it is difficult to put countries in boxes like liberal or electoral democracies; it would be more useful to evaluate them based on more or less democratic tendencies in different dimensions. One of the most important dimensions is equality among all citizens, especially minorities.

Tilly spoke specifically about the importance of equal inclusion of citizens in the political sphere. He argued that "democratization never occurs without at least partial realization of three large processes: integration of interpersonal trust networks into public politics; insulation of public politics from categorical inequalities; and elimination or neutralization of autonomous, coercion-controlling power centers in ways that augment the influence of ordinary people over public politics and increase the control of public politics over state performance."[8] Therefore, equal inclusion in public politics (together with the freedoms of expression, association, and demonstration, and other rights) is becoming more and more the fundamental element of democratization and democracy.

Diamond, another well-known scholar in democratic studies, speaks about the importance of substantive definitions of democracy. In particular, he considers four key elements in defining a system of government as a democracy: a political system for choosing and replacing the government through free and fair elections; the active participation of the people, as citizens, in politics and civic life; the protection of the human rights of all citizens; and the rule of law, in which the laws and procedures apply

---

[8] Ibid., p. 78.

equally to all citizens.[9] Together with Morlino, Diamond listed approximately eight dimensions along which democracies may vary in quality: freedom, the rule of law, vertical accountability, responsiveness, equality, participation, competition, and horizontal accountability.[10] Again, equality, participation, and, thus, inclusion of minorities are evidently becoming fundamental features of most definitions of democracy.

Finally, Acemoglu and Robinson recently argued that nations failed in the past and continue to fail today because of a lack of inclusiveness, which means the equal distribution of power in economic and political institutions.[11] They give the examples of South versus North Korea, Botswana versus Zimbabwe, and Congo versus Sierra Leone to explain why some democracies are flourishing countries while others are immersed in poverty and violence. They argue that it is not culture, geography, or history that leads to these outcomes but the differences in inclusiveness: where powerful elites define the rules to benefit themselves and seek exclusive control over government, they limit social progress and inclusion, culminating in a failed state.

Besides scholars of democratic studies, scholars of international relations (IR) theories also analyze the importance of inclusion of minorities. Mansfield and Snyder, for example, argue that emerging democracies are more likely to have instability, and even to initiate wars or intrastate conflict, because of different factions competing for power and nationalist ideology to rally support.[12] Walby maintains that to have modern states in our globalized world, we need to criminalize and delegitimize violence against women and minorities, and to do this we need to grant them more political representation for a deeper democracy based on equality.[13] Fareed Zakaria asserts that democracies are not always "free democracies," as a mix of elections and authoritarianism may produce illiberal democracies

---

[9] Larry Diamond, *Developing democracy: Toward consolidation* (Baltimore: Johns Hopkins University Press, 1999). Also: *What is democracy?* Lecture at Hilla University for Humanistic Studies, January 21, 2004. https://web.stanford.edu/~ldiamond/iraq/WhaIsDemocracy012004.htm.

[10] Larry Diamond and Leonardo Morlino, eds., *Assessing the quality of democracy* (Baltimore: Johns Hopkins University Press, 2005).

[11] Daron Acemoglu and James Robinson, *Why nations fail: The origins of power, prosperity, and poverty* (London: Profile books, 2013).

[12] Edward D. Mansfield and Jack L. Snyder, *Electing to fight: Why emerging democracies go to war* (Cambridge: MIT Press, 2005).

[13] Sylvia Walby, *Globalization and inequalities: Complexity and contested modernities* (Los Angeles: Sage Publications, 2009).

with consequences such as a majority of an electorate denying rights to minorities.[14] Finally, applying critical theory, Young argues that groups excluded based on gender, ethnicity, or class should instead be included because the characteristics of a modern polity should extend to social and economic interactions, giving more equality and justice to everyone.[15] Also in critical theory, the concept of "radical democracy" of Laclau and Mouffe[16] calls for a pluralism of diversity compared to liberal and deliberative democracies, which, in their attempts to build consensus, oppress diversity (similarly to Tocqueville's "tyranny of the majority").

Whatever definition of pluralist democracy we wish to use, the fact remains that to have substantive and not only formal democracies, minorities must be included in the civil and political life of the polity. The importance of inclusive citizenship, multicultural policies, and respect for minority rights therefore is evident not only in fledgling democracies—which need to search for equality and justice to have sustainable transitions, and specifically for Muslim countries of the Middle East that continue to struggle on their democratization path—but also in the maintenance of stable and peaceful societies in mature democracies that today are under stress from economic, identity, and political crises and migration processes.

For these reasons, this study uses a broad definition of democracy[17] that includes the equal participation of all parts of society and the respect for human rights and fundamental freedoms, including minority rights.

INCLUSION VERSUS EXCLUSION OF MINORITIES IN DEMOCRATIZATION PROCESSES

In the latter part of the twentieth and the beginning of twenty-first centuries, Western countries tried to encourage transitions to democracy in different places around the world based on the idea that democracy brings stability and peaceful cohabitation among various parts of society, including

---

[14] Fareed Zakaria, *The future of freedom: Illiberal democracy at home and abroad* (New York: W.W. Norton & Co., 2003).
[15] Iris Marion Young, *Inclusion and democracy* (New York: Oxford University Press, 2000).
[16] Ernesto Laclau and Chantal Mouffe, *Hegemony and socialist strategy: Towards a radical democratic politics* (London: Verso, 1985).
[17] For more broad definitions of democracy (not only minimalist definition of electoral democracy) see also Larry Diamond and Marc Plattner, *Democracy: A reader* (Baltimore: John Hopkins University Press, 2009).

different ethnic groups. However, this conviction—besides not producing a very diplomatic or legitimate foreign policy because of all the risk of "exporting democracy"—seems to forget that democracy is one thing but a transition to democracy is another. Actually, regarding the phase of transition to democracy, there is no consensus in the literature about whether this transition benefits minorities or, on the contrary, if democratization brings more conflict and violence to minorities. Of course, the political reality of this process is that it is not a binary outcome but rather a continuum of possibilities, for minorities as well.

As previously discussed, Mansfield and Snyder found evidence that new democracies are more likely to be unstable, and even to initiate wars or intrastate conflict, because their politics of democratizing are more likely to exhibit exclusionary nationalism and nationalist ideology and because democratization often precedes the institution-building necessary to create strong norms and the rule of law.[18] Bertrand and Haklai[19] instead argued recently that "democratization generally does not produce more violence. Yet it does not necessarily yield substantive equality for ethnic minorities."[20] Their findings, based on the works of many scholars, show that democratization in multiethnic societies is based mostly on procedural democracy, which produces a majority dominance and an ethnocentric leadership, more than liberal or substantive democracy with equal inclusion of all parts. However, they do not find a clear relationship between ethnic violence and democratization. They list three possibilities in the continuum of outcomes for minorities after democratization: violence, stability, or meaningful accommodation.[21] This third one is when minorities can negotiate some satisfaction of their requests, like more power to manage affairs or resources and cultural expression (similar to this study's concept of autonomization).

The very process of democratization therefore should bring minorities' requests to the political arena, with possibilities to create new parties, make free demonstrations, and file petitions to courts. In reality, it does not always happen, nor does the state react positively to these changes. Sometimes transitions make minority situations better, sometimes they

---

[18] Edward D. Mansfield and Jack L. Snyder, *Electing to fight: Why emerging democracies go to war* (Cambridge: MIT Press, 2005).
[19] Jacques Bertrand and Oded Haklai (eds.), *Democratization and ethnic minorities: Conflict or compromise?* (Abingdon: Routledge, 2014).
[20] Ibid., p. 1.
[21] Ibid., p. 3.

just maintain the same status quo from before the democratization, and sometimes they may fuel even more violent conflict. It depends on many factors, among which is whether democratization coincides with state-building, as in post-Communist Europe, with what Brubaker called the "nationalization of nationalism"[22] (that is, a dominant group trying to "own" the state during the transition period), and so with exclusionary policies that privilege the dominant nation.

Even though the topic of this research is not the analysis of the consequences of democratization for ethnic minorities, it is important to understand that democratization does not necessarily lead directly to their inclusion in the polity. This is the fundamental reason why this study is important: to understand the factors in a democratizing process that bring a state to include minorities, negotiating for a minority's autonomy, for example, after decades of violence, or to finally exclude the minority, choosing forms of securitization in order to definitively crush the possibility of an autonomous expression of the ethnic minority itself.

The last issue to consider when discussing democratization and minorities is that a democracy that respects minorities does not have to be a "Western-style" democracy. Different cultures and countries (including, to name just a few, India, Brazil, Senegal, and South Africa) may have different models and practices of democracies with significant variations with respect to the Western liberal democratic practices, even if these variations are not so strong as to transform the democracy into an illiberal or semi-authoritarian state. As a recent study from the Carnegie Endowment for International Peace argues, these democratic variations can be in different areas, including individual rights, economic justice, legal pluralism, power-sharing mechanisms, or alternative forms of civic action and representation. Notably absent from these areas is the treatment of minorities.[23]

One thing is certain: the idea of Fukuyama that Western liberal democracies would have spread around the world—besides risking an ethnocentric imposition of a model on the rest of the world—has been challenged by recent evidence.[24] Non-Western encounters with democracy vary

---

[22] Rogers Brubaker, *Nationalism reframed: Nationhood and the national question in the New Europe* (New York: Cambridge University Press, 1996): 60.

[23] Richard Youngs, *The puzzle of non-Western democracy* (Washington, DC: Carnegie Endowment for International Peace, 2015).

[24] Francis Fukuyama, *The end of history and the last man* (New York: Free Press, 1992).

widely.[25] In Islamic, Confucian and African cultures there is ground for equality but not necessarily based on rational individualism: other values like communal sharing might be more important than the individual rights of the Western concept of democracy.[26] Nonetheless, all democracies must have some form of inclusion of the different parts of societies, including ethnic minorities, in one way or another, in order to consider democratization a real process.

Strategies of Inclusion in Democracies

But how do democracies, either Western or non-Western style, create pluralistic and inclusive systems, in particular with their minorities? Several scholars have made proposals on how to "design democracy" for inclusion and pluralism, and many have argued that some type of "consensual" democracy, in contrast to majoritarian democracy, involves greater compromise and significant minority rights. This is because consensual practices would allow all parts of society to feel included and so to support and legitimize the democracy itself. Let us examine in more detail some of these scholars' works.

Arend Lijphart is one of most important theoreticians of the design of an inclusive system of state and government in ethnically divided societies.[27] Studying in particular the Dutch political system, he speaks about the importance of "politics of accommodation" as a good solution for pluralistic democracies based on cleavages, where ethnic divisions are particularly strong. Studying 36 democracies from 1945 to 1996,[28] he emphasized the "consociational" or "consensus" model of democracy as a better solution for states in which a traditional majoritarian or "Westminster" model of democracy might not work owing to deep ethnic, linguistic, or

---

[25] See on this also Christopher K. Lamont, Jan van der Harst, and Frank Gaenssmantel (eds.), *Non-Western encounters with democratization* (Surrey: Ashgate Publishing Limited, 2015).

[26] See on this, among many, Diego Von Vacano, "Is democracy a Western idea?" *Washington Post*, January 8, 2014, accessed September 30, 2017. https://www.washingtonpost.com/news/monkey-cage/wp/2014/01/08/is-democracy-a-western-idea.

[27] Arend Lijphart, *The politics of accommodation: Pluralism and democracy in the Netherlands* (Berkeley: University of California Press 1968).

[28] Arend Lijphart, *Democracy in plural societies: A comparative exploration* (New Haven: Yale University Press, 1977), and Arend Lijphart, *Patterns of democracy: government forms and performance in 36 countries* (New Haven: Yale University Press, 1999).

religious cleavages. This happens first of all, according to Lijphart, because the consensual model involves the presence of inclusive cabinet coalitions, inclusive governments based on a power-sharing system. This system acknowledges specific constitutional rights for minorities (as we can see, for example, in the cases of Switzerland and Belgium) in the implementation of multiparty systems, proportional electoral systems, minority veto, and constitutions protected by judicial review. These institutions guarantee that only an inclusive "supermajority" can control the policies of a state and that the state's ability to infringe on minority rights will be limited. Specifically, to avoid group polarization, the elites of major minority groups are given some form of representation, and the groups themselves are given some communal rights, giving both the elites the incentive to remain in the government and the population the incentive to avoid violent conflict.

Nevertheless, the division of power can not only happen at the governmental level with a power-sharing system, but it can also be distributed among separate political institutions.[29] This is the case, for example, of federal states, which can be either centralized or decentralized with local autonomies. Lijphart actually divides the 36 democracies that he analyzes between "unitary versus federal" and "centralized versus decentralized" states, creating four categories, with decentralization being either in a unitary state (like the Scandinavian states of Norway, Finland, Sweden, and Denmark, or like Japan) or in a federal state (like Switzerland, Belgium, Germany, Canada, the United States, and Australia). One of the case studies of this research, Indonesia, can be put in the category of decentralization in a unitary state. Therefore, a consociational system is characterized not only by power-sharing but also by a decentralization of authority to groups and regions, as well as some autonomy in the sphere of culture to minorities with cultural rights (such as language and educational rights). This is why the power-sharing theory of Lijphart is close to the autonomization concept expressed in this book and so is taken as its theoretical basis, as explained later in this chapter.

Another scholar who has argued that ethnically divided democracies must pay special attention to the problem of inclusion of minorities to prevent ethnic conflict is Donald Horowitz.[30] Democracy, according to

---

[29] Lijphart, 1999, pp. 185–200.
[30] Donald L. Horowitz, "Democracy in divided societies," *Journal of Democracy*, 4, 4 (October 1993): 18–38.

Horowitz, has progressed faster in Eastern European states with few ethnic cleavages (Hungary, Czech Republic, Poland) and slower in deeply divided states (Slovakia, Bulgaria, Romania, and the former Yugoslavia) precisely because of this lack of careful inclusive institution-building. Horowitz proposes not a consensual system like Lijphart but a "centripetal" system that promotes intercommunal alliances and discourages the polarization that will happen if ethnic identities are institutionalized (in some way, an ethnic version of the confessionalism evident, for example, in the case of Lebanon).

Andrew Reynolds, following the tradition of both Lijphart and Horowitz, focuses on how to design democracy in recent postconflict cases, including Iraq, Afghanistan, Sudan, Burma, and Lebanon, among a total of 66 countries.[31] For Reynolds, political inclusion utilizing constitutional engineering offers the best solution to resolve conflicts, including ethnic conflicts, even if there is no perfect solution valid for everyone: democracy must be home-grown and appropriate to a given society. John Dryzek is another scholar who argues that democratization is a matter of political inclusion of different groups and categories, not only in the state but in the polity in general.[32] In particular, he gives importance to "deliberative democracy" in divided societies, arguing that authentic deliberation, not mere voting, solves the problems stemming from the assertions of various communities, and the power-sharing system is the best solution.[33] Finally, Reilly, studying cases like Papua New Guinea, Sri Lanka, and Northern Ireland, argues that if political institutions promote political parties that have a broad base, inclusive of different ethnic groups and minorities, they can create healthy and moderate political competition to improve their democratic transitions.[34]

As we can see, according to several scholars, there are many possible channels and tools by which to build inclusive democracies, and even if we do not have conclusive evidence of which model is more suitable to avoid conflict and polarization and to increase stability in democratizing

---

[31] Andrew Reynolds, *Designing democracy in a dangerous world* (Oxford: Oxford University Press, 2011).

[32] John S. Dryzek, "Political inclusion and the dynamics of democratization," *American Political Science Review*, 90, 3 (September 1996): 475–487.

[33] John S. Dryzek, "Deliberative democracy in divided societies: Alternatives to agonism and analgesia," *Political Theory*, 33, 2 (April 2005): 218–242.

[34] Ben Reilly, *Democracy in divided societies: Electoral engineering for conflict management* (New York: Cambridge University Press, 2001).

countries, we must take into account the pluralistic needs of an inclusive democracy in divided societies. But to analyze the different models of inclusion of minorities in democratization processes is not the focus of this study. This study aims to analyze the variables that affect the exclusion or inclusion of minorities in states, specifically in Muslim-majority countries, during a democratization period. In particular, it examines two types of exclusion/inclusion of minorities: securitization and autonomization. Let us now examine the definitions of these terms more closely.

Outcomes of Theoretical Interest: Securitization and Autonomization

Securitization

McGarry and O'Leary argued that to manage pluralistic societies and regulate ethnic conflict, states resort either to the management of differences or to their elimination.[35] In the first case, they can chose between hegemonic control (such as ethnic minorities in Burundi or in the case of Northern Ireland between 1920 and 1972)[36], arbitration (as in the case of the European Community for Yugoslavia), cantonization or federalism (as in Switzerland, Belgium, and Canada), or finally consociationalism or power-sharing (the Lijphart system, such as for Western Europe but also Lebanon and Malaysia). When states want to eliminate differences, they can resort to partition or secession (as occurred with Bangladesh and Pakistan), assimilate the different ethnicities (as has occurred in the United States and the UK, or, among developing countries, in Burma, Sudan, and Iraq) or, in the worst scenario, states can either force mass population transfers (such as when Palestinians were expelled from Israel and today with Rohingya in Burma) or choose genocide (from the Holocaust to the Kurdish genocidal campaign in Iraq in 1988). However, states that opt for more centralization and exclusionary nationalism—what Mc Garry and O'Leary call "eliminating differences"—may also use a strategy of "securitization" of their minorities.

Securitization is a process of treating an issue outside the political arena, with only security means, in particular with a state-security orientation.

---

[35] John McGarry and Brendan O'Leary, *The politics of ethnic conflict regulation: Case studies of protracted ethnic conflicts* (New York: Routledge, 1993).
[36] Ibid., p. 23.

This concept of securitization is a constructivist theory based on a process of broadening security concepts, formulated by the Copenhagen School after the Cold War. Unlike the deepening of the security concept (also from the critical theory approach) that considers individuals, and no longer only states, as primary subjects of security (opening up space for the concept of "human security"), the broadening of security still considers states to be the main subject of security but expand the security arena of states. This is because, according to the Copenhagen School, the classical threat perception and traditional security studies could no longer represent the post-Cold War situation, with the growth of intrastate conflicts and global threats like migrations, pollution, and epidemics. International relations theory, including security, needed, therefore, to expand the security concept to other spheres.[37]

On this path the Copenhagen School described the "securitization theory," which argues that when a state labels something a "security" issue, it gives it a sense of urgency that justifies special measures to deal with it outside the political arena. In their famous book that launched this theory, Buzan, Wæver, and de Wilde described securitization as an "extreme version of politicization,"[38] a process that happens when one issue is promoted from the nonpoliticized (when the state does not deal with it) to the politicized arena (entering the sphere of public policy and governance) and is finally securitized (creating an existential threat that cannot be treated in the political arena but only through emergency measures). When this happens, the "securitizing actors" pass from the political sphere, the "marketplace of ideas" where everything can be negotiated and addressed by policies, to a nonpolitical but politicized space beyond the ordinary norms of the political domain that is based on extreme security measures. As Wæver puts it: "by uttering 'security,' a state-representative moves a particular development into a specific area, and thereby claims a special right to use whatever means are necessary to block it."[39]

Specifically, securitization is a process based on three elements[40]: (a) the referent objects, or objects that can be existentially threatened. First of all, it is the state and the nation (meaning sovereignty and identity) that

---

[37] Barry Buzan and Lene Hansen, *The evolution of international security studies* (Cambridge: Cambridge University Press, 2009): 187.

[38] Barry Buzan, Ole Waever, Jaap de Wilde, *Security: A new framework for analysis* (Boulder: Lynne Rienner Publishers, 1998).

[39] Ole Wæver, "Securitization and desecuritization," in *On security,* ed. R. Lipschutz (New York: Columbia University Press, 1995): 54–55.

[40] Barry Buzan, Ole Waever, Jaap de Wilde, *Security: A new framework for analysis* (Boulder: Lynne Rienner Publishers, 1998): 36

represent the traditional "middle-level limited collectivities"[41]; (b) the securitizing actors, like governments, political elites, and military or civil society, that perform the so-called security speech act,[42] declaring the referent object to be existentially threatened; and (c) the functional actors who influence decisions on security or who have a stake in the issue, like a private company or a political party that will benefit from the securitization process.

The securitization process generally happens in two stages.[43] The first stage is based on identifying an issue or an actor as an existential threat to the referent objects. In the second stage, the audience (public opinion, politicians, or other elites) is convinced by the securitizing actors, through a new narrative, the so-called speech act,[44] about the extraordinary measures needed. We could say that this second phase is more successful in dictatorial or militaristic states than in democracies, as propaganda tools are stronger in the creation of an "us-versus-them" narrative. But the speech act of stigmatization, and thus securitization of an issue, can happen in democracies as well. This study is based on the argument that this is what happened with the Kurdish issue in Turkey.

Regarding specifically the securitization of minorities, other than a few authors, the literature concentrates mostly on migrants, specifically in Western countries. Kymlicka[45] is one author who assesses the securitization of minorities using the concept of Weaver. According to Kymlicka, the securitization of minorities, and in general of ethnic relations, erodes both the democratic space and the possibility to respond to demands of minorities.[46] In particular, analyzing the countries in transition of Central and Eastern Europe in the 1990s, he argues that "there is enormous resistance in virtually every ECE[47] country to the idea of federalism or

---

[41] Ibid., 36.

[42] Ibid., 40.

[43] Ralf Emmers, "Securitization," in *Contemporary security studies,* ed. Allan Collins (Oxford: Oxford University Press, 2007): 111–113.

[44] The speech act is when the securitizing actor declares the referent object as existentially threatened. See Buzan et al., 40.

[45] Will Kymlicka, "Justice and security in the accommodation of minority nationalism," in *The politics of belonging: Nationalism, liberalism, and pluralism,* ed. Alain Dieckhoff (Lanham: Lexington Books, 2004).

[46] Will Kymlicka, *Politics in the vernacular: Nationalism, multiculturalism, and citizenship* (Oxford: Oxford University Press, 2002): 21.

[47] The term Central and Eastern Europe (CEE) has today displaced the alternative term East Central Europe (ECE) in the context of transition countries.

other forms of territorial autonomy to several national minorities."[48] This is also because of their "security objection," the national security issue that minorities represent, based on the notion that minorities are disloyal (collaborating with past, current, and potential enemies) and strong states need weak minorities. In this way they need to securitize them.[49]

To escape this vicious cycle of repression and delegitimization, therefore, a minority needs to be "desecuritized." The desecuritization process is supported by the Copenhagen School and in particular by Wæver as necessary in order to go back to the political arena in democracies.[50] Some scholars like Aras and Polat state that several factors can push towards desecuritization, among which is the pressure of international actors.[51] For example, the democratization process of a country, with the erosion of military power and the inclusion of civil society and media, or external actors such as the EU have been pushing Turkey in the direction of a more liberal and pluralistic approach to the minority issue.[52] This can be considered a desecuritization phase, on which more later.

But what scholars have treated the Kurdish case as being related to the securitization theory? One that has studied the securitization of Kurds in Turkey is Birdisli.[53] He argues that Turkish leaders have viewed Kurdish demands for autonomy and identity as a threat to national integrity, which is why the state has used extraordinary security measures during the history of the republic. These extraordinary measures have included first of all military intervention, with hundreds of thousands of Kurds forced to resettle in the western region or go in exile outside Turkey, in particular following military coups. Political restrictions have also been imposed, with 58 political parties banned between 1924 and 2009, 8 of which were related to the Kurdish minority. Finally, the state also pushed for the assimilation of Kurds through nationalist education, with the teaching of one nation, one language, and one identity.[54]

---

[48] Ibid., p. 131.
[49] Ibid., p. 138.
[50] Ole Wæver, "Securitization and desecuritization," in *On security*, ed. Ronny Lipschutz (New York: Columbia University Press, 1995): 46–86.
[51] Bülent Aras and Rabia Karakaya Polat, "From conflict to cooperation: Desecuritization of Turkey's relations with Syria and Iran," *Security Dialogue* 39(5) (2008): 495–515.
[52] Ibid., p. 499.
[53] Fikret Birdisli, "Securitization of Kurdish question in Turkey," *International Journal of Research in Social Sciences*, Vol. 4, No. 2 (June 2014): 1.
[54] Ibid., 9–10.

Another scholar who has analyzed the repression of Kurds during the history of the Turkish Republic is Kadıoğlu. In a situation resembling securitization, Kadıoğlu[55] applies Giorgio Agamben's argument about a permanent "state of exception"[56] to the Kurdish case. He argues that the state of exception was applied for the first time in 1925 after the first Kurdish rebellion, but since 1984 the military has used a "rhetoric of necessity" to reproduce this state permanently. This state of exception for the Kurds might resemble the securitization phase as, according to Kadıoğlu, after 1980's military coup it was based on the visible and active presence of armed forces in the so-called OHAL region,[57] on the imprisonment of many Kurdish intellectuals and activists, and on controlling the daily lives of Kurds, including extreme measures like the internal displacement of Kurdish citizens or the presence of "village guards" (that became paramilitaries of the state, often turning the villages into detention camps).[58] Almost 30,000 lives were lost, and "The Kurds of Turkey found themselves in a permanent state of exception."[59] After 1999, the state of exception might have given space to a so-called postexceptional state, but in reality the repression of Kurdish parties and the operations of Turkish armed forces demonstrated, as Kadıoğlu again says, that the policy still left Turkey's Kurdish issue in the security arena. Thus, Kadıoğlu concludes, in Turkey, "the rhetoric of the need to 'preserve a state with its nation' has consistently contributed to the justification of the state of exception."[60] Other scholars also speak about a state of exception. Kurban, for example, argues that "since the establishment of the Republic in 1923, some form

---

[55] Ayşe Kadıoğlu, "Necessity and the state of exception: The Turkish state's permanent war with its Kurdish citizens," in *Turkey between nationalism and globalization*, ed. Riva Kastoryano (London and New York: Routledge, 2013).

[56] Giorgio Agamben, *State of exception* (Chicago: University of Chicago Press, 2005). Agamben argues that the state of exception (Carl Schmitt's concept regarding the ability of a state to transcend the rule of law in the name of the public good) became in the twentieth century a normal phase of democratic governments instead of their "exception."

[57] The OHAL region (in Turkish: Olağanüstü Hâl Bölge Valiliği, English: Governorship of Region in State of Emergency) was a region in Kurdistan created by the Turkish state in 1987, after the state of emergency legislation was passed to deal with the Turkish–Kurdish conflict, until 2002.

[58] Kadıoğlu, *Necessity and the state of exception*, 150–151.

[59] Ibid., 153.

[60] Ibid., 156.

of state of exception was operative in Turkey most of the time."[61] The state of exception therefore can be considered one of the "extraordinary measures" typical of the securitization process, if not *the* extraordinary measure *par excellance*, that has been carried out with respect to the Kurdish minority in a continuum of Turkish history, because the most important feature of the securitization process is to put an issue above politics, and the state of exception is exactly that: to move an issue beyond the "game rules."

Therefore, using the Buzan, Wæver, and de Wilde structure, we can provide a brief application of the three elements of securitization to the Kurdish case. Regarding the referent objects—that is, objects that can be existentially threatened—in the Turkish case these objects have been represented by the sovereignty, the unity, and the identity of the country. Turkish sovereignty and identity are evidently existentially threatened by the Kurdish claim of autonomy and perhaps even independence in the future. Regarding securitizing actors, these have been primarily the Turkish government and its political elites, who have used the so-called security speech act to declare the referent objects as existentially threatened, in order to escalate the conflict with the PKK, stigmatize the political wings of the Kurdish minority, and marginalize them in the political arena. But the Turkish military, which performed the actual "security action" with the militarization of the Kurdish region and the conflict itself, has also been a securitizing actor. Finally, regarding the functional actors—the actors that influence decisions on security since they have a stake in the issue—these are represented by nonstate actors, first and foremost the mass media, which contributed to the creation of the narrative of "us-versus-them" and the delegitimization of the political factions of the minority as supporting terrorists or wanting separatism.[62] But the political parties that have benefited from the securitization process have also been functional actors; this means above all the political parties that ruled Turkey previously, like the Republican People's Party (CHP) and the Nationalist Movement Party (MHP), but also today's AKP, which has

---

[61] Dilek Kurban, "The Kurdish question: Law, politics and the limits of recognition," in, *Turkey's democratization process*, eds. C. Rodriguez, A. Avalos, H. Yilmaz, and A. Planet (Abingdon: Routledge, 2014), 346.

[62] See on this Derya Erdem, "The representation of the Democratic Society Party (DTP) in the mainstream Turkish media," in C. Gunes and W. Zeydanlioglu, eds., *The Kurdish question in Turkey: New perspectives on violence, representation and reconciliation* (Abingdon: Routledge, 2014).

benefited recently from resecuritization, as explained later on in the chapter. The political parties always compete for power and thus clearly strongly benefit from the securitization of a possible threat, like the Kurdish issue, in order to present themselves as the guardians of the security and safety of the people, the nation, and the state. The ten percent vote threshold for parliamentary elections in Turkey's proportional representation system—the highest threshold in the world—also gave existing parties strong incentives to keep the Kurdish issue in the security sphere, practically eliminating the possibility of a Kurdish party winning seats in Parliament (at least until 2015, when a Kurdish party gained seats in Parliament, becoming the third largest parliamentary group).

Autonomization

Following the method of management of differences of McGarry and O'Leary,[63] and in particular their case of cantonization or federalism, we can say that in addition, states can resort to some form of policies of regional autonomy in order to manage ethnic differences, especially after a period of repression/securitization of an ethnic conflict. Actually, in democratizing regimes, when states opt to manage minorities by decentralization, they face a dilemma of how much autonomy to give to the minority groups, particularly in peripheral regions. The solutions of possible conflicts with these minority groups to avoid secession (as happened in the former Yugoslavia, for example) range from a semi-independent state (such as the two administrative entities in Bosnia and Herzegovina) to some form of autonomy inside the state (as in the case of Kurdistan in Iraq or Northern Ireland in the UK).

This type of territorial autonomy, which eventually also becomes economic, political, and cultural autonomy—because the decentralization of governance allows the minority to manage some of its resources, protect its cultural identity, and have some form of local administration—could be called "autonomization" because sovereignty remains at the nation-state level. This study therefore defines the process of giving some type of autonomy as autonomization of the minority, as juxtaposed to its securitization, which is at the opposite end of the spectrum of methods of dealing with the incorporation of a minority. Autonomization can be defined as

---

[63] John McGarry and Brendan O'Leary, *The politics of ethnic conflict regulation: Case studies of protracted ethnic conflicts* (New York: Routledge, 1993).

the realization of policies of autonomy in relation to a minority, either through a peace-mediation process, after an ethnic conflict, or a reform process of decentralization of the state with more autonomy given to an ethnic minority. So what theoretical categories and scholars allow us to define this process of autonomization?

Already Dahl[64] had written about the importance of autonomy in pluralist democracies, arguing that all types of social organizations in a democracy require some form of independence or autonomy of communities besides control. He was referring to every type of inequality and diversity: "Like polyarchies, authoritarian regimes exist in countries with varying amounts of diversity…[and] potential cleavages appear to exist along every kind of difference that is familiar in democratic countries: language, ethnic group, race, religion, status, occupation, ideology."[65] Among the problems associated with pluralism, he listed functions of variations in national regimes, including conflict and cleavages. Diamond also argues that federalism and other forms of decentralization can strengthen democracy, with greater stability and unity that reduces the risk of secession. As illustrations he uses the examples of India, Spain, Mexico, and Nigeria versus Sudan and Sri Lanka, which instead experienced increasing conflict and refrained from granting more autonomy and decentralization. Incidentally, Diamond spoke about this also in a conference in Baghdad in 2004,[66] arguing for the importance of federalism in building a peaceful and democratic state in Iraq and avoiding the risk of breakup of the country. As is well known, instead of following the advice of a world expert on democracy, in 2006 the USA turned to al-Maliki as the candidate for the new government,[67] and things went quite bad after that.

As stated earlier, among studies of decentralization and policies of autonomy, the two most important scholars for the inclusion of minorities, one in the sense of minority rights the other in the sense of power-sharing

---

[64] Robert A. Dahl, *Dilemmas of pluralist democracy: Autonomy vs. control* (New Haven: Yale University Press, 1982).

[65] Ibid., p. 41.

[66] Larry Diamond, "Why decentralize power in a democracy?," Conference on Fiscal and Administrative Decentralization, 2/12/2004, accessed September 30, 2017. https://web.stanford.edu/~ldiamond/iraq/Decentralize_Power021204.htm.

[67] Warren Strobel, Missy Ryan, David Rohde, and Ned Parker, *Special report: How Iraq's Maliki defined limits of U.S. power*, Reuters, 6/30/2014, accessed September 30, 2017. http://www.reuters.com/article/2014/06/30/us-iraq-security-maliki-specialreport-idUSKBN0F51HK20140630.

and administrative decentralization, are Kymlicka in cultural studies and Lijphart in democratic studies. Kymlicka[68] argues that the practice of pluralistic democracies should be based on a multicultural approach to membership, a "diverse citizenship" that grants equal membership to political communities, including minority groups. Furthermore, Kymlicka[69] claims that community rights should supplement individual human rights, with some form of power-sharing or federalism, in order to guarantee justice for national minorities. According to Kymlicka, nationalism and multiculturalism or cosmopolitanism should not be considered opposite or incompatible, but instead as complementary in the creation of a "liberal nationalism," with either some form of "substate nationalism" for immigrated minorities or some form of cultural protection and self-government rights to indigenous minorities. This second form is the process defined as autonomization analyzed in this study.

Other authors agree with Kymlicka's position. Gutmann,[70] for example, argues that individual and group rights should both exist in a democracy, and identity politics should not be suppressed because they support justice and democracy for all groups. Miller[71] too agrees that nationalism and cosmopolitanism are not necessarily in conflict, as the principles of nationality can accommodate the demands of minority nations and does not necessarily lead to secession. This is an important claim for all modern countries, not only democratizing states, in this phase of migrations and crisis at different levels, but also in Western countries, where the failure of both assimilation and multiculturalism policies is pushing nations in the direction of old nationalisms and tribalisms.[72]

As noted earlier, Lijphart[73] has spoken about power-sharing systems for states and governments in ethnically divided societies. Regarding his concept of "consociational democracy" specifically, he claims that this type of inclusive democracy is based on power-sharing but also group autonomy,

[68] Will Kymlicka and W. J. Norman, *Citizenship in diverse societies* (Oxford: Oxford University Press, 2001).

[69] Will Kymlicka, *Politics in the vernacular: Nationalism, multiculturalism, and citizenship* (Oxford: Oxford University Press, 2002).

[70] Amy Gutmann, *Identity in democracy* (Princeton: Princeton University Press, 2004).

[71] David L. Miller, *Citizenship and national identity* (Cambridge: Polity, 2000).

[72] Koert Debeuf, "Tribalisation, or the end of globalization," *EU Observer*, December 8, 2015, accessed September 30, 2017. https://euobserver.com/opinion/131413.

[73] Arend Lijphart, *The politics of accommodation; pluralism and democracy in the Netherlands* (Berkeley: University of California Press 1968).

proportional system, and minority veto rights.[74] Autonomization processes therefore include legislative and executive systems and state decentralization, as analyzed by Lijphart, as well as a cultural approach to pluralism and inclusion, as emphasized by Kymlicka.

In the Aceh case, it is clear the autonomization process following the end of the armed conflict and negotiations led to the emergence of an autonomous region in Aceh and granted it cultural and social rights (including the possibility of applying Sharia law). Other examples of very successful autonomization events besides Aceh could be cited as well, in particular Northern Ireland, Kurdistan Iraq, and Macedonia. Lyon[75] gives the example of Macedonia to show how decentralization really can help to reduce ethnic discrimination in divided societies and multiethnic states and, by extension, the risk of conflict or secession. Political, administrative, and fiscal dimensions of decentralization are important, according to the author, but the fundamental factor in making decentralization and self-government successful is that it must be "substantive" and not only formal. Another interesting prospective case of autonomization is Morocco, which has considered autonomization for the Western Sahara since 2006. This case has several features that could make it emblematic. First of all, the ceasefire has remained in place since 1991 (the conflict started in 1976) thanks in part to the intervention of foreign countries and the United Nations. Second, the presence of a Moroccan Autonomy Plan, which is still under negotiation, allows for space and time to make it better and more sustainable. Finally, this process could benefit from further democratization of the Moroccan regime, which seems to be on the right path toward more reforms. Morocco is probably the only positive example of democratization efforts in the wake of the Arab Spring, together with Tunisia, because even if it is a constitutional monarchy, it has an elected parliament and an independent judiciary that were given more power following the protests. The process of autonomization of the Western Sahara could arrive at a final solution with this gradual reform process of the Moroccan state, but this book analyzes the autonomization process of Indonesia in its Aceh region and the securitization of Kurds in Turkey. Thus, let us now consider the theoretical basis of the four factors, or

[74] Arend Lijphart, "Constitutional design for divided societies," *Journal of Democracy*, Volume 15, Number 2 April 2004.
[75] Aisling Lyon, *Decentralization and the management of ethnic conflict: lessons from the Republic of Macedonia* (New York: Routledge, 2015).

independent variables, that this study analyzes to understand why one country went in one direction and the other in the opposite direction during their phases of democratization.

Independent Variables. Four Schools: Rationalism, Structuralism, Historical Institutionalism, and Critical Theory

This study examines four different sets of variables, based on four main theoretical approaches in comparative analysis, that may account for the difference between the securitization and autonomization of our cases. The first set is based on rational choice theory, the second on an international structuralist approach, the third on a historical-institutionalist approach, and the fourth on critical theory using a psychosocial-identity framework.

(1) Rational Choice Theory: Elites and Power Interests

There is a solid consensus in the literature that the power interests of the ruling elites decide what approach a state will take with respect to dealing with minorities and specifically to constructing minority identities and identity conflicts to take advantage of clashes (*divide et impera*, "divide and rule," from Latin). First of all, Fearon and Laitin[76] famously argued that ethnic identities are socially constructed to incite ethnic violence with the goal of enhancing elite power. Their argument is that elites compete with each other for power, so they deliberately construct ethnic identities with individual actions or with "supraindividual" discourses of ethnicity that motivate actions (similar to the speech act of securitization). But already ten years before them Paul Brass published his *Ethnicity and Nationalism: Theory and Comparison*,[77] in which he made two arguments: that ethnicity and nationalism were social and political constructions and that they were modern phenomena strictly related to the centralizing state. He presented, with a rationalist approach, the theory of "elite competition," arguing that in the early modernizing societies, both ethnicity

---

[76] James D. Fearon and David D. Laitin, "Violence and the social construction of ethnic identity," *International Organization*, Volume 54, Issue 04 (Autumn 2000): 845–877.

[77] Paul R Brass, *Ethnicity and nationalism: Theory and comparison* (Los Angeles: Sage Publications, 1991).

and nationalism were products of conflict between the leadership of centralized states and the elites of nondominant ethnic groups.

Besides constructing ethnicities, elites may promote national policies in order to maintain power. Some ethno-nationalist theorists argue that it is the elite interest that determines a state's approach to minorities. According to Marx,[78] for example, elites intentionally use nationalist policies to create inner group cohesion. Gill[79] instead argues that politicians and religious actors conduct a cost–benefit analysis and then decide on restrictions against religious minorities. In connection with the ethnic-cleansing politics of the former Yugoslavia, several authors show the importance of the construction of ethnic identity. Gagnon,[80] for example, illustrates how the political and economic elites in Yugoslavia created sectarian ethnic conflicts in order to block the dynamics of political change, manipulating populations that were threatening the existing structures of power. Kaufman[81] shows instead how the construction of identities was based more on symbolic narratives and symbolic politics. In particular, he argues that ethnic conflicts in the former Yugoslavia were based not on ancient hatreds but on "myths and symbols," the narratives that the ethnic groups tell about themselves. Finally, Petersen[82] argues that, precisely in order to escape the Western rational way of thinking based on "carrots and sticks," elites in the former Yugoslavia used emotions like fear, anger, and vengeance as resources for their political goals (similarly to Kalyvas and his analysis of the Algerian war).[83] Thus, as is evident, the elites have several tools at their disposal for constructing ethnic identities and formulating policies to repress or exclude minorities.

Furthermore, in the democratization phase, in particular when the transition starts, political elites may change strategies with respect to

---

[78] Anthony W. Marx, "The nation-state and its exclusions," *Political Science Quarterly* 117, No. 1 (2002): 103–126.

[79] Anthony Gill, "The political origins of religious liberty," *Interdisciplinary Journal of Research on Religion* 1 (2005).

[80] V. P. Gagnon, Jr., *The myth of ethnic war: Serbia and Croatia in the 1990s* (Ithaca: Cornell University Press, 2004).

[81] Stuart J. Kaufman, *Modern hatreds: The symbolic politics of ethnic war* (Ithaca: Cornell University Press, 2001).

[82] Roger Dale Petersen, *Western intervention in the Balkans: The strategic use of emotion in conflict* (New York: Cambridge University Press, 2011).

[83] Stathis N. Kalyvas, "Wanton and senseless? The logic of massacres in Algeria," *Rationality and Society*, 11, No. 3 (1999): 243–286.

minorities to gain advantages from the changed situation. Snyder[84] famously argued that elites promote nationalism once they fear the loss of power. For this reason, many democratic transitions often do not merely fail to prevent but actually cause nationalist conflicts, with elites appealing to parochial arguments to mobilize support, thereby creating more interethnic conflict. Rotchild[85] and Young[86] also argue that democratization can sometimes be associated with ethnic tensions and conflicts. Rotchild in particular argues that the Burundi civil war in 1993/1994 was a direct consequence of elites' attempts to make gains from the mobilization of ethnic identities stemming from democratization. Sometimes violence can come even from intragroup competition because democratization attracts more organizations that compete to represent an ethnic group.[87]

But elites do not always manipulate and reconstruct identities for political gain, nor do ethnic groups split into different political groups creating polarization that can cause more violence. Sometimes peaceful compromise can happen, in particular when elites strike a bargain for ethnic group representation, as in Taiwan's transition,[88] or when dominant elites limit democratization using ethnically based redistributive policies to avoid ceding power to extremist elites, which would create polarization. This was the case in Sri Lanka and Malaysia. Both started as highly inclusive democratic governments in their transitions, which coincided with their postcolonial independence, but as interethnic cooperation worsened, the elites used democratic competition to maintain their dominance with these

---

[84] Jack Snyder, *From voting to violence: Democratization and nationalist conflict* (New York: Norton, 2000).

[85] Donald Rotchild, "Liberalism, democracy and conflict management," in A. Wimmer et al (eds.), *Facing ethnic conflicts: Toward a new realism* (Lanham: Rowman & Littlefield, 2004).

[86] Crawford Young, "The heart of the African conflict zone: Democratization, ethnicity, civil conflict and the Great Lakes," *Annual Review of Political Science*, 9 (2006): 302–328.

[87] Jacquest Bertrand and Sanjay Jeram, "Democratization and determinants of ethnic violence: The rebel-moderate organization nexus," Ch. 6 in Jacques Bertrand and Oded Haklai (eds.), *Democratization and ethnic minorities: Conflict or compromise?* (Abingdon: Routledge, 2014).

[88] Andre Laliberte, "Democratization and recognition of difference in a Chinese society: The Taiwanese experience," Ch. 7 in Jacques Bertrand and Oded Haklai (eds.), *Democratization and ethnic minorities: Conflict or compromise?* (Abingdon: Routledge, 2014).

redistributive policies.[89] Nevertheless, these finally became exclusionary policies, in particular in Sri Lanka with the Tamil insurrection in the 1980s.

Therefore, we can state four main points of a rational choice approach to elites: (1) elites seek to preserve their status and power in a rational cost–benefit calculation; (2) elites craft policies toward minorities that seek to divide their opponents, and thus preserve power, sometimes even socially constructing ethnic identities; (3) because democratization creates pluralism, it can actually increase intragroup competition among minorities that skillful elites can exploit; and (4) growing ethnic tensions thus create incentives for autonomization or securitization.

(2) International Structure: International Factors/Geopolitical Situation

Since the breakthrough studies on geopolitics of Mackinder,[90] almost a century ago, IR theories have examined geography as a fundamental variable in their analyses. Without going to the extremes of environmental determinism, the concept of geopolitics has continued to this day to influence international studies and comparative politics. This perspective argues that there is no public policy, either international or domestic, that can disregard the fact that political processes are affected by geographical structures. Many political actions in the past and even today are justified on the basis of economic-geographical or political-geographical needs, from invasion and seizure of other lands, as in Ukraine, to the maintenance of the status quo without allowing territorial decentralizations, as in the Kurdish region of Turkey.[91]

Actually, the first factor that a casual observer of these two cases would say is important in the final different outcomes is the human and geographical one. The fact that Aceh represents only a small tip of the island

---

[89] Brian Shoup, "Ethnically based redistributive policies in democratizing bipolar states," Ch. 8 in Jacques Bertrand and Oded Haklai (eds.) *Democratization and ethnic minorities: Conflict or compromise?* (Abingdon: Routledge, 2014).

[90] Halford John Mackinder, *Democratic ideals and reality: A study in the politics of reconstruction* (New York: H. Holt and Company, 1919).

[91] Actually, Mackinder can also be considered a supporter of decentralization ante litteram, as he argued that modern human societies should return to more human-scale provinces and cities, like the ancient Greek city-states or Renaissance communes, so that national organization of the state can be based on decentralized and autonomous communities. See Mackinder 1919, Ch. 7, "The freedom of men."

of Sumatra with its small population, while the Kurdish region represents a big part of Turkish territory, with a gigantic population, could have had an influence on the political decisions regarding autonomy or securitization. But sometimes reality is a little more complex than just territory and population. Actually, while Kurdistan has no natural resources, Aceh has many, and while the Kurdistan region is very much underdeveloped compared with the rest of Turkey, the Aceh region was not so different in its development from many other areas of Indonesia. Usually, when a particular region is rich in natural resources and does well in general development, the state does not want to lose those resource to minorities, while minorities wants their independence so they can manage the resources within their territories (as one might argue was the case with Aceh). Instead, usually when a region has no resources and is rather poor, the state may be interested in some form of decentralization, but the minorities will not necessarily want that (as one might argue was the case with the Houthi in Yemen, but not in the Kurdish Turkish case). In addition, because differences in the sizes of populations and territories have always existed, this human and geographical variable cannot explain the policy changes between autonomization and securitization for both Turkey and Indonesia at different moments. Therefore, there is no clarity on how this geographical-material variable may have ultimately affected the two cases.

Nevertheless, there is evidence that human and political geography still matters in our cases, in particular because the regional situations may have affected the domestic treatment of minorities. In increasingly hostile regional environments like the Middle East, the fear of transnational support and spillover effects of minority conflicts can worsen the treatment of minorities, threatening the sovereignty of the nation-state. If minorities receive economic support from the diaspora community or other governments, or if they enjoy advocacy support from the international community, either governmental or nongovernmental, then these could also impact the state's treatment of those minorities.

In addition, if a minority dwells in several bordering states (as often happens), the state tends to feel threatened and so tends to favor repression over accommodation and securitization over autonomization. As noted earlier, a state rarely will be inclusive with respect to a minority if it feels that this minority represents the fifth column of a foreign country, as

Weiner argues.[92] An important scholar who analyzed how the regional situation and the foreign policies of a state affect its treatment of ethnic minorities is Harris Mylonas.[93] Studying the Balkan case, he explains systematically how the politics of ethnicity in the international arena can influence which ethnic minorities are assimilated, accommodated, or annihilated. He argues that the foreign policy of a state in the nation-building process—either revisionist or accepting the international status quo—and its relations with the external patrons of minority groups—either in alliance or rivalry—will influence policies towards ethnic minority groups. In particular, if the external patrons of an ethnic group are an enemy of the host state, then the state will undoubtedly use repression, whereas if it is an ally, then accommodation may be the policy of choice. Cederman, Girardin, and Gleditsch[94] also find that conflict is more likely when members of an excluded minority ethnic group have transnational kin in neighboring countries. While in the case-based literature ethnonationalist conflicts are often related to kin groups, quantitative studies treat ethnic conflicts only at the state level. These scholars instead integrate transnational links among minorities and find that transnational ethnic support can facilitate insurgencies, which are difficult for governments to target or deter. Therefore, in the case of minorities with relations in neighboring countries, there is a high possibility of ethnic conflict. This will be useful for our analysis of the Kurdish–Turkish case.

Regarding influences of the international community, there is no consensus in the literature about whether these system-level variables have an impact on the relationship between a state and its ethnic minorities. Nevertheless, in globalized times and with increasing interconnected regimes, the international arena remains important. This is also because today soft power, in addition to hard power, is an important tool of foreign policy. The prestige and acceptance of a state in the international community is of fundamental importance for the continuation of its power and the international status quo.

---

[92] Myron Weiner, "The Macedonian syndrome: An historical model of international relations and political development," *New Balkan Politics – Journal of Politics*, 2 (2001); originally published in World Politics (Vol. 23, No. 4, July 1971, pp. 665–683).

[93] Harris Mylonas, *The politics of nation-building: Making co-nationals, refugees, and minorities* (New York: Cambridge University Press, 2012).

[94] L.-E. Cederman, L. Girardin, and K. S. Gleditsch, "Ethno-nationalist triads: Assessing the influence of kin groups on civil wars," *World Politics* 61: 403–437 (2009).

Kymlicka,[95] for example, argues that international organizations and NGOs contribute to the diffusions of norms, but at the same time recent actions such as Russia's intervention in Ukraine demonstrate that the politics of great powers can be more influential than international regimes and norms. The many recent declarations of the international community on minority rights,[96] even if not enforceable, show that minority rights are considered an expression of human rights and, thus, universal principles recognized by the United Nations. This may influence the states to respect minority rights in some way. Nevertheless, the Turkish case does not appear to support such an argument, given the fact that Turkey did not listen to these UN declarations or even to the EU in its treatment of Kurdish minority. We will see in the chapter on international elements what factors have more impact for the Turkish and Indonesia cases.

(3) Historical Institutionalism: Nationalism and Citizenship

When the bipolar world was ending—actually, in the very year of the dissolution of the Soviet Union and Yugoslavia, 1991—some scholars published groundbreaking works on the relationship among nation-states, ethnic identity and citizenship, the crisis of nation-states, and at the same time the resurgence of nationalisms, from all different theoretic schools (realist, liberalist-institutionalist, constructivist, and critical theory). Academics proposed that we were at a crossroads, with one era, that of the nation-state as the Holy Grail for any structured societies, ending and a new one starting. The new one was the era of globalization but also localization, the era in which nation-states would have strained under tensions that would move them toward the creation of new polities, ones that were supranational, subnational, or transnational, to adapt to the evolving needs of changing societies. We still live in that era today, and we do not know how long it will last. This process of integration and fragmentation

---

[95] Will Kymlicka, *Multicultural odysseys: Navigating the new international politics of diversity* (Oxford: Oxford University Press, 2007).

[96] For example: UN Declaration on the Rights of Persons Belonging to National or Ethnic, Religious and Linguistic Minorities (1992), Council of Europe's European Charter for Regional or Minority Languages (1992), Council of Europe Framework Convention for the Protection of National Minorities (1995), UNESCO's Universal Declaration on Cultural Diversity (2001), UN Declaration on the Rights of Indigenous Peoples (2007).

has been defined by James Rosenau as "fragmegration,"[97] but it will take a long time before the transmutation is complete. Simply looking at the slow unification of Europe, the place where the nation-state was born, it has been more than 25 years since the Maastricht Treaty and more than 60 since the Treaty of Rome. Institutional innovation will be gradual and slow. At the same time, the current populist and nationalist movements in Europe show a resurgence of old nationalism and state sovereignty. But just as there are trends, there are also countertrends, so we don't know where the nation-state will end up.

In 1991, Etienne Balibar and Immanuel Wallerstein published *Race, Nation, Class: Ambiguous Identities*,"[98] a critical-theory approach to the exclusionary conditions of political rights in the formation of a nation-state. They argued that social structures—the nation-state, the division of labor, and the division between center and periphery in the world—were at the base of modern exclusion and that the crisis of the nation-state would coincide with a dangerous rise of nationalisms.

Rogers Brubaker, in 1992, following an institutionalist approach and looking at path dependency,[99] published *Citizenship and Nationhood in France and Germany*.[100] Deepening the analysis on the formation of the nation-state and studying specifically the cases of France and Germany, he argued that the concept of citizenship—and in particular the inclusion or exclusion of aliens—reflected the political culture of these two countries, one based on *jus soli* (France), and thus more open to naturalization among French aliens, and the other based on *jus sanguinis* (Germany), and so more exclusive regarding those born in Germany to foreign parents. The exclusion from political rights that passed through generations of resident aliens, according to Brubaker, was influenced by this concept of *jus sanguinis*.

---

[97] James N. Rosenau, *Distant proximities: Dynamics beyond globalization* (Princeton: Princeton University Press, 2003).

[98] Étienne Balibar and Immanuel Wallerstein, *Race, nation, class: Ambiguous identities* (London, New York: Verso, 1991).

[99] The path dependency theory, inside the theory of Historical Institutionalism, asserts that decisions one faces are limited by the decisions in the past, even though past circumstances may no longer be relevant. See T. Skocpol, P. Pierson, "Historical institutionalism in contemporary political science," in I. Katznelson, H. V. Milner (eds.) *Political science: State of the discipline* (New York: W.W. Norton, 2002).

[100] Rogers Brubaker, *Citizenship and nationhood in France and Germany* (Cambridge: Harvard University Press, 1992).

Finally, even if not in 1991 but a few years before, in 1983, Benedict Anderson published *Imagined Communities*,[101] masterfully explaining, using a constructivist approach, how national communities were based on their collective imaginations: "It is *imagined* because the members of even the smallest nation will never know most of their fellow members.... [I]t is imagined as a *community*, because regardless of the actual inequality and exploitation that may prevail in each, the nation is always perceived as a deep, horizontal comradeship."[102] People have imagined belonging to a socially constructed community since the birth of the nation-state, starting with the Industrial Revolution and its "print capitalism" (as he defines the process in which the vernacular languages created the concept of nation). This epochal shift affected the way people felt about themselves, and, as Anderson asserts, "ultimately it is this fraternity that made it possible, over the past two centuries, for so many millions of people, not so much to kill, as willingly to die for such limited imaginings."[103]

These studies have been very important for the purpose of conducting more in-depth analyses of the relationship between ethnic identity, nation-state formation, and the ensuing inclusive or exclusive citizenship. For this independent variable, therefore, it is crucial to understand how the inclusion of minorities in a full and equal citizenship may reflect the process of state formation. According to Tomas Hammar, a scholar of political culture who, like Brubaker, studied France and Germany,[104] when the state preceded the formation of the nation, as in the case of France, citizenship laws had a territorial base (reflected in the *jus soli* principle), whereas when the nation preceded the formation of the state, as in the German case, citizenship had a lineage base (reflected in the *jus sanguinis* principle). Following the historical-institutionalist theory, Hammar argued that the history of these two countries engendered a different approach to citizenship and, thus, to the inclusion of aliens as well. Germany was a nation in search of a state (that united quite late, in 1871), whereas France was a state in search of a nation (being a centralized state since Richelieu and the Peace of Westphalia in 1648). As a result, with respect to citizenship and

---

[101] Benedict Anderson, *Imagined communities: Reflections on the origin and spread of nationalism* (London, New York: Verso, 1983).

[102] Ibid., 6–7.

[103] Ibid., pp. 6–7.

[104] Tomas Hammar, *Democracy and the nation-state: Aliens, denizens, and citizenship in a world of international migration* (Aldershot, UK: Avebury, 1990).

national identity, Germany placed great emphasis on belonging to an ethnic nation, whereas France emphasized belonging to a state. This will be important later when we explain the differences between Turkey and Indonesian citizenship.

Another scholar, Stuurman, studying France and the Netherlands, argued that while in France the model of citizenship was historically "liberal-republican" based on individual rights, the Dutch model was "communitarian-liberal" based more on community rights.[105] With this model France moved in the direction of some form of cultural assimilationism, actually with a strong repression of minority languages in the nineteenth century, while the Netherlands (similarly to the UK) adopted some form of multiculturalism. In contrast to France, the Netherlands in its history of national identity has been more inclusive, in part because of the number of residents born in other nations, as Prak recalls,[106] which prompted the Dutch provinces to allow nonnatives to become citizens. As Earnest, following up the work of Prak, puts it: "Dutch citizenship is unique, then, in its combination of French republican liberalism, Protestant religious toleration, and colonial multiculturalism."[107] This has been reflected also in the Dutch colonies; Indonesia had a more communitarian model of citizenship, also thanks to the Netherlands' heritage.

In conclusion, the history of state formation shapes its institutions and laws of citizenship, in particular their relationship with the country's ethnic minorities. To put this in solidarity with Acemoglu and Robinson: "Different patterns of institutions today are deeply rooted in the past because once society gets organized in a particular way, this tends to persist."[108] Founding definitions of citizenship, then, continue to shape a state's treatment of ethnic minorities, including forms of autonomization or securitization during democratization processes.

---

[105] Stuurman, *Citizenship and cultural differences in France and the Netherlands*, 2004.
[106] Prak, 1997.
[107] David C. Earnest, *Old nations, new voters: Nationalism, transnationalism, and democracy in the era of global migration* (Albany: SUNY Press, 2008).
[108] Daron Acemoglu and James Robinson, *Why nations fail: The origins of power, prosperity, and poverty* (London: Profile Books, 2013) p. 44.

(4) Critical Theory: Ontological Security

Ontological Security

The ontological security concept was first coined by Anthony Giddens[109] and later transferred to the IR field in particular by Jennifer Mitzen and Brent J. Steele.[110] Ontological security in IR refers to the needs of states to have a secure notion of the "self" in the sense of its national identity. Every state has a different ontological interpretation of security depending on its history, geography, culture, and other factors. If this notion of the self and its position in the world is solid, a state enjoys stable ontological security; otherwise, the state's ontological security starts to falter. Ontological security may change over time; during some periods a state can feel a higher ontological security, while at other times it may feel a lower one, depending on internal or external threats. Usually, after the implosion of an empire or a federation of states, such as after the end of the Ottoman Empire or the Soviet Union, the heir of the previous powerful actor feels a low level of ontological security as it fears its own dismemberment and disappearance. Isolated countries may also feel low levels of ontological security because they tend to harbor feelings of mistrust owing to a lack of interaction with the international community and so tend to react with a defensive attitude (for example North Korea). Ontological security may be affected by the level of conflict a state experiences, feeling threatened in its existence and sovereignty when conflicts arise (for example, a state suffering through a civil war will obviously have a low level of ontological security). However, a recent book edited by Rumelili[111] that examines the cases of Cyprus, Northern Ireland, and Israel/Palestine argues that the prospects of peace can also generate anxieties in the ontological security of states, as peace may threaten the stability of self-narratives created in connection with the long-term conflicts. Nevertheless, it is evident that low levels of ontological

---

[109] Anthony Giddens, *Modernity and self-identity: Self and society in the late modern age* (Stanford: Stanford University Press, 1991).

[110] Jennifer Mitzen, "Ontological security in World politics: State identity and the security dilemma," *European Journal of International Relations*, Vol. 12, No. 3 (2006). Brent J. Steele, *Ontological security in international relations: Self-identity and the IR state* (Abingdon: Routledge, 2008).

[111] Bahar Rumelili, *Conflict resolution and ontological security: Peace anxieties* (New York: Routledge, 2015).

security make states fearful and, by extension, unaccommodating toward any demands for regional autonomy or decentralization. A state will not be inclusive and accommodating toward a minority in particular if it feels that this minority may collaborate with foreign countries against the nation-state, as Weiner argued with respect to the case of Macedonia.[112] Also, Kymlicka claims that one of the biggest obstacles to the autonomization of minorities is the fact that "minority groups are often seen as a kind of 'fifth column', likely to be working for a neighbouring enemy."[113] When seen as an internal threat connected with an external one, minority groups are stigmatized and as such disempowered.

Few studies exist on ontological security during democratization phases, but it seems that there is a consensus among scholars on the importance of this variable in general on the relationship between a country and its minorities. One may hypothesize that when states feel insecure, they may react in an exclusive and nationalist way, including by securitizing or repressing minorities. By contrast, when states enjoy a higher level of ontological security, they are more willing to consider and accept autonomization.

References

Agamben, Giorgio. 2005. *State of Exception*. Chicago: University of Chicago Press.
Anderson, Benedict. 1983. *Imagined Communities: Reflections on the Origin and Spread of Nationalism*. London/New York: Verso.
Balibar, Étienne, and Immanuel Wallerstein. 1991. *Race, Nation, Class: Ambiguous Identities*. London/New York: Verso.
Bertrand, Jacques, and Oded Haklai. 2014. *Democratization and Ethnic Minorities: Conflict or Compromise?* Abingdon: Routledge.
Bertrand, Jacques, and Sanjay Jeram. 2014. Democratization and Determinants of Ethnic Violence: The Rebel-moderate Organization Nexus. In *Democratization and Ethnic Minorities: Conflict or Compromise?* ed. Jacques Bertrand and Oded Haklai. Abingdon: Routledge.
Birdisli, Fikret. 2014. Securitization of Kurdish Question in Turkey. *International Journal of Research in Social Sciences* 4 (2): 1.

---

[112] Myron Weiner, "The Macedonian syndrome: An historical model of international relations and political development," *New Balkan Politics – Journal of Politics*, 2, 2001; originally published in *World Politics* (1971).
[113] Kymlicka, 2002, p. 19.

Brass, Paul. 1991. *Ethnicity and Nationalism: Theory and Comparison*. Newbury Park: Sage Publications.
Brubaker, Rogers. 1992. *Citizenship and Nationhood in France and Germany*. Cambridge: Harvard University Press.
———. 1996. *Nationalism Reframed: Nationhood and the National Question in the New Europe*. New York: Cambridge University Press.
Bülent, Aras, and Polat Rabia Karakaya. 2008. From Conflict to Cooperation: Desecuritization of Turkey's Relations with Syria and Iran. *Security Dialogue* 39 (5): 499.
Buzan, Barry, and Lene Hansen. 2009. *The Evolution of International Security Studies*. Cambridge: Cambridge University Press.
Cederman, L.-E., L. Girardin, and K.S. Gleditsch. 2009. Ethno-Nationalist Triads: Assessing the Influence of Kin Groups on Civil Wars. *World Politics* 61: 403–437.
Dahl, Robert A. 1971. *Polyarchy. Participation and Opposition*. New Haven: Yale University Press.
———. 1982. *Dilemmas of Pluralist Democracy: Autonomy vs. Control*. New Haven: Yale University Press.
———. 2005. What Political Institutions Does Large-scale Democracy Require? *Political Science Quarterly* 120 (2), Summer: 187–197.
Daron, Acemoglu, and James Robinson. 2013. *Why Nations Fail: The Origins of Power, Prosperity, and Poverty*. London: Profile books.
De Tocqueville, Alexis. 1835. *Democracy in America*. New York: Saunders and Otley.
Debeuf, Koert. 2015. *Tribalisation, or the End of Globalization*. EU Observer, December 8, 2015. https://euobserver.com/opinion/131413. Accessed 30 Sept 2017.
Diamond, Larry. 1999. *Developing Democracy: Toward Consolidation*. Baltimore: Johns Hopkins University Press.
———. 2004a. *Why Decentralize Power in A Democracy?* Conference on Fiscal and Administrative Decentralization, February 12, 2004. https://web.stanford.edu/~ldiamond/iraq/Decentralize_Power021204.htm. Accessed 30 Sept 2017.
———. 2004b. *What Is Democracy?* Lecture at Hilla University for Humanistic Studies, Iraq, January 21, 2004. https://web.stanford.edu/~ldiamond/iraq/WhaIsDemocracy012004.htm. Accessed 30 Sept 2017.
Diamond, Larry, and Leonardo Morlino, eds. 2005. *Assessing the Quality of Democracy*. Baltimore: Johns Hopkins University Press.
Diamond, Larry, and Marc Plattner. 2009. *Democracy: A Reader*. Baltimore: John Hopkins University Press.
Dryzek, John S. 1996. Political Inclusion and the Dynamics of Democratization. *The American Political Science Review* 90 (3): 475–487.

———. 2005. Deliberative Democracy in Divided Societies. Alternatives to Agonism and Analgesia. *Political Theory* 33 (2): 218–242.

Earnest, David. 2008. *Old Nations, New Voters: Nationalism, Transnationalism, and Democracy in the Era of Global Migration.* Albany: SUNY Press.

Emmers, Ralf. 2007. Securitization. In *Contemporary Security Studies*, ed. Allan Collins. Oxford: Oxford University Press.

Erdem, Derya. 2014. The Representation of the Democratic Society Party (DTP) in the Mainstream Turkish Media. In *The Kurdish Question in Turkey: New Perspectives on Violence, Representation and Reconciliation*, ed. C. Gunes and W. Zeydanlioglu. Abingdon: Routledge.

Fearon, James D., and David D. Laitin. 2000. Violence and the Social Construction of Ethnic Identity. *International Organization* 54 (04), Autumn: 845–877.

Fukuyama, Francis. 1992. *The End of History and the Last Man.* New York: Free Press.

Gagnon, V.P. 2004. *The Myth of Ethnic War. Serbia and Croatia in the 1990s.* Cornell: Cornell University Press.

Giddens, Anthony. 1991. *Modernity and Self-identity: Self and Society in the Late Modern Age.* Stanford: Stanford University Press.

Gill, Anthony. 2005. The Political Origins of Religious Liberty. *Interdisciplinary Journal of Research on Religion* 1: 1–35.

Gutmann, Amy. 2004. *Identity in Democracy.* Princeton: Princeton University Press.

Hammar, Tomas. 1990. *Democracy and the Nation-State: Aliens, Denizens, and Citizenship in a World of International Migration.* Aldershot: Avebury.

Horowitz, Donald. 1993. Democracy in Divided Societies. *Journal of Democracy* 4 (4): 18–38.

Kadıoğlu, Ayşe. 2013. Necessity and the State of Exception. The Turkish State's Permanent War With Its Kurdish Citizens. In *Turkey Between Nationalism and Globalization*, ed. Riva Kastoryano. London/New York: Routledge.

Kalyvas, Stathis. 1999. Wanton and Senseless? The Logic of Massacres in Algeria. *Rationality and Society* 11 (3): 243–286.

Kaufman, Stuart. 2001. *Modern Hatreds. The Symbolic Politics of Ethnic War.* Ithaca: Cornell University Press.

Kurban, Dilek. 2014. The Kurdish Question: Law, Politics and the Limits of Recognition. In *Turkey's Democratization Process*, ed. C. Rodriguez, A. Avalos, H. Yilmaz, and A. Planet, 345–360. Abingdon: Routledge.

Kymlicka, Will. 2002. *Politics in the Vernacular: Nationalism, Multiculturalism, and Citizenship.* Oxford: Oxford University Press.

———. 2004. Justice and Security in the Accommodation of Minority Nationalism. In *The Politics of Belonging: Nationalism, Liberalism, and Pluralism*, ed. Alain Dieckhoff. Lanham: Lexington Books.

———. 2007. *Multicultural Odysseys: Navigating the New International Politics of Diversity.* Oxford: Oxford University Press.

Kymlicka, Will, and W.J. Norman. 2001. *Citizenship in Diverse Societies.* Oxford: Oxford University Press.

Laclau, Ernesto, and Chantal Mouffe. 1985. *Hegemony and Socialist Strategy: Towards a Radical Democratic Politics.* London: Verso.

Laliberte, Andre. 2014. Democratization and Recognition of Difference in a Chinese Society: The Taiwanese Experience. In *Democratization and Ethnic Minorities: Conflict or Compromise?* ed. Jacques Bertrand and Oded Haklai. Abingdon: Routledge.

Lamont, Christopher K., Jan van der Harst, and Frank Gaenssmantel, eds. 2015. *Non-Western Encounters with Democratization.* Surrey: Ashgate Publishing Limited.

Lijphart, Arend. 1968. *The Politics of Accommodation; Pluralism and Democracy in the Netherlands.* Berkeley: University of California Press.

———. 1977. *Democracy in Plural Societies: A Comparative Exploration.* New Haven: Yale University Press.

———. 1999. *Patterns of Democracy. Government Forms and Performance in 36 Countries.* New Haven: Yale University Press.

———. 2004. Constitutional Design for Divided Societies. *Journal of Democracy* 15 (2): 96–109.

Lyon, Aisling. 2015. *Decentralization and the Management of Ethnic Conflict. Lessons from the Republic of Macedonia.* New York: Routledge.

Mackinder, Halford John. 1919. *Democratic Ideals and Reality. A Study in the Politics of Reconstruction.* New York: H. Holt and Company.

Mansfield, Edward D., and Jack L. Snyder. 2005. *Electing to Fight: Why Emerging Democracies Go to War.* Cambridge: MIT Press.

Marx, Anthony. 2002. The Nation-State and Its Exclusions. *Political Science Quarterly* 117 (1): 103–126.

McGarry, John, and Brendan O'Leary. 1993. *The Politics of Ethnic Conflict Regulation: Case Studies of Protracted Ethnic Conflicts.* New York: Routledge.

Miller, David L. 2000. *Citizenship and National Identity.* Cambridge: Polity.

Mitzen, Jennifer. 2006. Ontological Security in World Politics: State Identity and the Security Dilemma. *European Journal of International Relations* 12 (3): 341–370.

Mylonas, Harris. 2012. *The Politics of Nation-Building, Making Co-Nationals, Refugees, and Minorities Part of Problems of International Politics.* New York: Cambridge University Press.

Petersen, Roger Dale. 2011. *Western Intervention in the Balkans: The Strategic Use of Emotion in Conflict.* New York: Cambridge University Press.

Reilly, Ben. 2001. *Democracy in Divided Societies: Electoral Engineering for Conflict Management.* New York: Cambridge University Press.

Reynolds, Andrew. 2011. *Designing Democracy in a Dangerous World.* Oxford: Oxford University Press.

Rosenau, James. 2003. *Distant Proximities: Dynamics Beyond Globalization*. Princeton: Princeton University Press.
Rosenfeld, Michel, and Andrew Arato. 1998. *Habermas on Law and Democracy: Critical Exchanges*. Berkeley: University of California Press.
Rotchild, Donald. 2004. Liberalism, Democracy and Conflict Management. In *Facing Ethnic Conflicts: Toward a New Realism*, ed. Andreas Wimmer, Richard Goldstone, Donald Horowitz, Ulrike Joras, and Conrad Schetter. Lanham: Rowman & Littlefield.
Rumelili, Bahar. 2015. *Conflict Resolution and Ontological Security: Peace Anxieties*. New York: Routledge.
Shoup, Brian. 2014. Ethnically Based Redistributive Policies in Democratizing Bipolar States. In *Democratization and Ethnic Minorities: Conflict or Compromise?* ed. Jacques Bertrand and Oded Haklai. Abingdon: Routledge.
Skocpol, Theda, and Paul Pierson. 2002. Historical Institutionalism in Contemporary Political Science. In *Political Science: State of the Discipline*, ed. Ira Katznelson and Helen Milner. New York: W.W. Norton.
Snyder, Jack. 2000. *From Voting to Violence: Democratization and Nationalist Conflict*. New York: Norton.
Steele, Brent J. 2008. *Ontological Security in International Relations: Self-Identity and the IR State*. Abingdon: Routledge.
Strobel, Warren, Missy Ryan, David Rohde, and Ned Parker. 2014. Special Report: How Iraq's Maliki Defined Limits of U.S. Power. *Reuters*, June 30, 2014. http://www.reuters.com/article/2014/06/30/us-iraq-security-maliki-specialreport-idUSKBN0F51HK20140630. Accessed 30 Sept 2017.
Stuurman, Siep. 2004. *Citizenship and Cultural Differences in France and the Netherlands*. In *Lineages of European Citizenship: Rights, Belonging and Participation in Eleven Nation-States*, ed. Richard Bellamy, Dario Castiglione, and Emilio Santoro, 167–186. New York: Palgrave Macmillan.
Tilly, Charles. 2007. *Democracy*. New York: Cambridge University Press.
Von Vacano, Diego. 2014. Is Democracy a Western Idea? *Washington Post*, January 8, 2014. https://www.washingtonpost.com/news/monkey-cage/wp/2014/01/08/is-democracy-a-western-idea. Accessed 30 Sept 2017.
Wæver, Ole. 1995. Securitization and Desecuritization. In *On Security*, ed. Ronny Lipschutz. New York: Columbia University Press.
Walby, Sylvia. 2009. *Globalization and Inequalities: Complexity and Contested Modernities*. Los Angeles: Sage Publications.
Weiner, Myron. 2001. The Macedonian Syndrome: An Historical Model of International Relations and Political Development. *New Balkan Politics-Journal of Politics* 2: 665–683.
Young, Iris Marion. 2000. *Inclusion and Democracy*. New York: Oxford University Press.

Young, Crawford. 2006. The Heart of the African Conflict Zone: Democratization, Ethnicity, Civil Conflict and the Great Lakes. *Annual Review of Political Science* 9: 302–328.

Youngs, Richard. 2015. *The Puzzle of Non-Western Democracy*. Washington, DC: Carnegie Endowment for International Peace.

Zakaria, Fareed. 2003. *The Future of Freedom: Illiberal Democracy at Home and Abroad*. New York: W.W. Norton & Co.

CHAPTER 3

Research Design

RESEARCH METHOD AND SOURCES

To analyze securitization and autonomization, this book relies on case study analysis. The method of comparing cases aims to test hypotheses but, as Collier observes, can also "contribute to the inductive discovery of new hypotheses and to theory building."[1] This is the aim of the present study: to test an argument but also open up space for theory development, based on the findings.[2] That is why the research presented here has fewer cases than variables. Therefore, this study does not control for some confounding variables because the purpose of it is also theory building: to look at several factors in order to identify *if* and *how* these factors may affect the two different outcomes analyzed. Also, as Van Evera says, a good theory, besides having explanatory power and being falsifiable, parsimonious, and clearly framed, has "prescriptive richness. It yields useful policy recommendations."[3] The conclusions drawn from this study there-

---

[1] David Collier, "The comparative method", in: Ada W. Finifter, ed., *Political Science: The state of discipline II*, Washington, DC: American Political Science Association, 1993.
[2] See on this Alexander L. George and Andrew Bennett, *Case studies and theory development in the social sciences* (Cambridge: MIT Press, 2005).
[3] Stephen Van Evera, *Guide to methods for students of political science* (Ithaca: Cornell University Press, 1997) p. 21.

fore aim to bring some policy suggestions to fledgling democracies facing the challenge of inclusion of minorities.

There are several reasons to use qualitative analysis. First, a case study may be suitable for understanding the falsifiability of a theory because of its in-depth analysis. Qualitative research, as King, Keohane, and Verba argue, allows one "to explain as much as possible with as little as possible."[4] To do this, qualitative methodology uses descriptive analysis to understand the research problem in depth and with nuances that statistical analysis cannot give. In particular, case studies are important because they "provide an insightful description of complex events,"[5] an in-depth analysis to explain the causal relationships revealed in the research. Second, as this research seeks to explain the causes of the differences in treatments of minorities, the "causes-of-effects" approach of qualitative analysis is more appropriate to explain the specific outcomes of particular cases, rather than the quantitative "effects-of-causes" approach, which, according to Mahoney and Goertz (2006), "seeks to estimate the average effect of one or more causes across a population of cases."[6] Third, the narrative approach is more appropriate for the comparison of two discrete outcomes such as the securitization or autonomization of minorities. Understanding such outcomes requires an interpretation of facts that a statistical analysis cannot give. To show the relationship between the dependent and independent variables in this study, the best approach is qualitative analysis.

To make better causal inferences through qualitative analysis, this study uses the method of process tracing.[7] This methodology is based on dissecting a causal chain through the different causal mechanisms between the observed variables, looking in particular at the set of events and processes that build the cause–effect mechanism. As Bennett explains, process tracing involves empirical tests with evidence that have different kinds of probative value.[8] Usually process tracing requires original data based on field work or primary resources in the local language. However, because

[4] Gary King, Robert O. Keohane, and Sidney Verba, *Designing social inquiry: Scientific inference in qualitative research* (Princeton: Princeton University Press, 1994) p. 29.
[5] Ibid., p. 44.
[6] James Mahoney and Gary Goertz, "A Tale of Two Cultures: Contrasting Quantitative and Qualitative Research", *Political Analysis* 14 (2006): 230.
[7] Alexander George and Andrew Bennett, *Case Studies and Theory Development in the Social Sciences* (Cambridge: MIT Press, 2005).
[8] Andrew Bennett in "Process Tracing and Causal Inference" Chapter 10 of Henry Brady and David Collier (eds.) *Rethinking Social Inquiry* (Lanham: Rowman and Littlefield, 2010).

scholars have studied both Turkey and Indonesia, and both in their democratization processes and in their relationship with their ethnic minorities (in Turkey even more than in Indonesia), this study will rely on secondary resources. Also, because the two countries have been studied either separately or in comparison but without the question or the causal analysis proposed in this study (see Al Qurtuby,[9] for example), I consulted both scholarship analyzing the case studies and nonscholarly work (from government or NGOs/media reports) to find evidence in more factual sources. Finally, several informal interviews, conducted in both Turkey and Indonesia, contributed to this research, in particular to understand if the study could really make a case of securitization versus autonomization and analyze better the factors that may have affected the states' choice. This consultation with subject matter experts (in particular academics and activists) contributed to a deeper understanding of the issue.

Also, the research design is based on the "most similar systems"[10] and the "method of difference" (Mill's criteria).[11] In the most similar systems design, because common factors are controlled for, the differences in cases constitute the explanatory variables. This study follows the most similar systems because the two countries are Muslim-majority democracies with similar factors, as explained in the next section, and it is based on the method of difference because it deals with different outcomes in similar cases.

Case Study Choice and Selection Criteria

Why were these two case studies chosen and not others? The reason for this selection will be explained here. If Turkey and Indonesia have minority populations of very different sizes, both had 30 years of insurgency of the respective ethnic minority but with different results: Turkey is currently experiencing an escalating conflict, with an increase in the securitization of Kurds in the eastern region of the country and a democratic regression for Turkey. By contrast, the insurgency in Indonesia ended 10

---

[9] Al Qurtuby analyzes the dynamics of political reconciliation and attempts at conflict resolution and peacebuilding to understand the differences between Kurdish conflict and Acehnese conflict. See Sumanto Al Qurtuby, *Interethnic violence, separatism and political reconciliation in Turkey and Indonesia*, India Quarterly 71(2) (6/2015): 126–145.

[10] Adam Przeworski and Henry Teune, *The logic of comparative social inquiry* (New York: Wiley-Interscience, 1970).

[11] John Stuart Mill, *A system of logic* (Honolulu: University Press of the Pacific, 2002).

years ago with the autonomy of Aceh and a step forward in the "substantiveness" and meaningfulness of Indonesia's democracy. The purpose of the research presented here is to understand why two similar secular, modern, and relatively successful Muslim-majority democracies chose different strategies to deal with their ethnic minorities. The selection of the cases is based on a variation in the treatment of minorities (the dependent variable of the research) but also on a similarity in the following several factors. These factors represent the commonalities of the countries, the control variables of the study:

(1) <u>Ethnic versus religious heterogeneity</u>: Both nation-states have a dominant ethnic group (in Turkey, Turks make up around 70% of the population, in Indonesia, Javanese about 40%)[12] but also minorities with substantial populations (Kurds in Turkey, many groups in Indonesia). Islam is the predominant religion in both states: 98% in Turkey (majority of Sunni but a good part Shia Alevi[13]) and 88% in Indonesia, mostly Sunni.[14] While the Turks clearly define themselves as Sunni or Shia,[15] Indonesians define themselves mostly as nonsectarian. They all have strong traditions of mystic Sufism (from Rumi to Gulen in Turkey, and from Fansuri to Javanese court poets in Indonesia). In both countries Islam resisted Arabization, and in Turkey even more than in Indonesia (as the Ottoman Empire ruled over the Arab world).[16] But in Indonesia Islam was more pluralistic: as Geertz argued,[17] the Islam in Indonesia was born as a syncretistic religion that combined

[12] CIA World Factbook, 2015.

[13] There are no independent data on the numbers of Alevi (as well as Kurds): we go from 10% to 30% of the population. Another thing to take into account is that in Turkey every citizen automatically has Muslim as religious identity on the personal ID, and only if requested is that information removed.

[14] Pew Research Center, *Mapping the global Muslim population*, 2009, accessed September 30, 2017. http://www.pewforum.org/files/2009/10/Muslimpopulation.pdf.

[15] See Pew Research Center, *The world's Muslims: Unity and diversity*, Chapter 1: Religious Affiliation, 2012. Accessed September 30, 2017. http://www.pewforum.org/2012/08/09/the-worlds-muslims-unity-and-diversity-1-religious-affiliation/#_ftn9.

[16] Martin van Bruinessen, "Secularism, Islamism and Muslim intellectualism in Turkey and Indonesia: Some comparative observations", in Mirza Tirta Kusuma (ed.), *Ketika Makkah Menjadi* (Las Vegas: Agama, Jakarta: Gramedia, 2014).

[17] Clifford Geertz, *Islam observed: Religious development in Morocco and Indonesia* (New Haven: Yale University Press, 1968).

Hindu and polytheistic traditions, and as Hefner stated, in Indonesia, "Muslim politics…was varied from the start. At a few times and in a few places, there were pluralist tendencies not just in politics but in literature and religious practices as well."[18]

(2) Common constitutional secularism: Both Turkey and Indonesia are secular countries. Turkey has gradually imposed secularism since the birth of the republic in 1923, with Kemalist reforms that, from the constitution of 1924 on, led slowly to the final secularism based on the division between governmental and religious affairs. Secularism since then has always been strong in Turkey, but it has weakened with the moderate Islamist party AKP trying to influence politics with some Islamic values, even if without changing the constitution in that regard, at least for the time being.

By contrast, Indonesian secularism was not explicitly declared or forced by an ideology like Kemalism, but it comes from the five *Pancasila* values of tolerance and pluralism reflected in its history of diversity and in its constitution, since independence in 1945. Even if the level of secularism is debatable, as the first principle of Pancasila[19] is "the belief in the one and only God," and the constitution recognizes only six official religions, secularism in Indonesia is based on a public sphere that is separated from the private sphere of religion and a state that stands at an equal distance to all religions with equal rights.[20] Both Indonesia and Turkey uphold the separation of these public and private spheres.

---

[18] Robert Hefner, *Civil Islam: Muslims and democratization in Indonesia* (Princeton: Princeton University Press, 2000), p. 31.

[19] Islam in Indonesia is separate from nation building because of Pancasila (from Sanskrit: *Panca*, meaning five, and *sila*, meaning principles) the five principles at the base of the Indonesian state: (1) belief in the one and only God, (2) a just and civilized humanity, (3) a unified Indonesia, (4) democracy, guided by the wisdom of the representatives of the people, and (5) social justice for all Indonesians.

[20] See again Martin van Bruinessen, 2014. The separation between church and state is not very clear in many Western secular countries: England still has a state religion; in Germany the state collects church taxes on behalf of the church; in Norway the King is required to be a member of the Church of Norway, and the church is regulated by a special church law, unlike other religions; Italy had a state religion and compulsory teaching of Catholicism in public schools until recently, and the crucifix is still present in school buildings, even if the European Court of Human Rights judged it to be a violation of religious freedom as far back as 2009.

(3) Recent history of democratization with a unique path toward it: Turkey can be considered as having been fully democratized in 2002; for Indonesia democracy arrived in 1998. In Turkey the 2002 "democratization" was not seen as a break from the past (because the past had already experienced some form of electoral democracy), while for Indonesia the revolution brought democracy for the first time. One can date Turkish democratization to 2002 because that year marked the first time an Islamist, even if moderate, party won an election and the military did not intervene. Today both states are considered procedural democracies, even if scholars and well-known indices do not identify them as liberal democracies. Freedom House, for example, considers both "partly free" because they are still on a path to democratization. The Economist Intelligence Unit in its Democracy Index defines Turkey as a "hybrid regime" and Indonesia a "flawed democracy."[21] Finally, Democracy Ranking[22] scores them at 65 (Indonesia) and 69 (Turkey) among a total of 100 democracies. But they both represent a contrast with respect to their neighbors: Turkey is an exception with respect to the other Middle Eastern Muslim countries and Indonesia an exception with respect to Southeast Asian

[21] Freedom House considered Turkey and Indonesia as "partly free" (an "electoral" but not "liberal" democracy) even in its most recent evaluation of 2017, with the largest 10-year score decline in the entire world apart from the Central African Republic. Indonesia is in a better situation because, among other things, since 1998 it has changed president several times and in 2014 elected its first president that had not come from the country's political-military elite, while Turkey has had the same leadership and party since 2002. See *Freedom in the world 2017*, Freedom House, 2017, accessed September 30, 2017. https://freedomhouse.org/report/freedom-world/freedom-world-2017. The Economist Intelligence Unit defined Indonesia in 2016 as a "flawed democracy" and Turkey as "hybrid regimes," between democracy and autocracy. The Democracy Index analyzes 60 indicators with 5 categories: electoral process and pluralism; civil liberties; functioning of government; political participation; political culture. See The Economist Intelligence Unit's Democracy Index, *The Economist Group*, 2017, accessed September 30, 2017. https://infographics.economist.com/2017/DemocracyIndex/.

[22] Democracy Ranking is an initiative of the Democracy Ranking Association, located in Vienna, Austria, that creates an annual global ranking of democracies integrating some characteristics of a country's political system with nonpolitical dimensions like gender, economy, knowledge, health, and environment. The Democracy Ranking 2015 covers countries that were categorized by Freedom House as "free" or "partly free" in the years 2013 and 2014. Accessed September 30, 2017. http://democracyranking.org/ranking/2015/data/Scores_of_the_Democracy_Ranking_2015_A4.pdf.

countries. Regarding the impact of Muslim identity in the democratization process, in both Turkey and Indonesia, Muslim organizations and parties have played important roles in the transition to democracy. In Indonesia, the Muslim associations Muhammadiyah and Nahdlatul Ulama brought stability to the post-Soeharto transition; in Turkey the Islamic party AKP was able to implement important reforms since it won elections in 2002. The AKP is the first Islamist party, even if moderate, to win elections in a Muslim country and gain power in subsequent elections.[23]

(4) Armed independence struggle for both national independence and ethnic minority independence: In contrast to many other Muslim-majority nation-states, Turkey and Indonesia achieved independence after a prolonged armed struggle viewed as a fight against alien occupying forces, particularly in Turkey. This history also allowed the armed forces to retain a dominant role in politics for a long time to maintain a secular authority against Islamism or order against social rebellion.[24] Also, the two ethnonational groups[25] studied here, Kurds and Acehnese, picked up arms for their liberation movements in different periods (middle of 1970s and 1980s) because they did not find other efficient ways to fight for their self-determination. In both cases, the resistance to the national government is rooted not only in ethnic diversity and a lack of autonomy but also in the perception that the minority had not benefited from economic development, in the legacy of suffering as a result of government counterinsurgency operations, in the resentment toward social migration policies (in particular in Aceh), and in a rejection of the secular orientation of the state. Finally, both insurgencies were seen by their government and citizens as the most serious challenge to the respective territorial integrity, not as a legitimate tool for their self-determination, as was the case with respect to national independence.

---

[23] Martin van Bruinessen, 2014, p. 4.

[24] Martin van Bruinessen, 2014, p. 4.

[25] Ethno-national groups can be defined as "populations which express an ethnic identity and make a claim to being recognized as a nation. The ethnic identity is often grounded in region, common culture, religion or language, or a combination of some of these." See Ellis Cashmore, *Encyclopedia of race and ethnic studies* (London and New York: Routledge, 2004), p. 148.

The difference between the two cases, though, emerged during the democratization process. The Indonesian state increased its violent repression of the minority at the beginning of its democratic transition and after few years approached negotiations and autonomization with a final solution to the conflict. By contrast, the Turkish state started with an attitude of accommodation in the first few years, but suddenly the autonomization process was blocked and securitization restarted. Therefore, while in the Indonesian case the outcome is clear at this moment in time, since Aceh has been autonomous already since 2005, the Turkish case is still in process. Will policies of inclusion, decentralization, and autonomy take place sooner or later in the future? Or will securitization continue for a while, until the Kurdish issue disappears in Turkey (perhaps with the creation of a Kurdish state between Syria and Iraq and the migration of part of the Kurdish minority from Turkey to that new state)?

(5) <u>Non-Arabic Muslim countries with pluralistic cultural heritage</u>: Both Indonesia and Turkey are heirs to great civilizations. In Indonesia, these civilizations were the Buddhist Sriwijaya Empire of Sumatra, the Hindu Majapahit from Java, the Muslim sultanates of Aceh, Mataram, Banten, and other parts of the archipelago (as well as Christianity, which was spread by Portuguese and Dutch colonists). In Turkey the Hittite, Byzantine, and Roman empires, and after those the Seljuq and Ottoman empires, provide the country's civilizational heritage. Also, both states represent "bridge countries" among continents, cultures, and religions: Turkey between Europe and Middle East/Asia, Indonesia between Southeast Asia and Australia (but also India and China). Notwithstanding their pluralistic and inclusive heritage, these countries passed through securitization of their ethnic minorities but ultimately had different outcomes.

(6) <u>Growing economic, geopolitical, and strategic countries</u>: Both Turkey and Indonesia have made impressive progress in terms of improving the standard of living of their citizens, performing well in the Millennium Development Goals, and show great potential for further economic development. Turkey's GDP, for example, went from USD 200 billion in 2001 to USD 950 billion in 2013, while

Indonesia's grew from USD 95 billion in 1998 to USD 912 billion in 2013.[26] Both states belong to the G20 and are part of the so-called MINT group (Mexico, Indonesia, Nigeria, and Turkey)[27] and the Next Eleven group, identified by Goldman Sachs as having a high potential of becoming, along with Brazil, Russia, India, and China (the BRICs), among the world's largest economies in the twenty-first century.[28] Both also belie the myth that Muslim countries have a hard time with modernization, defined largely in terms of economic development. Finally, Turkey and Indonesia have growing geopolitical and strategic importance, reflected in their growing hard and soft power, ambitions for regional leadership, and their international roles. The point here is that even if they enjoyed economic growth during democratization, the countries chose at certain points to securitize their minorities and ultimately to go in different directions.

(7) <u>Close relationships with Western countries</u>: Both Turkey and Indonesia are strong partners of the USA, NATO, and the EU, though Turkey is more so than Indonesia: Turkey has been a NATO member since 1952, with long-time hopes of joining the EU. Indonesia is a strategic partner of the USA and a member of ASEAN and holds regular meetings with NATO (even though in the past it was the leader of the nonalignment movement). Both were anticommunist bulwarks during the Cold War, though Indonesia did massacre hundreds of thousands of "communists" in the 1960s. Though both countries have values close to Western values of minority rights, for example, their outcomes have been different.

To explain the study's case selection, Table 3.1 reports the four most important control variables (besides the indices on democracy by Freedom House and Economist Intelligence Unit) in 15 main democratizing Muslim-majority countries.

---

[26] The World Bank, "World Data." Accessed September 30, 2017. http://data.worldbank.org/indicator/NY.GDP.MKTP.KD.ZG. CIA, "World Factbook." Accessed September 30, 2017. https://www.cia.gov/library/publications/the-world-factbook/.

[27] Matthew Boesler, "The Economist Who Invented the BRICs Just Invented a Whole New Group of Countries: The MINTs," *Business Insider*, November 13, 2013.

[28] Eric Martin, "Goldman Sachs's MIST Topping BRICs as Smaller Markets Outperform," *Bloomberg Business*, August 7, 2012.

Table 3.1 Levels of democracy and principal control variables

States	Freedom house Index (2017)	EIU Index (2017)	Ethnic diversity	Religious diversity	Ethnic Fractionalization	Religious Fractionalization	Constitutional secularism	Recent democratization	Armed independence struggle	Self-determination armed conflict (minority struggle)
Bangladesh	Partly free	Hybrid regime	Low (Bengali 98%)	Low (Muslim 89%)	0.0454	0.2090	No (state religion)	1991	**Yes** 1971	
Burkina Faso	Partly free	Hybrid regime	**High**	High	0.7377	0.5798	Yes	2014	No	No
Indonesia	Partly free	Flawed democracy	High	Low (Muslim 88%)	0.7351	0.2340	Yes (but ambiguous)	1998	**Yes** (1945/49)	**Yes (Acehnese 74/04, Timorese 75/99, Papuans 61/today)**
Iraq	Not free	Hybrid regime	**High**	Low (Muslim 99%)	0.3689	0.4844	No (state religion)	2005	No	**Yes** (Kurds 1961/2005)
Kyrgyzstan	Partly free	Hybrid regime	**High**	Low (Muslim 86%)	0.6752	0.4470	Yes	2005/2011	No	No (but armed clashes between Uzbek and Kirgiz in 2010)
Lebanon	Partly free	Hybrid regime	Low (Arab 95%)	High	0.1314	0.7886	No (confessionalism)	1990	No	No (but 15 years civil war among different religions)
Malaysia (constitutional monarchy)	Partly free	Flawed democracy	**High**	High	0.5880	0.6657	No (state religion)	1991	No	No
Mali	Partly free	Hybrid regime	**High**	Low (95% Muslim)	0.6906	0.1820	Yes	1991	No	No (despite recent Tuareg rebellion 2012/2013)
Morocco (constitutional monarchy)	Partly free	Hybrid regime	Low (Arab-Berber 99%)	Low (99% Muslim)	0.4841	0.0035	No (state religion)	2011	No	**Yes** (Sahrawi rebellion in Western Sahara 1976/1991)

Nigeria	Partly free	Hybrid regime	High	0.8505	0.7421	**Yes**	1999/2011	No	No
Pakistan	Partly free	Hybrid regime	**High**	0.7098	0.3848	No (state religion)	2008	No	**Yes** (Balochistan conflict since 1948)
Senegal	Free	Flawed democracy	**High**	0.6939	0.1497	**Yes**	1991	No	**Yes** (Jola minority, also religious, 1982/2014)
Sierra Leone	Partly free	Hybrid regime	**High**	0.8191	0.5395	**Yes**	2002	No	No
Tunisia	Free	Flawed democracy	Low (Arab 98%)	0.0394	0.0104	No (state religion)	2011	No	No
Turkey	Partly free	Hybrid regime	**High**	0.3200	0.0049	**Yes**	2002	**Yes** (1919/1923)	**Yes (Kurds** 1984/today)

Turkey, by Alesina's indicator, has low fractionalization, probably because the Encyclopedia Britannica consulted by Alesina didn't consider the Kurds a minority, recognizing only the small minorities with legal status in Turkey: Jews, Greeks, and Armenians (same for Iraq)

Data sources: Ethnic/religious diversity: "CIA World Factbook 2017" (data vary from 2006 to 2017)

[a] Alberto Alesina et al. (2003) develop the "fractionalization scores" based on ethnicity and religious data from *Encyclopedia Britannica*

As we can see from Table 3.1, the two cases that have common ethnic diversity and religious homogeneity, as well as constitutional secularism, recent democratization, an armed independence struggle, and minority self-determination armed conflict, are Turkey and Indonesia. Actually, according to the index of Minorities at Risk, both the Kurds and Acehnese minorities are defined as "ethno-nationalist groups," both of which ramped up their armed rebellions after their democratic transition (together with other minorities like Mayans in Mexico or Chechens in Russia).[29] Obviously, the Aceh rebellion found a peaceful resolution, while the Kurdish one did not, the two cases represent different situations. Minority Rights Group International, for example, defined, in 2017 and preceding years, the Kurdish rebellion as an ongoing conflict and the Acehnese rebellion as a "contained armed conflict."[30] Actually, in the Global Peace Index 2017, of 162 countries, Indonesia was ranked 52 and Turkey was 146.[31] But it is still worthwhile comparing the two cases because in the first years of their democratization process they had ongoing armed ethnic conflicts that were finally resolved in two different ways.

CAUSAL MECHANISM TO RESEARCH IN THE TWO CASE STUDIES

As stated previously, this study's dependent variable, the state's treatment of ethnic minorities, is a variable with two different outcomes: securitization and autonomization. To test the four hypothesized explanations for

---

[29] Minorities at Risk (MAR) is a university-based research project that monitors and analyzes the status and conflicts of 284 politically active community groups around the world. MAR confirms that the Acehnese minority and the Kurdish minority are ethno-nationalist groups: "regionally concentrated peoples with a history of organized political autonomy with their own state, traditional ruler, or regional government, who have supported political movements for autonomy at some time since 1945." See "Minorities at Risk Dataset," MAR. Accessed September 30, 2017. http://www.mar.umd.edu/mar_data.asp.

[30] Minority Rights Group International is an international human rights organization founded in London in the 1960s. Their annual index, Peoples under Threat, ranks countries according to the degree of physical danger facing communities. In the 2015 index, of 70 countries, Turkey was ranked the 29th worst country, with 5 communities at risk (Kurds, Alevis, Roma, Armenians, and other Christians), while Indonesia was ranked 66th, with 5 communities at risk (Acehnese, Chinese, Dayaks, Madurese, and Papuans, besides religious minorities). Accessed September 30, 2017. http://peoplesunderthreat.org/.

[31] *Global Peace Index Report*, 2017, Institute for Economics and Peace. Accessed September 30, 2017. http://economicsandpeace.org/wp-content/uploads/2015/06/Global-Peace-Index-Report-2015_0.pdf.

the ethnic minority incorporation, this research operationalizes the measures for each of the four main theories in the following way.

(1) *Elite power interests.* This variable is related to rational choice theory.

According to this theory, political actors are motivated to stay in power, and so political elites often promote exclusive nationalist policies once they fear losing their power. This could be the case for Turkey, with a politically threatening minority, the Kurds, that for the first time had a party representing them in parliament, and Indonesia, without a politically threatening minority, with the ex-GAM party contesting only local elections. Another important actor is the army, which in Turkey is very strong and represents an obstacle to more constitutional rights and decentralization for minorities, while in Indonesia the army apparently did not block the final autonomization process.

The study of this book on elite interests in power suggests the following hypothesis:

Hypothesis 1: When elites face electoral or direct political challenges from minority groups, they are more likely to pursue securitization policies. Otherwise, they are more likely to pursue autonomization policies.

(2) *International* factors/*geopolitical situation*: These variables are related to international-structural theory.

Minority conflicts can also be a game of geopolitics, in particular in the case of the Kurdish conflict. At the end of World War I, the Kurds were denied a Kurdish state, but recently things have started to change, at least in Turkey's neighboring countries: in Iraq, with the autonomous Southern Kurdistan Region, and in Syria, with a corresponding Western Autonomous Region for Kurds. In Indonesia, the Acehnese minority does not present a geopolitical issue because, apart from the diaspora of some Acehnese, and even if it is strategically positioned at the Malacca Straight, there is no risk of spillover of the conflict, partly because Aceh is at the tip of Sumatra Island. Also important has been the role of the Western powers: Turkey is a NATO member and has been a candidate for membership since 1999, a state whose importance has grown during the Syrian migration crisis and instability in the Middle East. One can hypothesize that this increased importance has affected Turkey's treatment of its minorities. In the past, for example, Turkey might have been influenced by the EU on the Kurdish issue, but today it seems the opposite: facing the prospect of millions of refugees, the EU depends on Turkish decision makers and so does not pressure Turkey as it did in the past on minority issues.

Indonesia, even if it is an important country, is not so pivotal a country in terms of regional stability as Turkey is in its region. For this reason, it might have benefited from more independence in its decisions even if in reality international pressure has pushed Indonesia to accommodate its minorities, in particular in East Timor and Aceh. In addition, from the perspective of the self-determination movements, the Free Aceh Movement (GAM) was mostly free from external influences, avoiding negative consequences such as being labeled a terrorist organization by the West (as was the PKK in Turkey) but also positive ones (while Kurds have gained the advocacy of the EU, UN, and USA, in the case of Aceh, only international NGOs were interested in the conflict). At the same time, in the Aceh peace process, the role of third-party international actors is evident, with the Henri Dunant Center and especially the Finnish government during the negotiation phase. By contrast, with the Kurds there is no third party interested in the negotiations (apart from minor assistance from the Berghof Foundation) both because of Turkish rejection and the international community's cautious stance over falling into a very complex conflict with the risk of a quagmire. Also, it is important to analyze the role of the minority diaspora at the international level, because in the Aceh case it seemed to have played an important role, while in the Turkish case it did not. These studies therefore suggest the following subhypotheses:

Hypothesis 2A: When facing an external security threat, states are more likely to securitize minority demands for autonomy. In the absence of an external threat, states are more likely to choose policies of autonomization.

Hypothesis 2B: When external actors intervene in minority issues, states are more likely to grant autonomy to minorities. In the absence of pressure from external actors, states are more likely to securitize minority issues.

Hypothesis 2C: When a diaspora has an organized voice to support its cause, to advocate for its kinfolk inside the home country, and to lobby the international community to intervene, the state is pushed to start leaning toward accommodation.

(3) *Nationalism* and *citizenship*.[32] This variable is related to historical institutionalism and theories of path-dependent institutional development.

This variable examines how processes of decolonization and state formation have shaped conceptions of national identity in these democratizing Muslim societies, with particular attention paid to the role of elites in identity formation. Since the millet system in the Ottoman Empire, for example, Turkey has had constructions of citizenship based on nations of religions, not nations of ethnicities, and the system was divided among religious minorities, who were sometimes considered second-class citizens vis-à-vis Muslims. With the Western model of "monoethnic" nation-state building, the Turkish Republic was based on the Kemalist concept of one nation and one language, which is why the constitution granted legal status to non-Muslim small minorities but not to Muslim large minorities such as the Alevi (Shia) or Kurds (Sunni but with different ethnicity). Today, with the new Islamic nationalism of the AKP, Turkey still refuses to grant the Kurds the legal status of a recognized minority, even if during the early years of the AKP, for the first time the Turkish Republic granted cultural rights to Kurds.[33] By contrast, since the colonial era, Indonesia has had a different approach to minorities that combined the multinationalism of Dutch origins and the "unity in diversity" motto with the Pancasila principles in the Constitution of 1945. This, following the idea of path dependence, could have limited the ability of Turkey to implement inclusive policies or policies of autonomy for minorities.

These studies suggest the following hypothesis:

Hypothesis 3: States that form independently of former colonies tend to be more inclusive and are more likely to grant autonomy to minorities; when they evolve from traditional autochthonous institutions, they tend to be more exclusive and more likely to adopt policies of securitization.

---

[32] See, among others, Elizabeth Pisani, *Indonesia, etc.: Exploring the improbable nation* (New York: Norton, 2015). Sener Akturk, "Religion and nationalism contradictions of Islamic origins and secular nation-building: Turkey Algeria and Pakistan," *Social Science Quarterly*, Volume 96, Number 3, September 2015.

[33] Senem Aslan, "Different faces of Turkish Islamic nationalism", *New York Times*, February 20, 2015. Accessed September 30, 2017. https://www.washingtonpost.com/blogs/monkey-cage/wp/2015/02/20/different-faces-of-turkish-islamic-nationalism/.

(4) Ontological *security*: This variable is related to culturalist-social-identity critical theory.

Ontological security is the security of the self, the security of a national identity; it could be evaluated as low for Turkey (for its historical fear of invasion, siege, and risk of dismemberment) and high for Indonesia, an archipelago (or "maritime power" as defined recently by President Jokowi) that has never feared dismemberment or destruction by foreign conquest. Indonesia also is a state born of decolonization and not the implosion of a former empire invaded by foreigners. Nevertheless, ontological security may change over time, as it is related to the disruption of past routines that contribute to the challenges to self-identity, creating anxieties and fears, as discussed in Chap. 8.

Being related to the perception of self-identity, ontological security is also connected to the political ideology of both the state (being secular or with an Islamist ideology as in Turkey before and after democratization in the twentieth century) and minorities represented by separatist movements (either Marxist, like the PKK, or more liberal, like the GAM). In Turkey the political ideology of Kemalism and its assertive secularism and nationalism against any religious values in society and state contributed to the marginalization of minorities such as the Kurds (the first rebellion was carried out by a Shia cleric), with the army also playing a role in the repression of political Islam.[34] Also, the recent "conservative democracy" ruling in Turkey (with the moderate Islamist AKP), even if it led to reforms in minority rights, did not accept any form of power-sharing and after a failed attempt at negotiation resorted to securitization. On the other hand, the "national democracy" coalition currently in power in Indonesia, with President Joko Widodo at the helm, includes small Islamist moderate parties (National Awakening Party and National Mandate Party) in a secular government, as these parties do not push for more religion in politics but just use religion as inspiration. Also, as Cesari argues,[35] while Turkey has a

---

[34] See: John Esposito, Tamara Sonn, John O. Voll, *Islam and democracy after the Arab Spring* (Oxford: Oxford University Press, 2015). Jocelyn Cesari, *The awakening of Muslim democracies* (Cambridge: Cambridge University Press, 2014). Joshua Castellino and Kathleen Cavanaugh, *Minority rights in the Middle East* (Oxford: Oxford University Press, 2013).

[35] Jocelyne Cesari, "Religion and Politics: What Does God Have To Do with It?" *Religions*, 6 (2015): 1337.

"hegemonic Islam"—with exclusive legal, economic, and political rights denied to other religions—Indonesia (like Lebanon and Senegal) does not, even if discriminatory practices exist in the country. From these analyses one can derive the following hypothesis:

Hypothesis 4: As a state's ontological security worsens, it is more likely to adopt securitization policies. As its ontological security improves, it is more likely to pursue autonomization.

References

Akturk, Sener. 2015. Religion and Nationalism Contradictions of Islamic Origins and Secular Nation-Building. Turkey Algeria and Pakistan. *Social Science Quarterly* 96 (3): 778–806.

Al Qurtuby, Sumanto. 2015. *Interethnic Violence, Separatism and Political Reconciliation in Turkey and Indonesia. India Quarterly* 71 (2): 126–145.

Alesina, Alberto, Arnaud Devleeschauwer, William Easterly, Sergio Kurlat, and Romain Wacziarg. 2003. Fractionalization. *Journal of Economic Growth* 8: 155–194.

Aslan, Senem. 2015. Different Faces of Turkish Islamic Nationalism. In *Rethinking Nation and Nationalism*, Project on the Middle East and Political Science, POMPES studies n. 14, June 2, 2015, p. 10.

Bennett, Andrew. 2010. Process Tracing and Causal Inference. In *Rethinking Social Inquiry*, ed. Henry Brady and David Collier. Lanham: Rowman and Littlefield.

Boesler, Matthew. 2013. The Economist Who Invented The BRICs Just Invented A Whole New Group of Countries: The MINTs. *Business Insider*, November 13, 2013. http://www.businessinsider.com/jim-oneill-presents-the-mint-economies-2013-11. Accessed 2 Apr 2016.

Cashmore, Ellis. 2004. *Encyclopedia or Race and Ethnic Studies*. London/New York: Routledge.

Cesari, Jocelyn. 2014. *The Awakening of Muslim Democracies*. Cambridge: Cambridge University Press.

———. 2015. Religion and Politics: What Does God Have To Do with It? *Religion* 6 (4): 1330–1344.

CIA. *World Factbook*. https://www.cia.gov/library/publications/the-world-factbook/. Accessed 30 Sept 2017.

Collier, David. 1993. The Comparative Method. In *Political Science: The State of Discipline II*, ed. Ada W. Finifter. Washington, DC: American Political Science Association.

Democracy Ranking Association. *The Democracy Ranking 2015.* http://democracyranking.org/ranking/2015/data/Scores_of_the_Democracy_Ranking_2015_A4.pdf. Accessed 30 Sept 2017.

Esposito, John, Tamara Sonn, and John O. Voll. 2015. *Islam and Democracy After the Arab Spring.* Oxford: Oxford University Press.

Freedom House. *Freedom in the World 2017.* https://freedomhouse.org/report/freedom-world/freedom-world-2017. Accessed 30 Sept 2017.

Geertz, Clifford. 1968. *Islam Observed; Religious Development in Morocco and Indonesia.* New Haven: Yale University Press.

George, Alexander, and Andrew Bennett. 2005. *Case Studies and Theory Development in the Social Sciences.* Cambridge: MIT Press.

Global Peace Index Report. 2017. Institute for Economics and Peace. http://economicsandpeace.org/wp-content/uploads/2015/06/Global-Peace-Index-Report-2015_0.pdf. Accessed 30 Sept 2017.

Hefner, Robert. 2000. *Civil Islam: Muslims and Democratization in Indonesia.* Princeton: Princeton University Press.

Joshua, Castellino, and Kathleen Cavanaugh. 2013. *Minority Rights in the Middle East.* Oxford: Oxford University Press.

King, Gary, Robert O. Keohane, and Sidney Verba. 1994. *Designing Social Inquiry: Scientific Inference in Qualitative Research.* Princeton: Princeton University Press.

Mahoney, James, and Gary Goertz. 2006. A Tale of Two Cultures: Contrasting Quantitative and Qualitative Research. *Political Analysis* 14: 227–249.

Martin, Eric. 2012. Goldman Sachs's MIST Topping BRICs as Smaller Markets Outperform. *Bloomberg Business*, August 7, 2012. http://www.bloomberg.com/news/articles/2012-08-07/goldman-sachs-s-mist-topping-brics-as-smaller-markets-outperform. Accessed 2 Apr 2016.

Mill, John Stuart. 2002. *A System of Logic.* Honolulu: University Press of the Pacific.

Minorities at Risk Dataset, MAR. http://www.mar.umd.edu/mar_data.asp. Accessed 30 Sept 2017.

Peoples Under Threat, Minority Rights Group. http://peoplesunderthreat.org/. Accessed 30 Sept 2017.

Pew Research Center. *The World's Muslims: Unity and Diversity.* Chapter 1: Religious Affiliation, 2012. http://www.pewforum.org/2012/08/09/the-worlds-muslims-unity-and-diversity-1-religious-affiliation/#_ftn9. Accessed 30 Sept 2017.

———. *Mapping the Global Muslim Population.* Report 2009. http://www.pewforum.org/files/2009/10/Muslimpopulation.pdf. Accessed 30 Sept 2017.

Pisani, Elizabeth. 2015. *Indonesia, Etc.: Exploring the Improbable Nation.* New York: Norton.

Przeworski, Adam, and Henry Teune. 1970. *The Logic of Comparative Social Inquiry.* New York: Wiley-Interscience.
The Economist Group. *The Economist Intelligence Unit's Democracy Index 2017.* https://infographics.economist.com/2017/DemocracyIndex/. Accessed 30 Sept 2017.
The World Bank. *World Data.* http://data.worldbank.org/indicator/NY.GDP.MKTP.KD.ZG. Accessed 30 Sept 2017.
Van Bruinessen, Martin. 2014. Secularism, Islamism and Muslim intellectualism in Turkey and Indonesia: Some Comparative Observations. In *Ketika Makkah Menjadi, Las Vegas: Agama*, ed. Mirza Tirta Kusuma. Jakarta: Gramedia.
Van Evera, Stephen. 1997. *Guide to Methods for Students of Political Science.* Ithaca: Cornell University Press.

CHAPTER 4

Securitization and Autonomization in Turkey and Indonesia: A Brief History and Review of the Period of Democratization

THE KURDISH ISSUE IN TURKEY: A HISTORY OF EXCLUSION AND SECURITIZATION

The nation-states of the Middle East have long struggled to include minorities in their political communities. As Picard explains, the choice between majoritarian democracy (*Tocquevillian* democracy) and consensus democracy (*Lijphartian* democracy) shaped state–society relations—and by extension the state's relations with minorities—differently in each country of the region.[1] Therefore in this region, as Picard says, the "respect for minority rights has become—together with women's rights—the barometer of a successful transition to democracy."[2] That's why states and governments of the region have rarely attached importance to minorities' inclusion, and when they have, it has been mostly to maintain the dictatorial power of the ruling elites. Obviously, the historical legacy of the Ottoman Empire and especially the post-Ottoman period, with its lack of democracy and an external imposition of autocrats, has shaped the question of minorities in the Middle East in the direction of their exclusion. Kymlicka and Pföstl argue, for example, that three legacies created the

---

[1] Elizabeth Picard, "Nation-building and minority rights in the Middle East," in Roald, A. S. and Longva A. N. ed., *Religious minorities in the Middle East: Domination, self-empowerment, accommodation* (Leiden, Boston: Brill Academic, 2015).

[2] Ibid., p. 57.

current situation and struggle of minorities in the Middle East. The first is the millet legacy, the second the colonial legacy, and the final one the postcolonial nation-building legacy.[3]

Although Turkey did not pass through a period of Western colonization like the rest of the territories of the Ottoman Empire after World War I, the threat of Western powers dismembering the country had an impact on the state's future treatment of minorities. This danger of dismemberment convinced General Mustafa Kemal—later self-nominated *Atatürk*, the "father of the nation"—to fight a war of independence that lasted between 1919 and 1923, when the Turkish Republic was created. So the new republic, as a direct reaction to this foreign threat, was founded on a strong nationalism for a united and secular Turkish state, following the ideology of Kemalism,[4] with one people, one language, one state, and, thus, with the "Turkification" of all its population.

Actually, the two most important features of the new Turkish Republic identity since 1923, both diverging from the state's Ottoman origins, became "exclusionary nationalism" and "Western secularism"—and especially a particular form of the second one: an "assertive secularism" that aimed to explicitly exclude religion from the public sphere.[5] In fact, according to some scholars like Akturk,[6] Turkey was founded on a contradiction between its Islamic origins of war of independence and its secular nation-building. Much like Algeria and Pakistan, Akturk argues, Turkey was created on the basis of an Islamic mobilization against non-Muslim opponents, but when the "religious war" was won, its political elites chose a secular and nationalistic state model. Therefore, since Turkey's foundation, the nationalistic state has always struggled with the inclusion of

---

[3] Will Kymlicka and Eva Pföstl, "Minority politics in the Middle East and North Africa: The prospects for transformative change," *Ethnic and Racial Studies* (2015) Vol. 38, No. 14, 1–10.

[4] The six fundamental pillars of the Kemalist ideology (from Turkish Republic founder Mustafa Kemal Ataturk) are republicanism, populism, nationalism, secularism, statism, and reformism. See on Kemalism, among many others, Umut Azak, *Islam and secularism in Turkey: Kemalism, religion and the nation state* (New York: I. B. Tauris, 2010).

[5] See on this Ahmet T. Kuru, "Passive and Assertive Secularism: Historical Conditions, Ideological Struggles, and State Policies toward Religion," *World Politics*, Volume 59, No. 4, July 2007, pp. 568–594.

[6] Sener Akturk, "Religion and Nationalism: Contradictions of Islamic Origins and Secular Nation-Building in Turkey, Algeria, and Pakistan," *Social Science Quarterly*, 96, 3 (2015): pp. 778–806.

minorities, religious ones[7] and, even more, ethnic ones.[8] Nevertheless, the Turkish treatment of minorities changed through its history, with periods of more accommodation and near inclusion alternating with periods of repression and total exclusion. Actually, we can separate Turkish history into three main phases for the treatment of the Kurds:

(1) The original phase of repression and securitization during the twentieth century, in different degrees and by different means, from the foundation of the republic to the late 1990s (in particular since the PKK full-scale insurgency since August 1984)
(2) A phase of desecuritization, dating from the PKK ceasefire declared in September 1999; the start of Turkish candidacy for full membership in the EU in December 1999; and the AKP's victory in the 2002 elections with new propositions to include Kurds in Turkish society. This phase lasted until 2011/2015
(3) Finally, the current phase of resecuritization began in some sense in 2011, with the resumption of hostilities, but especially since the summer of 2015, upon completion of the peace process that had started in 2013, and further increased following the failed coup in July 2016[9]

Regarding the first phase, the new Turkish Republic granted legal status only to small numbers of ethnic and non-Muslim minorities: Armenian Catholics, Greek Orthodox, and Jews. The Kurds were left out because Turkey refused to recognize any large ethnic minority within its borders, on the belief that this could have threatened the nationalist model of the Turkish state. Founders of the Turkish Republic believed that an ethnically heterogeneous society was the main reason behind a weak state, just as it

---

[7] Ramazan Kilinc, "International Pressure, Domestic Politics, and the Dynamics of Religious Freedom. Evidence from Turkey," *The Journal of comparative politics*, Volume 46, No. 2 (January 2014): 127–145.

[8] Mesut Yegen, "Turkish nationalism and the Kurdish question," *Ethnic and Racial Studies*, Volume 30, Issue 1 (2007) pp. 119–151.

[9] According to some reports, Turkey's state of emergency following the coup made the situation with the Kurds even more repressive. For example, the Ministry of Interior seized control of 28 elected municipalities in the weeks following the coup, mostly run by the Kurdish Democratic Regions Party, in the name of saving democracy. See on this Naomi Cohen and Nuhat Mugurtay, "Kurds are paying the price of Turkey's post-coup crackdown," *Middle East Eye*, September 20, 2016. http://www.middleeasteye.net/columns/turkeys-kurdish-question-turns-new-page-894865406.

had been behind the end of Ottoman Empire. For this reason, they wanted the new Turkish Republic to follow the nationalist European model of one language, one nation, and one state, which found wide acceptance at the Paris peace talks that ended World War I and led to the founding of the League of Nations.

Ethnic Albanians, Pontics, Kurds, Arabs, Bosniaks, Circassians, and Chechens—many of them coming from the lands lost by the Ottoman Empire—also started to be considered Turkish under Turkish law, assimilating in the Turkish identity even if they were still ethnically different from Turks.[10] The new republic also expected Kurds to assimilate in this way. Therefore, since the beginning of the Turkish state, Kurds started to lose their language and identity, in a process of assimilation, or acculturation as some scholars define it,[11] in the Turkish nation, meaning through a kind of "Turkification." Nevertheless, according to Mesut Yeğen,[12] Turkish state officials before the foundation of the republic, needing the support of Kurds for the war of independence, declared that they would have recognized them as an ethnic group, with minority rights, as reflected in the Amasya Protocol of 1919.[13] Instead, since the mid-1920s, the state denied not only their rights but their very existence, at least until the end of the twentieth century. Yeğen argues that for several reasons this changed during the century: Turkish nationalism mostly saw the Kurdish issue in terms of a rivalry between the backward and tribal past and the prosperous present and future in the first half of the nineteenth century; in the 1950s and 1960s it was more a tension between the peripheral economy and the national market; and in the 1970s the Kurdish rebellion was seen as a communist incitement. But the assimilation had always the same goal: that Kurds would have become Turks sooner or later. To do this, the state also implemented small-scale population relocations to reduce concentrations of Kurds in areas where some nationalist uprisings could have happened.

---

[10] Stephen Kinzer, *Crescent and Star: Turkey between two worlds* (New York: Farrar, Straus and Giroux, 2008).

[11] Heper, for example, argues that the concept of acculturation is more proper than that of assimilation in the Kurdish case in Turkey, given the centuries of amicable relations between the state and the Kurds. See Metin Heper, *State and Kurds in Turkey: The Question of Assimilation* (New York: Palgrave Macmillan, 2007).

[12] Mesut Yeğen, "The Kurdish question in Turkey: Denial to recognition," in Marlies Casier and Joost Jongerden, *Nationalisms and politics in Turkey: Political Islam, Kemalism, and the Kurdish issue* (New York: Routledge, 2011): pp. 67–84.

[13] Ibid., p. 127.

When and where such uprisings happened, the government neutralized nationalist movements with deportations and arrest or execution of leaders, dismemberment of traditional institutions, and, finally, support to the Kurdish feudal landowning class and tribal leaders (ağas) and leaders of Sufi orders (şeyhs) to block any nationalist desire in their communities.[14]

The Kurds were not the only minority excluded since the founding of the republic. If Kurds were the ethnic minority excluded from the construction of the Turkish Republic, the Alevis (considered "heterodox" Muslim since they were part of the Shia tradition) were the religious minority excluded (and sometimes the two discriminations went hand in hand) as the only form of Islam recognized in Turkey was the Sunni denomination. Nonetheless, their religious exclusion included some efforts at cultural inclusion. As Tambar explains,[15] the cultural inclusion of Alevis within the ethno-national imaginary of Turkey was based on "public display," as an example of Turkish diversity—in particular with the Alevi "revival" in the 1980s and 1990s—but not for substantive political incorporation. In Turkish Republican history, there has always been tension and ambiguity between, on the one hand, the recognition of cultural rights of minorities like the Alevis, as "an element of Turkey's folkloric heritage,"[16] and, on the other hand, sectarian religious and political hostility toward them. This tension exists even today, if we consider that the majority of the people repressed in the Gezi Park protests in 2013, for example, were Alevi.[17]

Anyway, as a reaction to Kurdish exclusion and securitization, in 1925 Sheikh Said—a famous Sufi Naqshbandi religious and Kurdish leader—mobilized tens of thousands of people in a rebellion against the Turkish government. Two years later another Kurdish rebellion, this time secular nationalist, broke out in Agri (Ararat). The state violently repressed these rebellions, resulting in thousands of casualties, as they were considered

---

[14] Denise Natali, *The Kurds and the State: Evolving National Identity in Iraq, Turkey and Iran* (Syracuse: Syracuse University Press, 2005).

[15] Kabir Tambar: *The Reckoning of Pluralism: Political Belonging and the Demands of History in Turkey* (Palo Alto: Stanford University Press, 2014).

[16] Ibid., p. 21.

[17] *Hurriyet Daily News*, "78 percent of Gezi Park protest detainees were Alevis: Report," November 25, 2013. Accessed September 30, 2017. http://www.hurriyetdailynews.com/78-percent-of-gezi-park-protest-detainees-were-alevis-report-.aspx?PageID=238&NID=58496&NewsCatID=341.

threats to the foundation of the new republic.[18] Between 1937 and 1938, the Turkish military also killed thousands of people to repress the rebellion in the Kurdish Alevi region of Dersim, for which Recep Tayyip Erdogan asked forgiveness when he was Turkish prime minister.[19] Since World War II and the start of a multiparty system in Turkey, political parties have tried to engage with Kurdish leaders in order to form political alliances,[20] but they have not allowed Kurds to have their "Kurdishness" represented in the Parliament. This lack of political opportunity for the Kurdish minority contributed later to the creation of the *Partiya Karkaren Kurdistan*, or Kurdish Workers Party (PKK), which was also building on the revolutionary left movements in Turkey. In fact, as a reaction to assimilation and repression, half a century after the founding of the republic, in 1974 a group of Kurdish activists called the Revolutionaries of Kurdistan started a campaign for Kurdish rights, and following the government crackdown on this movement in 1978, the PKK was founded. A few years later, in 1983, during a period of military rule, a new law (2932) was incorporated into the constitution that prohibited the use of the Kurdish language "in the expression and dissemination of thought" (Art. 28) aiming for the final assimilation of Kurds, this after, in 1982, the setting of the highest threshold for a party to enter a parliament in the world: ten percent. This renewed offensive against Kurdish identity, together with armed clashes and crackdowns by the government, made the PKK decide on a full-scale insurgency in 1984.

Since then, between 30,000 and 40,000 people have been killed, and the war has passed through several periods of escalation, with an increased involvement of the civilian population in the Southeastern region.[21] Besides casualties, the conflict has created many refugees and internally displaced people. The displacement of Kurdish citizens, with many forced out of villages under attacks or curfews, has increased the asymmetrical

---

[18] Ayse Kadioğlu, "Necessity and the state of exception. The Turkish sate's permanent war with its Kurdish citizens," in: Riva Kastoryano ed. *Turkey between nationalism and globalization* (Abingdon: Routledge, 2013): 145.

[19] *BBC News*, "Turkey PM Erdogan apologizes for 1930s Kurdish killings," November 23, 2011, http://www.bbc.com/news/world-europe-15857429.

[20] Henri J. Barkey and Graham E. Fuller, *Turkey's Kurdish question* (Lanham: Rowman & Littlefield Publishers, 1998): 77.

[21] Crisis Group, *Turkey's PKK Conflict: The Death Toll*, July 20, 2016, accessed September 30, 2017, https://www.crisisgroup.org/europe-central-asia/western-europemediterranean/turkey/turkey-s-pkk-conflict-death-toll.

power relationship between the state and the Kurdish population, which is often caught in the middle of the conflict between the state and the PKK. The number of Kurdish villages depopulated in Turkey between the 1980s and 1990s is estimated at around 3000, with the displacement of almost 400,000 people.[22] But in total, the total number of Kurdish refugees is around three million people today, an estimated million of which were still internally displaced as of 2013.[23] The causes of the depopulation and displacement included village raids and forced evacuations by the Turkish state's military operations and the PKK attacks against unsupportive Kurdish clans (and even the destructions of Kurdish towns like Cizre, Sur, and Silopi by Turkish security forces). Aside from the conflict, the poverty of the Southeastern region made many Kurds migrate to other parts of the country or abroad, though mostly the reasons are to be found in the armed conflict between the Turkish army and the PKK. Therefore, as we can see, the militarization of the Turkish–Kurdish conflict—and with it the securitization of the Kurdish issue—fluctuated for a long time but intensified from 1984 until the end of the century. As Unver argues, in the 1990s the Kurdish question was reduced to a terrorist problem and territorial threat, an issue of concern solely to the military forces.[24] Only Turkish President Turgut Özal approached the conflict differently, viewing it not just as a military issue, and seemed open to a new inclusiveness. Unfortunately, he died while in office in 1993, under suspicious circumstances.[25]

The second phase in the treatment of the Kurdish minority by the Turkish state started with the rise in November 2002 of the AKP, the first Islamist, even if moderate, party to attain power in Turkey without an immediate response from the military. Since the beginning it seemed that

[22] Human Rights Watch, *Turkey Report*, March 2005, p. 3, accessed September 30, 2017, https://www.hrw.org/reports/2005/turkey0305/3.htm#_Toc97005223.
[23] Internal Displacement Monitoring Center, *Turkey: Internal displacement in brief*, as of December 2013, accessed February 12, 2016, http://www.internal-displacement.org/europe-the-caucasus-and-central-asia/turkey/summary.
[24] Akin Unver, *Turkey's Kurdish question: Discourse and politics since 1990* (London: Routledge, 2015) p. 98.
[25] *Hurriyet Daily News*, "Turkish President Ozal's death suspicious," June 13, 2012, accessed September 30, 2017, http://www.hurriyetdailynews.com/turkish-president-ozals-death-suspicious-state-audit-board-.aspx?pageID=238&nID=23053&NewsCatID=338.
Rasim Ozan Kutahyali, "Who Poisoned Former Turkish President Ozal?," *Al Monitor*, August 22, 2013, accessed September 30, 2017. https://www.al-monitor.com/pulse/originals/2013/08/turkey-president-ozal-poisoned.html.

the new trend toward democratization in Turkey could finally bring about a real process of inclusion, not only of the very pious and conservative Islamist people excluded at the founding of the republic, but also of ethnic minorities, in particular the Kurds. Owing in part also to its increased interest in EU membership, the AKP started to speak a language of "diversity within unity" (like the European motto) and proposed to accept the religious, linguistic, and ethnic differences of the country in a vision of a new pluralist society.[26] It can be asserted that, as early as 1999, Turkey had already passed through a phase of desecuritization, also thanks to its EU candidacy.[27] Supporters of an accommodative approach to the Kurdish question, like former Prime Minister (between 1997 and 1999) Mesut Yilmaz, started to express the need for a reduction of the old Kemalist structures.[28] With the AKP things improved even more. The new AKP elites represented the so-called Black Turks, the more religious Turks coming from Anatolia, unlike the secular republican elites of the western Turkish cities (so-called White Turks) and more similar to the pious people of the Kurdistan region. The AKP, and in particular Erdogan, decided therefore to start to recognize Kurdish identity, granting it the "rights of difference."

An important moment for the shift of strategy was the historic visit of Erdogan (who at that time was prime minister) to Diyarbakir in 2005. With the new AKP in power, Kurdish-language books became legal, even if the government controlled them, and Kurdish broadcasting was allowed on TRT (the state television station), even if for only 30 minutes a week, until 2009, when a government-run Kurdish language TV channel launched. Finally, parents could once again call their children by their Kurdish names, though not "subversive" ones or containing letters like q, w, or x, which do not exist in the Turkish alphabet.[29] The AKP even drew up a partial amnesty law aimed at PKK militants and introduced the Return

[26] Ali B. Soner, "The Justice and Development Party's policies towards non-Muslim minorities in Turkey," *Journal of Balkan and Near Eastern Studies* 12, no. 1 (2010): 23–40.

[27] Bülent Aras and Rabia Karakaya Polat, "From Conflict to Cooperation: Desecuritization of Turkey's Relations with Syria and Iran," *Security Dialogue* 39(5) (2008): p. 499.

[28] Hakan Yavuz, "Five Stages of the Construction of Turkish Nationalism in Turkey," *Nationalism and Ethnic Politics* 7(3) (2001): 1–24.

[29] David Romano, "The long road toward Kurdish accommodation in Turkey: The role of elections and international pressures," Ch. 9 in Jacques Bertrand and Oded Haklai (eds.) *Democratization and Ethnic Minorities: Conflict or Compromise?* (Abingdon: Routledge, 2014): 175–176.

to Village and Rehabilitation Project for the repatriation of internally displaced Kurds.[30] Therefore, a clear line was drawn between the PKK (a security problem) and Kurdish minority rights (a political problem), under a desecuritization process.[31]

This shift in attitude and policies toward accommodation increased even more starting in 2009, when local elections in the southeast part of the country were lost by the AKP. At that point, the AKP understood that identity and autonomy were very important for the Kurdish electorate, and so something had to be done to engage, not repress, them (that year the Democratic Society Party, the main pro-Kurdish party, was also shut down). The PKK leader Abdullah Ocalan, in jail since 1999, proposed a Road Map, based on ten principles, including the the Democratic Nation Principle, Common Homeland Principle, Inseparability of the Individual and Collective Rights Principle, and Ideological Independence and Freedom Principle.[32] Following secret talks between the AKP and the PKK between 2009 and 2011, known as the Oslo Process,[33] in March 2013 Ocalan announced the end of armed struggle and the start of a ceasefire and peace talks with the government. As the International Crisis Group concluded,[34] in 2013 and 2014 favorable conditions, including strong leadership on both sides, broad public legitimacy, a unilateral PKK ceasefire, a mutual understanding that neither side could win a military victory, and well-established principles for negotiations, were preparing the road for a successful peace process. But in reality, military hostility had already restarted in 2011. The situation became more difficult in 2014,

---

[30] Özlem Pusane, "Turkey's Kurdish Opening: Long Awaited Achievements and Failed Expectations," *Turkish Studies* 15(1) (2014): 81–99.

[31] Tarik Oğuzlu, "Soft Power in Turkish Foreign Policy," *Australian Journal of International Affairs* 61(1) (2007): 81–97.

[32] See on this Abdullah Ocalan's three-phase Road Map, Partiya Karkeren Kurdistan, accessed September 30, 2017, http://www.pkkonline.com/en/index.php?sys=article&artID=114. See also Akin Unver, *Turkey's Kurdish question: Discourse and politics since 1990* (London: Routledge, 2015) p. 160.

[33] Hugh Pope, "Turkey, Syria and Saving the PKK Peace Process," *The International Crisis Group*, December 10, 2014, accessed September 30, 2017, http://www.crisisgroup.org/en/regions/europe/turkey cyprus/turkey/op-ed/pope-turkey-syria-and-saving-the-pkk-peace-process.aspx.

[34] *International Crisis Group*, "Turkey and the PKK: Saving the Peace Process," Europe Report No. 234, November 6, 2014, accessed September 30, 2017, http://www.crisisgroup.org/en/regions/europe/turkey-cyprus/turkey/234-turkey-and-the-pkk-saving-the-peace-process.aspx.

also due to a spillover of the Syrian civil war, and in July 2015 the peace process definitively collapsed after the PKK interrupted the ceasefire and Turkey started to bomb PKK positions in Iraq as a response to the Suruç bombing attack (which targeted leftist Kurdish activists). With the military conflict, the civilian population was once again affected, finding itself caught between the two sides, the curfews, and the radicalized youth affiliated with the PKK (i.e., *Yurtsever Devrimci Gençlik Hareketi*, the Patriotic Revolutionary Youth Movement/YDGH) that declared autonomy in cities like Cizre. Therefore, since the end of the peace process in 2015, which also coincided with the first seats in Turkey's parliament for the Kurdish party as the third political force, the Turkish securitization of the Kurdish issue had restarted: the Kurdish minority had become again only a security problem. Renewed alienation and polarization between the Kurds of the southeast region of Turkey and the Turkish Republic led to demonstrations and political assassination and even a crackdown on media and academicians supporting the Kurdish cause, who were considered terrorists.

So what went wrong? Why did Turkey revert to securitization of the Kurdish nationalist movement and the Kurdish minority in Turkey's Southeastern region? Why have hundreds of civilians again been killed[35] and cities destroyed since July 2015? And why is the Kurdish issue as far as ever from being resolved in a peaceful and negotiated way? The fact is that since the beginning, the freedoms and rights granted to the Kurds by the AKP were intended as "negative freedoms," in the sense that they were designed to, at most, end the oppression of Kurdish society and identity, but not necessarily as "positive freedoms," in the sense of real recognition of a different nationality, territory, or political body with decentralization and autonomization, as the Kurdish political movement sought. As Murat Tezcur rightly points out, "in the long run, it is unreasonable to expect that the Kurds in Turkey would be satisfied with the status quo while their ethnic kin in Iraq and Syria enjoy political and cultural autonomy."[36]

But this study, rather than seeking to understand what the inclusion of Kurds in the Turkish state would look like or analyze the point of view of

---

[35] Human Rights Watch, December 22, 2015, *Turkey: Mounting Security Operation Deaths, Scores of Civilians Among Hundreds Killed in Southeast*, accessed September 30, 2017, https://www.hrw.org/news/2015/12/22/turkey-mounting-security-operation-deaths.

[36] Gunes Murat Tezcur, "Prospects for Resolution of the Kurdish Question: A Realist Perspective," *Insight Turkey,* accessed September 30, 2017, http://file.insightturkey.com/Files/Pdf/15_2_2013_tezcur.pdf.

the minority, investigates the causes that may have shifted the state's strategy toward the minority during the democratization years, from an engaging and accommodating one to a repressive and securitizing one. Before answering these questions on the basis of an analysis of the four hypotheses, what follows is a brief discussion of recent developments in Turkish democracy, which will help to put the resecuritization in perspective.

Turkish Democracy: Recent Developments

Since the second part of the twentieth century, many Western scholars have considered Turkey favorably as a democracy, even if only a formal one. The country started to hold democratic elections in 1950, but even though it has been a multiparty system since that time, the elections were not enough to demonstrate the democratic identity of Turkey; moreover, on several occasions since then, the military seized power when elites became concerned that, for example, Islamism or communism might threaten the foundations of the republic, with its nationalism, secularism, and capitalist system. Military coups occurred in 1960 and 1980, and military memoranda, or "soft coups," that deposed elected governments happened in 1971 and 1997. While in 1980 the target of the coup were the communists, in 1996 Turkey had its first pro-Islamic government since 1923, and so the military blocked it with a "soft coup," deposing Prime Minister Necmettin Erbakan, and a Constitutional Court ban of Islamist parties until 2002.

As we can see, even though Turkey is one of only two countries in the Middle East to go down the path of democracy since the early 1900s, with the Young Turk Revolution in 1908 (the other country being Iran with its Persian Constitutional Revolution in 1905), it was only at the dawn of the twenty-first century that the Turkish state truly found itself on the right track headed toward a real and substantive democracy, when the popular vote was respected and the military remained in the barracks. Therefore, even though, compared to other Muslim countries of the Middle East, Turkey had developed some type of democratic institutions or policies, the idea that this system was truly democratic was a myth. The population was not free to choose who would govern, even though it was a multiparty system, and did not benefit from the liberal elements of a democracy like freedom of speech, press, or assembly. So why, according to many Western scholars, was Turkey considered to be the only Muslim democracy, and how was the concept of Turkey as a "model" of Muslim democracy built?

Bernard Lewis has been an important scholar making this claim.[37] He started from the point of view that Turkey had never been colonized; on the contrary, it won its war of independence and so learned by itself how to build democratic institutions (unlike countries that have seen these institutions imposed after a war or left after decolonization). Second, Turkey, like Tunisia, had been strongly connected with the West, so it had a westward political orientation, first of all with its experiment in parliamentary power that dates back to the nineteenth century (since the First Constitutional Era in 1876, which created a constitutional monarchy), then with its secularism since Ataturk and Turkish independence in 1923, and finally with its NATO membership starting in 1952. These elements therefore meant that Turkey's political institutions closely resembled a European democratic system.

Nevertheless, Turkey introduced democracy gradually, in small but increasing steps, with stronger trade unions, a freer press, the presence of civil society organizations, and so forth. This is also because Turkey put in one of the strongest economic performances in the MENA region in the twentieth century, thanks to natural resources, its strategic geopolitical position, and strong institutions. This wealth created a broad middle class that started to push for an active civil society without which democratic institutions cannot work. But it was not until the twenty-first century that Turkey attained a much higher level in its democratic status. It was in 2002 when the Justice and Development Party/AKP attained power, representing the first moderate Islamist party (though the party prefers to define itself as "conservative democrat") to be elected in the country without a subsequent intervention of the army or the Constitutional Court. The AKP has been ruling Turkey these first few years very successfully, both in terms of politics and the economy. Nevertheless, to keep winning elections is not exactly a good sign for democracy, as Przeworski[38] and others showed, since a healthy democracy will generally see transfers of power (in particular if the use of power becomes increasingly exclusionary and authoritarian, as in the Turkish case). Turkish democracy therefore started to become again a *de facto* dominant-party system (even if not a

---

[37] Bernard Lewis, "Why Turkey Is the only Muslim Democracy," *Middle East Quarterly*, March 1994, pp. 41–49.

[38] Adam Przeworski, Michael E. Alvarez, Jose Antonio Cheibub, and Fernando Limongi, *Democracy and development: Political institutions and well-being in the world, 1950–1990* (Cambridge: Cambridge University Press, 2000).

single-party one) as the AKP held office for four terms, including the most recent one, which started in November 2015. AKP leader Recep Tayyip Erdogan has been prime minister for three terms and is currently the Turkish president in a new presidential system, which was created following the April 2017 referendum, which could allow him to stay in office for many more years. This process of democratic erosion and "authoritarianization" has produced an increasingly "sick" Turkish democracy (even if it is happening in a very healthy Turkish economy), starting especially with the elections of 2015, the failed coup in 2016, and, finally the referendum on the presidential system in 2017. So how did Turkey arrive at this point in recent years?

In brief, Erdogan and the AKP came to power in the 2002 on a moderate Islamic-based platform that promised to build a gradual "conservative democracy" based on government accountability and civic pluralism. Since then the AKP has kept growing in power, in part because of the impressive economic growth that Turkey has seen under the AKP: between 2002 and 2014 the Turkish economy tripled in size, reaching USD 1.4 trillion (with an annual average real GDP growth between 2002 and 2011 of 5.2 percent).[39] But the economic growth was accompanied by a democratic reversal after the first few years. The AKP at the beginning of its rule avoided confrontations with the traditional powers of judiciary and military actors. However, in the 2007 election, when the AKP gained more electoral support, the party and its elites started trying to reduce the power of the old secular and nationalist Kemalist establishment and infiltrated the civilian and military institutions. This process was also accompanied by suspected "internal enemies" of the AKP and Erdogan. Classical claims about the "deep state" and conspiracy theories against the AKP have emerged in particular since 2007, when hundreds of people, especially retired military personnel, were arrested for the alleged "Ergenekon" plot to topple the AKP government.[40] Unfortunately, even if the scandal started as a preoccupation with the existence of a secret group of military

---

[39] From: "World Economic Outlook," April 2012, Turkish Statistical Institute, retrieved September 30, 2017, http://www.propertyturkey.tv/Pages.aspx?ID=2.

[40] *Al Jazeera*, "Timeline: Turkey's Ergenegon trial," August 5, 2013, accessed September 30, 2017, http://www.aljazeera.com/news/europe/2013/08/20138512358195978.html.

The Economist, "Justice or revenge?," August 10, 2013, accessed September 30, 2017, http://www.economist.com/news/europe/21583312-harsh-verdicts-are-handed-down-ergenekon-trial-justice-or-revenge.

actors, intelligence officers, judges, and others, it ended with the persecution and imprisonment of AKP opponents, among whom were journalists, academics, and politicians from the opposition.[41] This raised serious concerns both about the democratic elements of the AKP and the quality and independence of judicial institutions, with the start of the authoritarian drift of the Erdogan regime with respect to the media and political opponents.[42]

Also, after 2007, the AKP gradually worked for a new social contract with the people, to rewrite a civilian constitution in collaboration with various forces, since Turkey's last constitution was written by the army in 1982. But after the elections in 2011, when the AKP realized that its growing power could soon attain an absolute majority in parliament, it postponed the writing of the new constitution, opting to wait for a majoritarian position in order to have sole authority to revise the constitution. This plan was temporarily blocked in the elections of July 2015 owing to the success of the pro-Kurdish People's Democratic Party (*Halkların Demokratik Partisi*/HDP), the first Kurdish party to win seats in parliament and even becoming the country's third political force. The HDP is also a leftist secular party that gave voice not only to the Kurds but also to the younger segment of the population, which was worried about the authoritarian and Islamist, even if moderate, drift of the regime. This was one of the main turning points in the strategy of the AKP with respect to the Kurdish minority, caused in particular by the elites' perceived risk of losing power, as this study will explain later in Chap. 5 regarding the elites' power struggle.

In the parliamentary elections of 2011 and 2015, 87 percent and 84 percent of Turks voted respectively, compared with 79 percent in the 2002 elections that brought the AKP to power. But even as the turnout at the polls increased, the ability to contest politics has been reduced, and Turkey eventually became in practice the dominant-party democracy we see today. Erdogan centralized and strengthened his power and that of the AKP, founded by him after his term as mayor of Istanbul in the 1990s, in partnership with various figures, in particular Abdullah Gul and Bulent Arinc,

---

[41] E. P. Licursi, "The Ergenekon Case and Turkey's Democratic Aspirations," Freedom House, February 7, 2012, accessed September 30, 2017, https://freedomhouse.org/blog/ergenekon-case-andturkey%E2%80%99s-democratic-aspirations.

[42] Ted Piccone, *Five Rising Democracies and the Fate of the International Liberal Order* (Washington: Brooking Institution Press, 2016): p. 185.

the other two founders of the AKP, and later with Ahmet Davutoglu, a diplomat and academic who represented the good face of Turkey abroad, at least until he was on the same track as Erdogan. When Davutoglu started to disagree with Erdogan, in particular about the presidential system, he was forced to resign as prime minister and was replaced by Binali Yildirim in June 2016. Erdogan left the post of prime minister to become president in 2014 in a direct election by the population, a result from the 2007 constitutional referendum that changed the constitution, introducing a direct national vote for the president, as Erdogan himself wanted. Following that election, Erdogan started to transform the presidency from a ceremonial role to the most important and powerful actor of the state, in order to arrive at a referendum to codify this new balance of power leaning toward presidentialism.[43] As president, he started to exercise his increasing power with a strong hand, curtailing freedom of speech and assembly, attacking critical journalists, human rights activists, and even international actors.

But this shift in strategy since 2011, and increasingly every year since then, was caused not only by his success at the polls but also by two international events that occurred around that time: the Arab Spring and the civil war in Syria, from which arose ISIS (the Islamic State of Iraq and Syria) in 2013. The Arab Spring caused the AKP government to worry about possible internal repercussions, in particular with the increased internal tensions with the Gulen movement[44] and the Gezi Park protests in 2013, which reflected the growing frustration of the youth with the Turkish regime (actually the overwhelming majority of Gezi Park protesters were Alevis, and this could have affected the way the government

[43] Tim Arango, "Turkish Leader, Using Conflicts, Cements Power," *New York Times*, October 31, 2014 accessed September 30, 2017, http://www.nytimes.com/2014/11/01/world/europe/Erdogan-uses-conflict-to-consolidatepower.html?emc=edit_th_20141101&nl=todaysheadlines&nlid=41699871&_r=1.

[44] The Gulen movement is a religious and social movement, with a strong impact in education, both nationally and internationally, guided by a Turkish Islamic scholar Fethullah Gulen. At the beginning of the AKP government, Gulen was a supporter and friend of Erdogan but over time the relationship deteriorated. See the next chapter, which deals with the relationship between these two elites. Today Gulen is exiled in the USA, the movement is referred to by the Turkish government as the Gülenist Terror Organization (FETO), accused by Erdogan of being a "parallel state" that aims to weaken the AKP government (for example, Erdogan has blamed Gulen's followers for orchestrating the 2013 government corruption scandal). Also a state administrator has been running the Gulen newspaper, the only antigovernment newspaper, *Today's Zaman*, since March 2016.

reacted, but that is a separate topic of research). But the situation created by ISIS in Syria and Iraq has been even more important as it threatened not only the AKP government but the Turkish state itself, first of all ontologically (see Chap. 8 on ontological security) because suddenly it was possible for an independent proto-state to be born inside another state as a type of "cancer" (actually in this case supported also by the same Turkey as a tool against the Assad regime). Second, ISIS threatened the Turkish state materially, because the Syrian war made space for Kurdish autonomy with the creation in 2013 of the Rojava region (also known as Western Kurdistan or Syrian Kurdistan), which facilitated collaboration between the Syrian Kurdish forces (known as the PYG) and the PKK in Turkey. The AKP, therefore, was pushed to return to authoritarianism and repression of diversity, to maintain a strong unified state and protect the country from a possible implosion, for example, with the birth of a Kurdish area inside the state. But this process, besides facilitating the resecuritization of Kurds, reopened old polarizations in the country, first between young forces in civil society, often more liberal and left-oriented, and old establishment elites who were more conservative. The second polarization was between precisely the two main "nationalist souls" in Turkey, that is, those who consider themselves predominantly Turks and those who consider themselves predominantly Kurds. This increased polarization can be seen also between those who support the Kurdish demand for some form of self-rule—like public education in the Kurdish language and regional autonomy—and those who believe that these demands represent the greatest threat to Turkish unity and national identity.

Therefore, regarding the level of democracy in Turkey, scholars today no longer consider Turkey to be a very effective and substantive democracy, nor do well-known international indices of democracy. As stated earlier, the Economist Intelligence Unit defined Turkey as a "hybrid regime" between democracy and autocracy in its 2017 Democracy Index, while Freedom House (FH) considered Turkey a "partly free" country ("electoral" but not "liberal" democracy) in its 2017 index. The evaluation of FH is due to the state's political interference in the legislative and judiciary system as well as in media, academia, and civil society, in particular owing to the repercussions of the attempted coup in July, which led the government to declare a state of emergency and carry out mass arrests and firings of civil servants, academics, journalists, and other perceived enemies. The ISIS fight at the Turkish border since 2014 also pushed the AKP to deal with very important national security threats, as did the state failure of its two bordering countries, Syria and Iraq. In this scenario, as Kinzer says, "taboos that limit the freedom of ethnic groups and other minorities remain strong,"[45] and so the relationship between the Turkish state and the Kurds has deteriorated. The ceasefire that started in 2013 broke down in 2015, restarting what has on many occasions been a "securitization" process of this minority.

But such has not always been the case under AKP rule. As stated earlier, in 2002 the AKP started a process of including two segments of society that had traditionally been excluded by the Turkish secular Kemalist philosophy: the Islamist segment, the conservative pious people, with the symbolic elimination of the ban on headscarves and other policies in favor of a moderate Islam, and the Kurdish minority, with the enactment of new laws that allowed, for example, the Kurdish language to be used for the first time in private schools and broadcasting. As Cavanaugh and Hughes put it, the AKP, together with the HDP, brought the Kurdish issue back into politics from the "political cold."[46] But while the first process of inclusion of the conservative segment of society worked successfully and is still ongoing, the second one—the inclusion and equal participation of the Kurdish minority in the Turkish polity—which seemed eventually to lead to a peace process with the PKK, reversed course in 2011 and even more in 2015, with a resecuritization process put in place by the same AKP that had started the Kurds' inclusion.

This started to affect not only the level of inclusiveness and thus of substantiveness and meaningfulness of Turkish democracy, but also the process of Turkish integration in the EU, a long-running process that has also been delayed because of the Turkish treatment of minorities. Actually, the most recent EU reports of progress in Turkey's candidacy from 2014 to 2016 states that the dialogue between the government and representatives of minorities continued but is not enough.[47] With respect specifically to the Kurdish population, the report states that "the settlement of the Kurdish issue through a political process is the only way forward; reconciliation and reconstruction are also becoming key issues for the authorities

---

[45] Stephen Kinzer, *Crescent and Star: Turkey between two worlds* (New York: Farrar, Straus and Giroux, 2008), xiv.

[46] Kathleen Cavanaugh and Edel Hughes, "A Democratic Opening? The AKP and the Kurdish Left," *Muslim World Journal of Human Rights,* De Gruyter; 12(1): 53–74 (2015).

[47] European Commission, *Turkey 2017 Report,* accessed September 30, 2017, https://ec.europa.eu/neighbourhood-enlargement/sites/near/files/pdf/key_documents/2016/20161109_report_turkey.pdf.

to address."[48] And regarding the crackdown following the attempted coup, the report clarifies that the Kurdish issue has deteriorated: "the crackdown has continued since and has been broadened to pro-Kurdish and other opposition voices."[49] The report contains a special section also on the situation in the Eastern and Southeastern regions of the country that "remained one of the most critical challenges for the country"[50] and expresses concern about the political repression: "the adoption in May of a law allowing the immunity of a large number of deputies to be lifted and the ensuing detentions and arrests of several HDP Members of Parliament, including the two Co-Chairs, in November is a matter of grave concern."[51]

Some International NGOs, like Human Rights Watch and Amnesty International, went even further, denouncing human rights violations and civilian casualties carried out by the Turkish government in recent years. This "lighter" pressure of the EU today on Turkey, with respect to other representatives of the international community, stems from various causes, above all the refugee crisis in Europe, which requires the support of Turkey, but also the conflict with ISIS, which requires that Turkey serve as a bulwark against this threat (see Chap. 6 on international factors involved in this situation). Thus, it is clear that the EU keeps pushing Turkey toward more inclusion of minorities, in particular the Kurdish community, to improve its standing for possible future integration. However, there has been no strong criticism or condemnation of some acts that may have permanently jeopardized the democratization process in Turkey, such as the continued securitization of the Kurdish minority, which is often caught in the middle of the conflict between the PKK and the Turkish government. The next section therefore will examine in detail how the Turkish state has carried out the resecuritization of the Kurdish minority.

Turkish Resecuritization of the Kurdish Minority

It is difficult to say exactly which side first broke the truce, derailing the peace process between Turkey and the PKK in 2015, as information from the isolated Eastern region of Kurdistan is never easy to come by. However, the government is always the actor that should keep negotiations alive, in

[48] Ibid., 6.
[49] Ibid., 9.
[50] Ibid., 28.
[51] Ibid., 10.

order to arrive at a peace agreement sooner or later, and it is the government that finally decided to go back to the securitization of Kurdish issues and the Kurdish minority, including its main representative political actor, the HDP.

The first thing that President Erdogan did, since the election results of June 2015 blocked the AKP from forming a new government by itself, was to jeopardize the possibility of a coalition government and call for a snap election in November, as usually snap elections result in increased majorities for the party already in power. The goal of Erdogan in the meantime was to launch a forceful campaign against the HDP, based on the delegitimization and stigmatization of a party that, according to the AKP, was not clearly detached from the violent struggle of the PKK. Furthermore, by restarting the conflict with the PKK in July 2015, Erdogan sought to make the Turkish population afraid of instability and insecurity and attract large numbers of votes to the nationalist party in power, the AKP.[52] To help with this strategy, the worst terrorist attack in Turkish history occurred in Ankara during the electoral campaign on October 10, on a rally held by several trade unions and the HDP to protest the growing conflict between the Turkish armed forces and the separatist PKK. In the attack, more than a hundred people died, including two HDP candidates. The event had the effect of blocking definitively the HDP from leading rallies during the campaign and contributed to an increase in polarization and extremism in Turkey.[53] ISIS was held responsible for the attack, even though the HDP accused the government of being behind it and similar previous attacks against Kurdish targets. The results of this strategy of targeting the HDP party and in general the Kurdish minority of Eastern Turkey have been that the elections of November 2015 could not be considered "free and fair" as in the past

---

[52] Ceylan Yeginsu, "Strikes on Kurd Militias Elevate Tensions in Turkey," *New York Times*, July 26, 2015, accessed September 30, 2017, http://www.nytimes.com/2015/07/27/world/europe/heightened-tensions-in-turkey-afterstrikes-on-kurdish-militants-in-iraq.html.

Sarah Almuhtar and Tim Wallace, "Why Turkey Is Fighting the Kurds Who Are Fighting ISIS," *New York Times*, August 12, 2015, accessed September 30, 2017, http://www.nytimes.com/interactive/2015/08/12/world/middleeast/turkey-kurds isis.html.

[53] *The Economist*, "Turkish extremism. Heightening the contradictions," October 17, 2015.

because media freedom was strictly controlled by the Erdogan regime.[54] The HDP lost votes, even though it maintained a presence in parliament, and the AKP regained its absolute majority. The strategy worked well as the AKP attained its goal of changing the constitution toward a presidential system with the new phase of resecuritization.[55]

This case study starts from the premises that Turkey during its period of democratization shifted its strategy with respect to the Kurds, from an engagement based on desecuritization of the traditional repression of the Kurdish minority to a resecuritization of this minority. Thus, let us look in detail at the elements of this resecuritization. Regarding the extraordinary measures taken by securitizing actors, these have been first of all the restarting of the war with the PKK and second the "state of exception" (a state of emergency) that was recreated for the Kurdish minority in the Kurdish region. Since the end of the peace process in 2015, this state of emergency in the Southeastern region has had several consequences: the killing of hundreds of civilians besides the PKK fighters, the destruction of parts of Kurdish cities (in particular Cizre[56] but also others like Sur and Silopi[57]), the application of curfews in many towns, and the forced displacement of populations. This prompted the intervention of international human rights organizations, which asked the government to stop the abusive use of force in Kurdish areas.[58] However, as stated earlier, the EU and the rest of the international community were more reluctant to criticize Turkey because of the need for Turkey's support in the refugee crisis and the war against ISIS.

---

[54] Kareem Shaheen, "Turkish election campaign unfair say international monitors," *The Guardian*, November 2, 2015.

[55] Even though to make constitutional changes, which require either two-thirds of Parliament or 331 MPs plus a referendum (AKP got 316 MPs), the AKP needed the support of other parliamentarians and had to win a referendum.

[56] Dominique Soguel, "Residents Return to Turkish Town of Cizre, Find It Destroyed," ABC News, March 2, 2016, accessed September 30, 2017, http://abcnews.go.com/International/wireStory/turkey-rolls-back-curfew-kurdish-town-37327505.

[57] For the reconstruction of these towns there is a crowd-funding campaign. See Room4life in Turkey, accessed September 30, 2017, https://www.generosity.com/emergencies-fundraising/room4life-in-turkey-support-rebuilding-sur-cizre.

[58] Dominique Soguel, "Rights group urges Turkey to stop 'abusive' use of force in Kurdish areas, investigate deaths," *Associated Press/US News,* 22 December, 2015, accessed September 30, 2017, http://www.usnews.com/news/world/articles/2015-12-22/rights-group-civilian-deaths-rise-in-turkeys-kurdish-areas.

Other extreme measures taken by the regime included the targeting of pro-Kurdish political parties,[59] in particular with judicial attempts to eliminate them, something that had already started with the ban on the Democratic Society Party (KCK) trials in 2009[60] and continued with charges filed by Erdogan against the HDP in 2015, accusing the HDP of supporting terrorism.[61] The reduction of HDP's power in parliament continued with the arrest of the two leaders of HDP, Selahattin Demirtas and Figen Yuksekdag, and other party members in November 2016, with the accusation of spreading propaganda for militants fighting against the Turkish state.[62]

Actually, thousands of Kurdish politician-activists have been imprisoned (and hundreds murdered) for supporting the Kurdish cause just in recent decades. As Watts argues,[63] Kurdish parties used the legal political system to promote the Kurdish national agenda in recent decades, and they have been an integral part of Turkish politics, benefiting Turkish democratization, but their incorporation into the system did not necessarily bring moderation to their position. For this reason, the Turkish state has justified its repression of the Kurdish minority out of fear of Kurdish independence. The problem is that the 2006 modifications to the Anti-Terror Law failed to distinguish peaceful political dissent from the promotion of violence, which is why the state has applied the law broadly against young Kurdish demonstrators to restrict their freedoms of expression and association.[64] Therefore, respect for the principles of a fair trial, *habeas*

---

[59] Derya Bayir, 2014, "The role of the judicial system in the politicide of the Kurdish opposition," in Gunes C. and Zeydanlioglu W. ed., *The Kurdish question in Turkey: New perspectives on violence, representation and reconciliation* (Abingdon: Routledge, 2014).

[60] The KCK, *Koma Civakên Kurdistan*, or Group of Communities in Kurdistan, was an organization founded to put into practice Öcalan's ideology of Democratic Confederalism. Thousands of people were arrested, on dubious charges of propaganda of a "terrorist organization."

[61] After the HDP won seats in Parliament in June 2015, its 80 parliamentarians elected had been reported by Erdogan to the judiciary on an accusation of supporting terrorism so that they would lose immunity and be processed. See Roberta Zunini, "Demirtas: la violenza? È colpa di Erdogan. Parla il leader del partito filo-curdo," *L'Espresso*, August 13, 2015.

[62] BBC, "Turkey pro-Kurd HDP party condemns arrest of leaders," accessed September 30, 2017, http://www.bbc.com/news/world-europe-37875605.

[63] Nicole Watts, *Activists in office: Kurdish politics and protest in Turkey* (Seattle: University of Washington Press, 2010).

[64] Human Rights Watch, *Protesting as a Terrorist Offense: The Arbitrary Use of Terrorism Laws to Prosecute and Incarcerate Demonstrators in Turkey*, November 1, 2010, accessed

corpus, and other human rights, required also by the Copenhagen Criteria, have been in decline in Turkey. The EU actually criticized Turkey for its definition of terrorism.[65] Therefore, one can also consider as extreme measures the targeting of parties, human rights groups, civilian organizations, and bar associations, all of which have come under increasing attack by Erdogan's regime since 2011 and especially 2015. This targeting also opened the door to more political violence, which resulted in the suspected killings of lawyers, such as that, in March 2015, of prosecutor Mehmet Selim Kiraz,[66] who was involved in the investigation of a death in the Gezi Park protests, or the assassination in November 2015 of the prominent Kurdish lawyer Tahir Elci, who one month prior had been arrested for saying that the PKK was not a terrorist organization.[67] Therefore, today in Turkey the state views the Kurds in the Southeastern region once again as a security threat, not only as guerillas and militants (which could be explained on the basis of national security), but also as activists, political parties, media, and generally as a civilian population protesting against the militarization of the region. Even academicians have been targeted: hundreds of them were placed under investigation and arrested in early 2016 for signing a petition asking the government to stop the violence in the Southeastern region.[68] The attack and delegitimization of nonmainstream media that have criticized the regime's implementation of policies against the Kurdish minority or other issues happened first of all with the incarceration of journalists critical of the regime, such as those

September 30, 2017, https://www.hrw.org/report/2010/11/01/protesting-terrorist-offense/arbitrary-use-terrorism-laws-prosecute-and.

[65] International Crisis Group, "Turkey: The PKK and a Kurdish Settlement," *ICG Europe Report No. 219*, September 11, 2012, accessed September 30, 2017, http://www.crisisgroup.org/en/regions/europe/turkey cyprus/turkey/219-turkey-the-pkk-and-a-kurdish-settlement.aspx.

[66] Suspected members of the Revolutionary People's Liberation Party-Front (a Marxist party in Turkey considered a terrorist group) took prosecutor Kiraz hostage demanding that the police announce the names of members of the security services who they said were connected to the death of a young boy during Gezi Park protests. The police intervened and the lawyer was killed as a result of the operation.

[67] Erdogan accused the PKK of carrying out the killing, but many people protested in the capital declaring it a "homicide of the regime," as there was no reason why the PKK should have killed someone who was legitimizing the PKK itself.

[68] Elizabeth Redden, "Turkish Academy Under Attack," *Inside Higher Education*, February 12, 2016, accessed September 30, 2017. https://www.insidehighered.com/news/2016/02/12/more-1000-turkish-scholars-are-under-criminal-investigation-signing-petition.

from *Cumhuriyet*, starting in 2015 and escalating in the aftermath of the 2016 attempted coup.[69] Additionally, other tools have been used, for example, *Zaman*, a journal supported by the Gulen movement, besides the arrest of some of its journalists, came under the supervision of a state administrator in March 2016 (with the unsurprising result that the journal is no longer critical of the government).

Today, the AKP actually openly asserts that there is a terrorist issue, not a Kurdish issue, in Turkey. The process of securitizing the Kurdish minority aimed therefore at reducing the Kurdish issue to a security-militarization problem, a "terrorist" problem, concentrating on attacking the militant organization coming from this minority, the PKK, and delegitimizing the rest of the minority, in its social and political aspects, both repressing the civilian population of the region and attacking the political expression of the party. Obviously, the PKK does not have a monopoly on representing Turkey's Kurdish population; indeed, many Kurds consider it a terrorist organization too. More conservative Kurds cannot support a Marxist-Leninist group like the PKK, and many independent Kurdish factions, asking for cultural rights and regional autonomy, oppose the PKK's ideological rigidity. But the government's focus on the PKK has helped Turkey to erase any elements of legitimacy of Kurdish demands, based on a "value rationality" of dignity and self-identity, as Varshney[70] defined it, blocking any possibility for Kurds to channel their demands and abandon the armed struggle for political inclusion. This process actually reflects a common trend in Middle Eastern states that since the end of the Ottoman Empire has delegitimized and securitized minority requests, framing the issue as being attached to militant groups that fought for their self-determination (from Hezbollah to Hamas) and fighting them as "terrorist organizations."

As stated earlier, the securitization of Kurds has been under observation especially because of Turkey's candidacy for EU membership; it has not been viewed positively by the EU. Unfortunately, the end of the ceasefire in 2015 coincided with the ISIS crisis and the refugee crisis in Europe. Thus, the EU started to close its eyes Turkey's treatment of the Kurds, viewing the country as a bastion against ISIS expansion and a buffer zone

---

[69] *The Guardian*, "Turkey detains editor and staff at opposition Cumhuriyet newspaper," October 31, accessed September 30, 2017, https://www.theguardian.com/world/2016/oct/31/turkey-detains-editor-and-staff-at-opposition-cumhuriyet-newspaper.

[70] Ashutosh Varshney, "Nationalism, Ethnic Conflict, and Rationality," *Perspective on Politics*, 1 (1), 2003, pp. 85–100.

for millions of refugees. This, indirectly, also contributed to giving Turkey more leeway in the recent resecuritization of the Kurdish minority, but it will not be very helpful for the growth of democracy in Turkey, just as US support for the El-Sisi military regime in Egypt undermined democracy there. The process of securitization of the Kurdish minority by the Turkish government is not only currently making the domestic situation unstable, but it is also causing a dangerous reversal of Turkish democratization. The fact that the HDP has been heavily targeted by the crackdown under Turkey's state of emergency following the attempted coup in 2016 shows how political regression in Turkey occurs, perhaps especially as a result of the repression and securitization of the Kurdish minority and its social and political expressions.

Subsequent chapters will analyze the possible causes of the initial autonomization policy toward the Kurdish minority and resecuritization, in an attempt to explain why Turkey chose one path while Indonesia chose a different one.

The Acehnese Issue in Indonesia: A History Between Autonomization and Securitization

Indonesia is an emblematic case in Southeast Asia of the treatment of minorities, as it had different approaches in different times. At the institutional level, Indonesia has been a highly centralized state, much like Turkey, already since its time as a Dutch colony, despite Dutch efforts to decentralize their structure at specific points in time—like, for example, with the 1903 Decentralization Law of the Netherlands Indies. Also, with independence in 1948, the Indonesian state, fearing the loss of national control over parts of the vast archipelago, refrained from granting any form of autonomy to its regions or provinces. It is at precisely this point that the Acehnese case begins.

Actually, during the Indonesian national revolution for independence, Aceh supported the nationalist movement in the expectation that it would be able to retain some form of autonomy following independence. But things turned out differently, so in 1953, many pious Acehnese joined an Islamist rebellion led by Daud Beureu'eh from the *Darul Islam* (House of Islam) movement, a national Islamist movement that aimed at the establishment of an Islamic state of Indonesia. The rebellion ended only in 1959 when Aceh obtained a "Special Region" status, with the right to enact Islamic laws.

Both the Turkish and Indonesian rebellions were rooted in religion and directed against a secular state. Aceh is the most religious part of the country, as it was the first region of what is now Indonesia to become Muslim in the thirteenth century, with the founding of the Kingdom of Aceh Darussalam (in Arabic *Dar as Salam* means House of Peace or House of Islam). But while Turkey, because of its history and geography, was worried about identity, Indonesia was more worried about territory, and so the later rebellion is connected more to territorial concerns. This is because Indonesian security was traditionally based on a concept of social order guaranteed by the state, which could not allow any loss of sovereignty. This concept had already been developed in the Dutch East Indies under the principle of "peace and order" (*rust en orde*),[71] and later under Suharto, when the New Order of his dictatorship, starting in 1967, revitalized the concept, calling it "safety and order" (*keamanan dan ketertiban*). This had been one of the main drivers of rebellions in several Indonesian regions: the failure of a centralized Indonesian state to address regional demands because it sought to assure the centralization of safety and order as well as a monopoly over resources. Therefore, the Aceh case is peculiar in this sense because at the beginning of Indonesian independence, Aceh wanted a federalist system in order to have some control in particular over natural resources and cultural and religious issues, but Jakarta resisted. Therefore, after the *Darul Islam* rebellion and the semi-autonomous status of the region was established, another rebellion started, this one in 1976 with the Free Aceh Movement (GAM), which demanded full independence.[72]

Specifically, the causes of the secessionist rebellion in Aceh were a mix of factors based on repression and exploitation, rather than accommodation toward minority demands. According to Larry Niksch, in a quite detailed report of the US Congressional Research Service, the separatism in Aceh was a combination of at least four factors: (1) distinct history as an independent kingdom from the fifteenth century until the beginning of the twentieth century, (2) progressive alienation of the population in reaction to the policies of Indonesian governments, (3) extensive human rights abuses by the Indonesian military, and (4) transfer of Aceh's wealth

---

[71] Benedict Anderson, *Language and Power: Exploring Political Cultures in Indonesia* (Ithaca: Cornell University Press, 1990) p. 119.
[72] Olle Törnquist, "Dynamics of peace and democratization. The Aceh lessons," *Democratization*, 18: 3 (2010) 823–846.

to the central government.[73] These facts make the Acehnese case quite different from the Kurdish one because, as stated previously, the Aceh rebellion has been more a question of sovereignty than of identity[74] (even if religious identity played a role in the first insurrection), but also because in the pluralistic approach of the Indonesian state, language rights and other cultural features were more respected and accepted than in the Turkish case.

The Acehnese independence movement was related, therefore, mostly to territorial and political control,[75] whereas the Kurdish one was related, yes, to territory but also to identity recognition and even national participation in the public sphere, in the political arena and national government. This is important to take into consideration because these differences may have affected, at least in part, the type of response of the national government and the type of ontological security that the country had, as Chap. 8 will explain.

The Acehnese rebellion also had at least three phases, like the Kurdish one: as stated earlier, the first one was the *Darul Islam* rebellion, a religious rebellion with the goal of establishing an Islamist state in Indonesia, fighting together with other regions like West Java and South Sulawesi between 1953 and 1959.[76] This rebellion was fought for two main reasons; the first was a rejection of the new nationalist and "secular" (or at least not only Islamic) Republic of Indonesia, and the second was the Indonesian government's decision in 1950 to deprive Aceh of its status as a province, with its privilege of applying Islamic laws differently from the rest of the country, but also blocking free trade between Aceh and foreign countries.[77] The result was an acceptance by the Indonesian state of a

[73] Larry Niksch, "Indonesian separatist movement in Aceh," in E. McFlynn, *Economics and Geopolitics of Indonesia* (New York: Nova Science Publishers, 2002); Larry Niksch, "Indonesian Separatist Movement in Aceh," *CRS Report for Congress.* January 12, 2001.

[74] Edward Aspinall, *Islam and nation: Separatist rebellion in Aceh, Indonesia* (Palo Alto: Stanford University Press, 2009).

[75] Anthony, Reid, ed., *Verandah of Violence: The Background to the Aceh Problem* (Seattle: University of Washington Press, 2006).

Sultan Barakat, David Connolly, and Judith Large, "Winning and Losing in Aceh: Five Key Dilemmas in Third-Party Intervention," *Civil Wars,* 5, no. 4, (2002): 1–29.

Kirsten E. Schulze, "The Free Aceh Movement (GAM): Anatomy of a Separatist Organization," *Policy Studies,* No. 2 (Washington DC: East-West Center, September 2004).

[76] Ibid.

[77] Leo Suryadinata, *The making of Southeast Asian Nations: State, ethnicity, indigenism and citizenship* (Singapore: World Scientific, 2015) p. 149.

form of autonomy, with a peace deal and the "Special Region" status granted in 1959.

The second phase started in 1976, when a former *Darul Islam* member, Hasan di Tiro,[78] created the Free Aceh Movement (*Gerakan Aceh Merdeka*-GAM) and started an insurrection that concentrated on attacks against Mobile Oil Company, in response to the Indonesian government's centralization of recently discovered oil and gas reserves and the consequent lack of readjustment of their incomes. This rebellion therefore was not the continuation of the earlier *Darul Islam* one, but more the continuance of the war against the Dutch and the Japanese, a national struggle to regain sovereignty for Aceh, which lay dormant for a few years during the euphoria of the earlier days of Indonesian independence and the twelve years of the *Darul Islam* conflict. Even though leaders of GAM tried to win support by saying that secession would turn the province into another Brunei,[79] the rebellion failed to garner popular support, either locally or internationally. This phase of securitization lasted a short time, though, as the rebellion was repressed just one year later, when Hasan di Tiro was shot in the leg in a military ambush and fled to Malaysia.[80]

In 1989 GAM tried again, this time better equipped with some funds from Iran and Libya[81] and with hundreds of GAM fighters returning from Libya after military training. However, the Indonesian state organized strong counterinsurgency operations that lasted until 1996, with many casualties and human rights violations.[82] During this time, the Indonesian government considered the area one of the "Military Operation Zones," which allowed it to impose heavy repression, again a "state of exception," an extraordinary measure of the securitization phase. However, this also

---

[78] According to someone, he was a descendent of the last sultan of Aceh before the Dutch conquer; according to others, he was the eighth-generation descendant of the great di Tiro family of *ulemas* (religious leaders). Whatever the truth may be, he was an aristocrat and Western-educated businessman.

[79] Michael Ross, *Oil, Drugs, and Diamonds: How Do Natural Resources Vary in Their Impact on Civil War?* (New York: International Peace Academy, Project on Economic Agendas in Civil Wars, June 5, 2002).

[80] Eric Morris, *Islam and Politics in Aceh: A Study of Center-Periphery Relations in Indonesia*. Unpublished PhD dissertation, Cornell University, 1983.

Kenneth Conboy, *Kopassus: Inside Indonesia's Special Forces* (Sheffield: Equinox Publishing, 2002).

[81] Michael L. Ross, *Resources and Rebellion in Aceh*, Indonesia, The World Bank (2007).

[82] Tim Kell, *The roots of Acehnese rebellion 1989–1992* (Ithaca: Cornell Modern Indonesia Project, 1995).

increased the local population's support for GAM, making it a symbol of resistance,[83] particularly when government forces tortured and killed many innocent civilians.

As we see, unlike the Kurdish case, the Acehnese case comprises some aspects of autonomization and some parts of securitization, stemming as it did from a different history and different causes of the rebellions. But how has this minority been treated during Indonesian democratization and what made the final autonomization possible?

Indonesian Autonomization of the Acehnese Minority

After 1998, with the fall of the dictatorship of Suharto, and the so-called New Order, and the start of the democratization process, Indonesia feared the opposite of what it had feared during the dictatorship: that without granting some autonomy to the regions, secessionist forces could disintegrate the state in a kind of Balkanization.[84] Therefore, one year after the *Reformasi*, in 1999, Indonesia created eight new provinces when the national parliament approved two laws on decentralization: Law 22 concerning administrative decentralization, and Law 25, concerning financial administration. Today Indonesia has a total of 34 provinces, of which 5 have special administrative status, but this does not mean that the process has always been beneficial to the country's minorities.

As Duncan argues,[85] for example, sometimes ethnic minorities in Indonesia, instead of going back to local forms of land and resource management, have faced the exploitation of local governments that started resource extraction exactly as the Dutch and Indonesian central states had done. Another scholar, Vedi Hadiz,[86] criticizes the neo-institutionalist per-

---

[83] Jacques Bertrand and Sanjay Jeram, "Democratization and determinants of ethnic violence: The rebel-moderate organization nexus," Ch. 6 in Jacques Bertrand and Oded Haklai (eds.) *Democratization and Ethnic Minorities: Conflict or Compromise*? (Abingdon: Routledge, 2014): p. 112.

[84] "Regional autonomy in Indonesia," IDEA International, accessed September 30, 2017: http://www.idea.int/publications/country/upload/6_regional_autonomy.pdf.

[85] Christopher R. Duncan, "Mixed Outcomes: The Impact of Regional Autonomy and Decentralization on Indigenous Ethnic Minorities in Indonesia," *Development and Change*, 38, 4 (July 2007): 711–733.

[86] Vedi R. Hadiz, "Decentralization and Democracy in Indonesia: A Critique of Neo-Institutionalist Perspectives," *Development and Change*, 35, 4, (September 2004): 697–718.

spective supporting decentralization in Indonesia, arguing that decentralization has often failed to reach higher levels of democracy and good governance because of power interests and struggle, as in the Indonesian case. And although the process of decentralization and autonomization made Indonesian democracy more viable, stable, and sustainable, in practice liberal localization also fostered conflictual politics.[87]

Nevertheless, decentralization and autonomy have been important policies for the inclusion of minorities in the national polity of the new democratic Indonesia, even as the Indonesian state treated differently the three main regions that fought for independence with armed guerrillas: Timor-Leste, Aceh, and West Papua. The first received its independence in 2002, the second received its autonomy as a Special Region in 2005 in the form of partial "self-government,"[88] while the third situation still awaits resolution, with the longest conflict, which has been going on since the 1960s between the Indonesian government and the Free Papua Movement, with hundreds of thousands of casualties.[89]

Aceh today is one of the five provinces in Indonesia that have a special status, together with Papua and West Papua (for their implementation of sustainable development), the city of Yogyakarta (as a special "sovereign monarchy" within Indonesia), and the city of Jakarta (as the capital region). But Aceh is really the only semiautonomous region of Indonesia. The Law on Governing Aceh was passed by the Indonesian House of Representatives on July 11, 2006, and signed by President Susilo Bambang Yudhoyono on August 1, 2006, translating the Aceh peace agreement of 2005 into law. Soon thereafter, in 2006, GAM's former intelligence chief, Irwandi Yusuf, was elected governor, and after him, in 2012, another GAM representative, Zaini Abdullah, became governor (until 2017, when Yusuf was reelected). This process of autonomization allowed the region to have local parties, retain 70 percent of its natural resource revenues, and

---

[87] Henk Schulte Nordholt, "Decentralisation in Indonesia: Less State, More Democracy?" in *Politicising Democracy The New Local Politics of Democratisation*, edited by Harriss, J., Stokke, K., Törnquist, Olle, p. 29/50 (New York: Palgrave Macmillan, 2005).

[88] During the Helsinki negotiations, Indonesia didn't want to discuss independence, and GAM rejected autonomy, so "self-government" was agreed to as a workable compromise. See on this Nur Djuli and Nurdin Abdul Rahman, "Reconfiguring politics: The Indonesia-Aceh peace process," Conciliation Resources, Accord Issue: 20, 2008.

[89] Jennifer Robinson, "The UN's chequered record in West Papua," Al Jazeera, 3/21/2012, accessed September 30, 2017, http://www.aljazeera.com/indepth/opinion/2012/03/201232172539145809.html.

implement some cultural and religious laws, in particular Sharia law as its regional law, which has been criticized recently, raising concerns regarding the respect in Aceh for the democratic and liberal values of Indonesia.[90] However, other opportunities were missed in Helsinki to secure an agreement on fiscal policy and on investigations into human rights abuses (thousands of crimes against humanity remain unresolved). Aceh today is still one of the poorest regions of Indonesia,[91] but the fact that it represents a successful story of the policy of autonomy makes it an interesting case to analyze, to understand why, unlike Turkey, the Indonesian democratic government chose autonomization when faced with a long-standing rebellion of a minority.

In Aceh, with the start of the democratization of Indonesia in 1998, several actors tried to take the lead in the situation.[92] First were some religious leaders, as in the 1950s but nonviolently this time, in particular with Daud Beureueh, an *ulama* who was the first governor of Aceh following Indonesia's independence. Nevertheless, the *ulama* had already lost their legitimacy as fighters for independence in Acehnese society and could not accomplish much. Another group that tried to take on a leadership position was the middle class of Acehnese working in universities, government positions, and businesses who opposed independence and supported autonomy. Nevertheless, they did not enjoy the support of the population, in particular the local technocratic and parliamentary representatives, because of their past connections to the Suharto regime. Finally, Syamsuddin Mahmud, the governor of Aceh since 1993, and some Jakarta-based Acehnese also tried to assume leadership of the region, proposing to the Indonesian parliament autonomy for Aceh and securing passage of the special autonomy law of 2001, but it was already too late.[93] GAM was the actor best able to take up leadership again on the issue of

---

[90] Mohshin Habib, "Sharia Law Swallowing Indonesia," Gatestone Institute, February 7, 2013, accessed September 30, 2017, http://www.gatestoneinstitute.org/3579/indonesia-sharia.

[91] Edward Aspinall, Ben Hillman, and Peter McCawley, *Governance and capacity-building in post-crisis Aceh*, a report by Australian National University Enterprise, UNDP, Jakarta, 2012.

[92] Rodd McGibbon, "Local leadership and the Aceh conflict," in A. Reid (ed.) *Verandah of violence: The background to the Aceh problem* (Seattle: University of Washington Press 2006).

[93] Ibid. See also: Jacques Bertrand, *Nationalism and ethnic conflict in Indonesia* (Cambridge: Cambridge University Press, 2004).

the Acehnese demand for independence following democratization, and so it started the third phase of the Acehnese rebellion, but this time being more organized and powerful than it had been the previous time.

However, this time there were also new Indonesian democratic governments, with a new approach to the Acehnese case, guided before by the transitional president Habibie, between 1998 and 1999, and then by the first elected president Abdurrahman Wahid, between 1999 and 2001. Habibie sought to address grievances and undermine GAM's leadership role by granting some political concessions without conferring autonomy and complete independence to the region. At the same time, he supported the adoption of Islamic law in Aceh, with Law 44 (1999), and removed the status of "theater of military operations" from Aceh.[94] Thus, as we see, the desecuritization phase was implemented very clearly, with the end of the "state of exception" for Aceh. Habibie also visited Aceh to apologize for past abuses and appointed an independent commission to investigate those abuses. Finally, he passed a regional autonomy bill, Law 22, in April 1999, promising more power and government funds to the provinces.[95]

President Wahid at the beginning of his presidency implemented Law 22 on Regional Autonomy, also apologized to the peoples of East Timor, Aceh, and West Papua for past misdeeds of the army, and pledged to withdraw troops and hear local grievances.[96] He also signed a temporary ceasefire (called a "humanitarian pause") with Aceh to bring aid to the Acehnese people in May 2000, opening up room for negotiations but also reigniting in the Indonesian state a fear of "national disintegration."[97] Wahid's plan in Aceh was to give the people a referendum on various modes of autonomy rather than to decide on independence as in East Timor. However, the military believed GAM was taking advantage of the ceasefire, and President Wahid failed to forge an agreement between Aceh and the Indonesian government. Therefore, Wahid, one year after the "humanitarian pause" that had continued the autonomization phase, issued a presidential instruction in April 2001, restarting the repression of the insurgency by deploying 25,000 and resecuritizing the minority, caus-

---

[94] Angel Rabasa and John Haseman, *The military and democracy in Indonesia: Challenges, politics and power*, RAND, National Security Research Division, 2002, p. 103.

[95] Bertil Lintner, "Centrifugal Forces Stir in Indonesia," *Jane's Intelligence Review*, May 31, 2000, accessed September 30, 2017, https://www.library.ohiou.edu/indopubs/2000/05/31/0002.html.

[96] Ibid.

[97] Ibid.

ing many losses and much suffering among the civilian population as well.[98] By July, Wahid even asked Susilo Bambang Yudhoyono, the Coordinating Minister for Politics and Security, to declare a state of emergency. When Yudhoyono refused, Wahid suspended him, but at that point Wahid had lost the support of the military and finally agreed to resign. He was succeeded by Megawati Sukarnoputri, who was appointed the first woman president of Indonesia on July 23, 2001. Megawati, daughter of Sukarno, had founded a few years earlier the Indonesian Democratic Party of Struggle, heir to one of the only three political parties recognized by President Suharto during the New Order (actually the party's center-left ideology is based on the concept of *Pancasila* and is the same party in power today with Joko Widodo).

Megawati, who would remain president until October 2004 when the first direct presidential elections were held in Indonesia, adopted a strategy similar to that of Wahid at the beginning, of allowing some autonomy and at the same time imposing military repression. As soon as she was elected, she signed the Special Autonomy Law for Aceh (Law 18 of 2001), for example; however, the law, which was approved by the parliament, fell short of expectations and the new revenues coming from natural resources opened the door to corruption while the conflict remained unresolved. Thus, in December 2002, two months after the Bali bombing that led to GAM's being labeled a terrorist group, the Indonesian government and GAM signed a Cessation of Hostilities Agreement in Geneva, organized by a Swiss-based NGO, the Henri Dunant Centre (or Centre for Humanitarian Dialogue/HDC, the same group that facilitated the humanitarian pause in 2000), and supported by foreign countries that sought a more stable Indonesia. Unfortunately, a wide gap in the interpretation of the terms of the agreement and a weak monitoring capacity (only 150 foreign and domestic observers) soon led to its collapse and, once again, to the resecuritization of the minority. According to some scholars, as often happens, the agreement was used by both conflicting parties as a pretext for regrouping and reconsolidating their positions.[99]

Therefore, the government once again proclaimed a military emergency in May 2003, and President Megawati signed the emergency decree to impose martial law. Megawati, like Wahid, rejected GAM's request for

---

[98] Rabasa and Haseman, *The military and democracy in Indonesia*, 2002.
[99] Olle Törnquist, "Dynamics of peace and democratization. The Aceh lessons," 2010, p. 832.

independence, after having already permitting East Timor's independence in 2002, and so allowed a final strong offensive of the Indonesian army in 2003–2004 that severely disabled the rebel movement with many deaths but also impacted the population. Some scholars argue that the consequent reduction of GAM's control of areas contributed to the decision of GAM to drop the demand for full independence and to be more accommodating during the post-tsunami negotiations.[100] It seems likely that the government's strategy of ceasefires and later crackdowns on the rebel movement (which seems similar to the tactics used by Turkey against the PKK) played a role in the decision of the two parties to finally engage in constructive negotiations. The stalemate actually caused both parties to understand that they would not have been able to win by force, and this is one important difference with the Turkish case, where neither the PKK nor the Turkish state thought that.

But besides GAM's new leadership and strong resurgence, and despite the government's most violent repression in the history of the conflict, the democratization process introduced a new positive element in Indonesia: an empowered and mobilized civil society. Student groups and NGOs had formed starting in 1998 to ask for justice over past atrocities and to call for a referendum on the autonomy of the region, in particular on the wave of the East Timor referendum of 1999. SIRA (*Sentral Informasi Referendum* or Referendum Information Centre) in particular, founded by local activists and students, organized large demonstrations in November 1999 and January 2000, with hundreds of thousands of people participating. This represented a moderate nonviolent alternative to the armed rebellion, at least initially, even if later SIRA lost its appeal because of its lack of organization and the increased crackdown of the government, and did not want to create a party as in the case of Turkey with the HDP. SIRA started to align its position with that of GAM, as both finally had the same goal—Acehnese independence or at least a strong autonomy[101]—but they were not repressed like HDP supporters. Therefore, it may be asserted that under democratization the Acehnese rebellion lived through its most violent episode, but during these years moderate democratic forces of civil society emerged, too, and were accepted by the national administration. Even if the alternative nonviolent leadership of civil society was not able to

---

[100] Edward Aspinall, "The Helsinki Agreement: A More Promising Basis for Peace in Aceh?," *Policy Studies* 20, Washington, DC: East-West Center, 2005.

[101] Rabasa and Haseman, *The military and democracy in Indonesia*, 2002, p. 112.

gain any more legitimacy than GAM, it likely drove the resolution of the Acehnese issue, at least from the Acehnese perspective, toward a final autonomization of the region.[102]

Thus, in 2004, the first-ever direct presidential election brought to power the retired General Susilo Bambang Yudhoyono and the businessman Jusuf Kalla as his deputy. The new government started to adopt peaceful means to end various regional, ethnic, and religious conflicts. Kalla and Yudhoyono already had experience with peace agreements: Kalla, as Coordinating Minister for Social Welfare, had negotiated peace agreements in 2001 and 2002 in the provinces of Central Sulawesi and the Moluccas with the consent of Yudhoyono (at that time the Coordinating Minister of Political and Security Affairs).[103] The times seemed to start to really change at the national level, and suddenly in December the tragedy of the tsunami happened in Aceh, with tens of thousands of deaths and tremendous levels of destruction. One month after the tsunami, in January 2005, the Crisis Management Initiative (CMI) of Helsinki, chaired by former Finnish President Martti Ahtisaari, offered a new mediation effort, later backed also by the EU. After six months of negotiations, the Helsinki Memorandum of Understanding (MoU) was signed on August 15, 2005, by the Indonesian government and GAM, ending a bloody 30-year conflict that had caused around 15,000 deaths.[104] The core content of the peace agreement was the self-government rule for Aceh, as expressed in the MoU (Chapter 1.1.2 a):

> Aceh will exercise authority within all sectors of public affairs, which will be administered in conjunction with its civil and judicial administration, except in the fields of foreign affairs, external defense, national security, monetary and fiscal matters, justice and freedom of religion, the policies of which belong to the Government of the Republic of Indonesia in conformity with the Constitution.[105]

---

[102] An interesting comparison would be with the West Papua region, where the moderate faction, supported by the local Christian bishops (West Papua is majority Christian) and stronger than the rebels, assumed leadership. But today the region, divided into two provinces, has a flawed autonomy and the discontented people keep the conflict going.

[103] Olle Törnquist, "Dynamics of peace and democratization. The Aceh lessons," 2010.

[104] Human Rights Watch and Amnesty International estimated that between 10,000 and 20,000 people were killed.

[105] "Memorandum of Understanding between the Government of the Republic of Indonesia and the Free Aceh Movement," CMI, 2006, accessed September 30, 2017, http://www.acehpeaceprocess.net/pdf/mou_final.pdf.

Unfortunately, only around one-third of the clauses were later introduced into the Law on Governing Aceh (UUPA No.11/2006), and this is one of the criticisms of the application of the peace process. Among those implemented are the creation of regional parties for the regional government and the possibility of retaining 70 percent of revenues from natural resources. Even if the incomplete implementation of the MoU puts at risk the success of Aceh's autonomization, as some external observers argue, the result is that after 30 years of civil war in Aceh, the democratizing Indonesian state, after a few phases of engagement in autonomization and resecuritization, finally implemented a process of autonomization. The Aceh region won its autonomy, and the guerrilla group became a political party, even if it split up into different factions with different candidates for the governorship.[106] So what factors brought the Indonesian government, willing or not, to accept Acehnese autonomy?

Briefly we can say that from the perspective of the Acehnese rebels, the repression by the Indonesian military forces and the tsunami of December 2004 that caused 120,000 deaths played an important role. Actually, the tsunami, some say, triggered the negotiations and the necessity to reach an agreement as soon as possible to allow massive assistance from the international community to be distributed without hindrance. From the perspective of the state, the Helsinki MoU of 2005 was also the result of the democratization process and the subsequent decentralization process that started with the new century. Without the *Reformasi* in 1998 that ended the Indonesian dictatorship, Aceh would not have won its autonomy for some time to come. The new democratic Indonesia initially engaged in increased repression of this independence movement but later opted for the path of negotiations, decentralization, and inclusion. This is in contrast to Turkey, which, even though it chose a similar path at certain moments of its democratization process, failed to achieve the same results and resorted to resecuritization. It is evident that for the Indonesian government the costs of the insurgency in terms of human lives —whether the lives of soldiers, policemen, civil servants, or ordinary Acehnese people— could no longer be ignored in the era of democracy and a free press. Also, the world financial crisis that hit Indonesia very severely made military spending more difficult: in 2004, the newly elected President Yudhoyono

---

[106] Today there are still many problems of corruption, internal conflict, and other issues, both inside the Aceh party (former GAM party) and in the other smaller Acehnese parties, but the important thing is that they are functioning.

told the nation that a peaceful solution was the only way to end the conflict in Aceh. His deputy, Jusuf Kalla, said that the war in Aceh had become too expensive to continue. "Peace is cheaper," he said.[107] But this book aims to understand what role was played by four more important variables related to the main theories of comparative studies. The next four chapters, therefore, will attempt to explain the different outcomes in Turkey and Indonesia using four theoretical perspectives: elite power, international factors, historical institutions, and ontological security.

References

Akturk, Sener. 2015. "Religion and Nationalism: Contradictions of Islamic Origins and Secular Nation-Building" in Turkey, Algeria, and Pakistan. *Social Science Quarterly* 96 (3): 778–806.

Al Jazeera. 2013. *Timeline: Turkey's Ergenegon Trial*. August 5, 2013. http://www.aljazeera.com/news/europe/2013/08/20138512358195978.html. Accessed 30 Sept 2017.

Almukhtar, Sarah, and Tim Wallice. 2015. Why Turkey Is Fighting the Kurds Who Are Fighting ISIS. *New York Times*, August 12, 2015. http://www.nytimes.com/interactive/2015/08/12/world/middleeast/turkey-kurds   isis.html. Accessed 10 Apr 2016.

Anderson, Benedict. 1990. *Language and Power. Exploring Political Cultures in Indonesia*. Ithaca: Cornell University Press.

Arango, Tim. 2014. Turkish Leader, Using Conflicts, Cements Power. *New York Times*, October 31, 2014. http://www.nytimes.com/2014/11/01/world/europe/Erdoğan-uses-conflict-to-consolidatepower.html?emc=edit_th_20141101&nl=todaysheadlines&nlid=41699871&_r=1. Accessed 30 Sept 2018.

Aspinall, Edward. 2005. The Helsinki Agreement: A More Promising Basis for Peace in Aceh? *Policy Studies* 20. Washington, DC: East-West Center.

———. 2009. *Islam and Nation: Separatist Rebellion in Aceh, Indonesia*. Palo Alto: Stanford University Press.

Aspinall, Edward, Ben Hillman, and Peter McCawley. 2012. *Governance and Capacity-Building in Post-Crisis Aceh*. A Report by Australian National University Enterprise, UNDP, Jakarta.

Azak, Umut. 2010. *Islam and Secularism in Turkey: Kemalism, Religion and the Nation State*. New York: I. B. Tauris.

Barakat, Sultan, David Connolly, and Judith Large. 2002. Winning and Losing in Aceh: Five Key Dilemmas in Third-Party Intervention. *Civil Wars* 5 (4): 1–29.

---

[107] Yuji Uesugigi, *Peacebuilding and Security Sector Governance in Asia*, LIT Verlag, Geneva Centre for the Democratic Control of Armed Forces (DCAF) 2014, p. 34.

Barkey, Henri J., and Graham E. Fuller. 1998. *Turkey's Kurdish Question*. Lanham: Rowman & Littlefield Publishers.

Bayir, Derya. 2014. The Role of the Judicial System in the Politicide of the Kurdish Opposition. In *The Kurdish Question in Turkey: New Perspectives on Violence, Representation and Reconciliation*, ed. C. Gunes and W. Zeydanlioglu. Abingdon: Routledge.

BBC News. 2011. *Turkey PM Erdogan Apologizes for 1930s Kurdish Killings*. November 23, 2011. http://www.bbc.com/news/world-europe-15857429. Accessed 30 Sept 2017.

———. 2017. *Turkey pro-Kurd HDP Party Condemns Arrest of Leaders*. November 4, 2017. http://www.bbc.com/news/world-europe-37875605. Accessed 30 Sept 2017.

Bertrand, Jacques. 2004. *Nationalism and Ethnic Conflict in Indonesia*. Cambridge: Cambridge University Press.

Bertrand, Jacques, and Sanjay Jeram. 2014. Democratization and Determinants of Ethnic Violence: The Rebel-Moderate Organization Nexus. In *Democratization and Ethnic Minorities: Conflict or Compromise?* ed. Jacques Bertrand and Oded Haklai. Abingdon: Routledge.

Bülent, Aras, and Polat Rabia Karakaya. 2008. From Conflict to Cooperation: Desecuritization of Turkey's Relations with Syria and Iran. *Security Dialogue* 39 (5): 499.

Cavanaugh, Kathleen, and Edel Hughes. 2015. A Democratic Opening? The AKP and the Kurdish Left. *Muslim World Journal of Human Rights*, De Gruyter 12 (1): 53–74.

Ceylan, Yeginsu. 2015. Strikes on Kurd Militias Elevate Tensions in Turkey. *New York Times*, July 26, 2015. http://www.nytimes.com/2015/07/27/world/europe/heightened-tensions-in-turkey-afterstrikes-on-kurdish-militants-in-iraq.html. Accessed 30 Sept 2017.

Cohen, Naomi, and Nuhat Mugurtay. Kurds Are Paying the Price of Turkey's Post-coup Crackdown. *Middle East Eye*. http://www.middleeasteye.net/columns/turkeys-kurdish-question-turns-new-page-894865406. Accessed 30 Sept 2017.

Conboy, Kenneth. 2002. *Kopassus: Inside Indonesia's Special Forces*. Sheffield: Equinox Publishing.

Crisis Group. 2016. *Turkey's PKK Conflict: The Death Toll*, July 20, 2016. https://www.crisisgroup.org/europe-central-asia/western-europemediterranean/turkey/turkey-s-pkk-conflict-death-toll. Accessed 30 Sept 2017.

Djuli, Nur and Nurdin Abdul Rahman. 2008. *Reconfiguring Politics: The Indonesia-Aceh Peace Process*. London: Conciliation Resources. Accord Issue: 20.

Duncan, Christopher R. 2007. Mixed Outcomes: The Impact of Regional Autonomy and Decentralization on Indigenous Ethnic Minorities in Indonesia. *Development and Change* 38 (4): 711–733.

European Commission. *Turkey 2017 Report.* https://ec.europa.eu/neighbourhood-enlargement/sites/near/files/pdf/key_documents/2016/20161109_report_turkey.pdf. Accessed 30 Sept 2017.

Habib, Mohshin. 2013. Sharia Law Swallowing Indonesia. *Gatestone Institute*, February 7, 2013. http://www.gatestoneinstitute.org/3579/indonesia-sharia. Accessed 16 Apr 2016.

Hadiz, Vedi. 2004. Decentralization and Democracy in Indonesia: A Critique of Neo-Institutionalist Perspectives. *Development and Change* 35 (4): 697–718.

Heper, Metin. 2007. *State and Kurds in Turkey: The Question of Assimilation.* New York: Palgrave Macmillan.

Human Rights Watch. 2005. *Turkey Report.* March 2005, p. 3, https://www.hrw.org/reports/2005/turkey0305/3.htm#_Toc97005223. Accessed 30 Sept 2017.

———. 2010. *Protesting as a Terrorist Offense: The Arbitrary Use of Terrorism Laws to Prosecute and Incarcerate Demonstrators in Turkey.* November 1, 2010. https://www.hrw.org/report/2010/11/01/protesting-terrorist-offense/arbitrary-use-terrorism-laws-prosecute-and. Accessed 30 Sept 2017.

———. 2015. *Turkey: Mounting Security Operation Deaths, Scores of Civilians Among Hundreds Killed in Southeast.* December 22, 2015. https://www.hrw.org/news/2015/12/22/turkey-mounting-security-operation-deaths. Accessed 30 Sept 2017.

Hurriyet Daily News. 2012. *Turkish President Ozal's Death Suspicious.* June 13, 2012. http://www.hurriyetdailynews.com/turkish-president-ozals-death-suspicious-state-audit-board-.aspx?pageID=238&nID=23053&NewsCatID=338. Accessed 30 Sept 2017.

———. 2013. *78 Percent of Gezi Park Protest Detainees Were Alevis: Report.* November 25, 2013, http://www.hurriyetdailynews.com/78-percent-of-gezi-park-protest-detainees-were-alevis-report-.aspx?PageID=238&NID=58496&NewsCatID=341. Accessed 2 Feb 2016.

Internal Displacement Monitoring Center. 2013. *Turkey: Internal Displacement in Brief,* as of December 2013. http://www.internal-displacement.org/europe-the-caucasus-and-central-asia/turkey/summary. Accessed 12 Feb 2016.

International Crisis Group. 2012. *Turkey: The PKK and a Kurdish Settlement.* ICG Europe Report No. 219, September 11, 2012. http://www.crisisgroup.org/en/regions/europe/turkey cyprus/turkey/219-turkey-the-pkk-and-a-kurdish-settlement.aspx. Accessed 30 Sept 2017.

———. 2014. *Turkey and the PKK: Saving the Peace Process.* ICG Europe Report No. 234, November 6, 2014. http://www.crisisgroup.org/en/regions/europe/turkey-cyprus/turkey/234-turkey-and-the-pkk-saving-the-peace-process.aspx. Accessed 18 May 2016.

Kadıoğlu, Ayşe. 2013. Necessity and the State of Exception. The Turkish State's Permanent War with Its Kurdish Citizens. In *Turkey Between Nationalism and Globalization,* ed. Riva Kastoryano. London/New York: Routledge.

Kell, Tim. 1995. *The Roots of Acehnese Rebellion 1989–1992*. Ithaca: Cornell Modern Indonesia Project.

Kilinc, Ramazan. 2014. International Pressure, Domestic Politics, and the Dynamics of Religious Freedom. Evidence from Turkey. *The Journal of Comparative Politics* 46 (2): 127–145.

Kinzer, Stephen. 2008. *Crescent and Star: Turkey Between Two Worlds*. New York: Farrar, Straus and Giroux.

Kuru, Ahmet T. 2007. Passive and Assertive Secularism: Historical Conditions, Ideological Struggles, and State Policies Toward Religion. *World Politics* 59 (4): 568–594.

Kutahyali, Rasim Ozan. 2013. Who Poisoned Former Turkish President Ozal? *Al Monitor*, August 22, 2013. https://www.al-monitor.com/pulse/originals/2013/08/turkey-president-ozal-poisoned.html. Accessed 30 Sept 2017.

Kymlicka, Will, and Eva Pföstl. 2015. Minority Politics in the Middle East and North Africa: The Prospects for Transformative Change. *Ethnic and Racial Studies* 38 (14): 1–10.

Lewis, Bernard. 1994. Why Turkey Is the Only Muslim Democracy. *Middle East Quarterly* 1: 41–49.

Licursi, E.P. 2012. The Ergenekon Case and Turkey's Democratic Aspirations. *Freedom House*, February 7, 2012. https://freedomhouse.org/blog/ergenekon-case-andturkey%E2%80%99s-democratic-aspirations. Accessed 30 Sept 2017.

Lintner, Bertil. 2000. Centrifugal Forces Stir in Indonesia. *Jane's Intelligence Review*, May 31, 2000. https://www.library.ohiou.edu/indopubs/2000/05/31/0002.html. Accessed 11 Oct 2016.

McGibbon, Rodd. 2006. Local Leadership and the Aceh Conflict. In *Verandah of Violence: The Background to the Aceh Problem*, ed. Anthony Reid. Seattle: University of Washington Press.

Memorandum of Understanding between the Government of the Republic of Indonesia and the Free Aceh Movement, CMI, 2006. http://www.acehpeaceprocess.net/pdf/mou_final.pdf. Accessed 14 Oct 2016.

Morris, Eric. 1983. *Islam and Politics in Aceh: A Study of Center-Periphery Relations in Indonesia*. Unpublished PhD Dissertation, Cornell University, 1983.

Natali, Denise. 2005. *The Kurds and the State: Evolving National Identity in Iraq, Turkey and Iran*. Syracuse: Syracuse University Press.

Niksch, Larry. 2001. Indonesian Separatist Movement in Aceh. *CRS Report for Congress*. January 12, 2001.

———. 2002. Indonesian Separatist Movement in Aceh. In *Economics and Geopolitics of Indonesia*, ed. E. McFlynn. New York: Nova Science Publishers.

Nordholt, Henk Schulte. 2005. Decentralisation in Indonesia: Less State, More Democracy? In *Politicising Democracy the New Local Politics of Democratisation*, ed. J. Harriss, K. Stokke, and Olle Törnquist, 29–50. New York: Palgrave Macmillan.

Ocalan, Abdullah. *Three-phases Road Map*. Partiya Karkeren Kurdistan. http://www.pkkonline.com/en/index.php?sys=article&artID=114. Accessed 23 Sept 2016.

Oğuzlu, Tarik. 2007. Soft Power in Turkish Foreign Policy. *Australian Journal of International Affairs* 61 (1): 81–97.

Picard, Elizabeth. 2015. Nation-building and Minority Rights in the Middle East. In *Religious Minorities in the Middle East: Domination, Self-Empowerment, Accommodation*, ed. A.S. Roald and A.N. Longva. Boston: Brill Academic.

Piccone, Ted. 2016. *Five Rising Democracies and the Fate of the International Liberal Order*. Washington, DC: Brooking Institution Press.

Pope, Hugh. 2014. Turkey, Syria and Saving the PKK Peace Process. *The International Crisis Group*, December 10, 2014. http://www.crisisgroup.org/en/regions/europe/turkey cyprus/turkey/op-ed/pope-turkey-syria-and-saving-the-pkk-peace-process.aspx. Accessed 30 Sept 2017.

Przeworski, Adam, Michael E. Alvarez, Jose Antonio Cheibub, and Fernando Limongi. 2000. *Democracy and Development: Political Institutions and Wellbeing in the World, 1950–1990*. Cambridge: Cambridge University Press.

Pusane, Özlem. 2014. Turkey's Kurdish Opening: Long Awaited Achievements and Failed Expectations. *Turkish Studies* 15 (1): 81–99.

Rabasa, Angel, and John Haseman. 2002. *The Military and Democracy in Indonesia. Challenges, Politics and Power*. RAND, National Security Research Division.

Redden, Elizabeth. 2016. Turkish Academy Under Attack. *Inside Higher Education*, February 12, 2016. https://www.insidehighered.com/news/2016/02/12/more-1000-turkish-scholars-are-under-criminal-investigation-signing-petition. Accessed 2 Mar 2016.

Regional Autonomy in Indonesia, IDEA International. http://www.idea.int/publications/country/upload/6_regional_autonomy.pdf. Accessed 30 Sept 2017.

Reid, Anthony, ed. 2006. *Verandah of Violence. the Background to the Aceh Problem*. Seattle: University of Washington Press.

Robinson, Jennifer. 2002. *The UN's Chequered Record in West Papua*. Al Jazeera March 21, 2002. http://www.aljazeera.com/indepth/opinion/2012/03/201232172539145809.html. Accessed 16 Apr 2016.

Romano, David. 2014. The Long Road Toward Kurdish Accommodation in Turkey: The Role of Elections and International Pressures. In *Democratization and Ethnic Minorities: Conflict or Compromise?* ed. Jacques Bertrand and Oded Haklai. Abingdon: Routledge.

Ross, Michael. 2002. *Oil, Drugs, and Diamonds: How Do Natural Resources Vary in Their Impact on Civil War?* New York: International Peace Academy, Project on Economic Agendas in Civil Wars, June 5.

———. 2007. *Resources and Rebellion in Aceh*. Indonesia: The World Bank.
Schulze, Kirsten E. 2004. *The Free Aceh Movement (GAM): Anatomy of a Separatist Organization*. Policy Studies, No. 2. Washington, DC: East-West Center.
Shaheen, Kareem. 2015. Turkish Election Campaign Unfair Say International Monitors. *The Guardian*, November 2, 2015.
Soguel, Dominique. 2015. Rights Group Urges Turkey to Stop 'Abusive' Use of Force in Kurdish Areas, Investigate Deaths. *Associated Press/US News*, 22 December, 2015. http://www.usnews.com/news/world/articles/2015-12-22/rights-group-civilian-deaths-rise-in-turkeys-kurdish-areas. Accessed 30 Sept 2017.
———. 2016. Residents Return to Turkish Town of Cizre, Find It Destroyed. *ABC News*, March 2, 2016. http://abcnews.go.com/International/wireStory/turkey-rolls-back-curfew-kurdish-town-37327505. Accessed 30 Sept 2017.
Soner, Ali B. 2010. The Justice and Development Party's Policies Towards Non-Muslim Minorities in Turkey. *Journal of Balkan and Near Eastern Studies* 12 (1): 23–40.
Suryadinata, Leo. 2015. *The Making of Southeast Asian Nations. State, Ethnicity, Indigenism and Citizenship*. Singapore: World Scientific.
Tambar, Kabir. 2014. *The Reckoning of Pluralism: Political Belonging and the Demands of History in Turkey*. Palo Alto: Stanford University Press.
Tezcur, Gunes Murat. Prospects for Resolution of the Kurdish Question: A Realist Perspective. *Insight Turkey*. http://file.insightturkey.com/Files/Pdf/15_2_2013_tezcur.pdf. Accessed 2 Feb 2016.
The Economist. 2013. Justice or Revenge? August 10, 2013. http://www.economist.com/news/europe/21583312-harsh-verdicts-are-handed-down-ergenekon-trial-justice-or-revenge. Accessed 30 Sept 2017.
———. 2015. Turkish Extremism. Heightening the Contradictions, October 17, 2015.
The Guardian. Turkey Detains Editor and Staff at opposition Cumhuriyet Newspaper. October 31. https://www.theguardian.com/world/2016/oct/31/turkey-detains-editor-and-staff-at-opposition-cumhuriyet-newspaper. Accessed 30 Sept 2017.
Törnquist, Olle. 2010. Dynamics of Peace and Democratization. The Aceh Lessons. *Democratization* 18 (3): 823–846.
Turkish Statistical Institute. 2012. *World Economic Outlook*, April 2012. Retrieved on September 30, 2017. http://www.propertyturkey.tv/Pages.aspx?ID=2.
Uesugigi, Yuji. 2014. *Peacebuilding and Security Sector Governance in Asia*. Geneva: Geneva Centre for the Democratic Control of Armed Forces (DCAF).
Unver, Akin. 2015. *Turkey's Kurdish Question: Discourse and Politics Since 1990*. London: Routledge.

Varshney, Ashutosh. 2003. Nationalism, Ethnic Conflict, and Rationality. *Perspectives on Politics* 1 (1): 85–100.
Watts, Nicole. 2010. *Activists in Office: Kurdish Politics and Protest in Turkey*. Seattle: University of Washington Press.
Yavuz, Hakan. 2001. Five Stages of the Construction of Turkish Nationalism in Turkey. *Nationalism and Ethnic Politics* 7 (3): 1–24.
Yegen, Mesut. 2007. Turkish Nationalism and the Kurdish Question. *Ethnic and Racial Studies* 30 (1): 119–151.
———. 2011. The Kurdish Question in Turkey: Denial to Recognition. In *Nationalisms and Politics in Turkey: Political Islam, Kemalism, and the Kurdish Issue*, ed. Marlies Casier and Joost Jongerden, 67–84. New York: Routledge.
Zunini, Roberta. 2015. Demirtas: la violenza? È colpa di Erdoğan. Parla il leader del partito filo-curdo. *L'Espresso*, August 13, 2015.

CHAPTER 5

Political Elites' Power Interest and Rational Decision Making

INTRODUCTION

The first hypothesis that this study examines to explain the different treatment of minorities during a democratization period—that is, early securitization and later autonomization for Indonesia and early autonomization (or at least desecuritization) and later securitization for Turkey—concerns the struggle of elites for power. According to rational choice theory, the political elites in charge of decision-making about ethnic minorities analyze costs and benefits to decide what policies to implement. State elites are motivated to satisfy their political and economic interests; therefore, they often promote exclusive nationalist policies when they fear losing power.

The evidence presented in this chapter shows that at the beginning of democratization in Turkey, the inclusive and accommodative approach toward the Kurds likely was caused by the shift of ruling elites among the nationalist, Kemalist, and military elites and the moderate Islamist elites, who had in Islam an important commonality with the Kurds. Later, the resecuritization of the Kurdish minority started because of the risk of power loss by the Islamist elites, represented in particular by the AKP, which prompted a change in strategy of the AKP with a rebalancing of strategies between the Islamist elites and the military–Kemalist ones. Nevertheless, even if the surge of the AKP as a political party at the beginning and slight subsequent decline are fundamental to understanding this policy change, the most important explanatory factors for these outcomes are how the AKP elites interacted with other elite groups. We cannot understand the electoral strategies of the AKP without understanding the power struggle with the other national elites. How these other elite groups responded (or failed to respond) to the rise of Islamist elites with the AKP explains the change in strategies and the processes of autonomization versus securitization toward the Kurdish minority.

For Indonesia, by contrast, initially the state increased repression because the military and nationalist elites were still strong: the change in the balance of power among elites in Indonesia has been more gradual than in Turkey. Later, when the military and nationalist elites started to lose their power to new civilian elites, the state started to use processes of autonomization toward minorities and in particular the Aceh region. Instead, Islamist elites in Indonesia have not been as decisive as in Turkey, not having a corresponding political party that could have reached the national government.

Theoretical Background

As Collier argues, political elites can be defined either as incumbents—including oppositions to government—or leaders.[1] For the second group, she refers to the classical definition of Burton, who identifies political elites as "persons who are able, by virtue of their strategic positions in powerful organizations, to affect national political outcomes regularly and substantially. Elites are the principal decision makers in the largest or most resource-rich…organizations and movements in a society."[2] This study, therefore, following Burton and Collier, defines political elites as actors either within the state or in society who are leaders because of their position in deciding or impacting political outcomes. Actors in the state are represented by the ruling segments of the state political institutions, either civilians or military, who set national polices. This includes the highest ranks of the government, parliament, judiciary, and military as well as the highest ranks of the political parties that are in charge of the government, as often they are in interchangeable positions. Political elites outside the

---

[1] Ruth Collier, *Paths toward Democracy: The working class and elites in Western Europe and South America* (New York: Cambridge University Press, 1999), p. 18.

[2] Michael Burton, Richard Gunther, and John Higley, "Introduction: Elite Transformations and Democratic Regimes," in *Elites and Democratic Consolidation in Latin America and Southern Europe*, edited by John Higley and Richard Gunther (London: Cambridge University Press, 1992) p. 8. Cited in Collier, *Paths toward Democracy*, p. 18.

state, by contrast, are represented by business, religious, or civil society leaders who have enough economic clout to influence politics.

Regarding the main interests of the government elites, both the civilian political elites and the military ones want to rise to and remain in power to acquire, above all, political power, second, material resources, and finally, status or ideational resources (such as social esteem or prestige). Geddes argues that some elites "value office because they want to control policy, some for the pure enjoyment of influence and power, and some for the illicit material gains that come with office in some countries."[3] Nonstate business elites have instead as their main interest to acquire as much revenue from the market or subsides from the state (if they are rent-seekers) as possible.

To pursue their interests, elites conduct cost–benefit analyses before making decisions; this is the basis of rational choice theory, borrowed by political science from economic science.[4] This theory is not to be confused with "elite theory,"[5] which argues that a minority of economic and political elites have power independently of formal state institutions. Rational choice theory claims instead that patterns of behavior in societies reflect the choices made by rational individuals as they try to maximize their benefits and minimize their costs. It is a utilitarian approach based on perfect information, cognitive ability, and time to weigh all choices against each other. From this perspective, elites also calculate costs and benefits before making decisions. Political science has used rational choice theory extensively for several decades, though it has also been criticized, so this is the first theory used in our analysis.[6]

With respect to democratic studies, Dahl in the 1970s spoke about "costs of repressions" and "costs of toleration" in a regime's decision to "liberalize" or not, which means to move toward democracy or maintain

---

[3] Barbara Geddes, "What do we know about democratization after twenty years?," *Annual Review of Political Science*, 2:115–44, 1999, p. 129.

[4] Patrick Dunleavy, *Democracy, Bureaucracy and Public Choice: Economic Models in Political Science* (London: Pearson, 1991).

[5] The Elite Theory was developed at the end of the nineteenth century by the so-called Italian School of Elitists. In 1956, Charles Wright Mills retook the concept in *The Power Elite*, arguing about a system of power in the USA based on political, economic, and military groups that make ordinary citizens powerless in the hands of these groups.

[6] Donald P. Green and Ian Shapiro, *Pathologies of Rational Choice Theory: A Critique of Applications in Political Science*. (New Haven: Yale University Press, 1994).

authoritarianism.[7] Dahl specifically argued that when there is a power shift from a dictatorship to a democracy, it is because the dictator calculates that the costs of repression of the opposition parties or the people who want more freedom are higher than the costs of tolerating the same opposition and people's demands. Therefore, the cost of repression is the cost of maintaining the dictatorship, while the cost of toleration is how much power the elites lose to accept the transition—the cost of democracy. More recently, other scholars such as Weingast have analyzed how the difference between these two types of political costs is fundamental in elites' decision to engage in a democratization process or not.[8] In particular, Weingast claims that if public officers have incentives to respect the limitations on their behaviors without resorting to repression, democracies have more stability based on the rule of law. If there are no such incentives, democracies are more unstable because of the lack of group cohesion, a collective action problem, as Mancur Olson would characterize it.[9] Besides a lack of incentives, according to Weingast, ethnic divisions also increase collective action problems, in particular with respect to the appropriate role of the state, and undermine democratic stability. This is related to the difficulty of transitioning to democracy in pluralistic societies, as this study argued in Chap. 3, with the literature review on democracy in divided societies. Finally, Bueno de Mesquita also supported rational choice theory in a famous book on economic development.[10] According to Bueno de Mesquita, political leaders pay attention in their policies first of all to the people and systems that allow them to remain in power because they are foremost power maximizers and second wealth maximizers. Therefore, their economic policies are the ones that satisfy the winning coalition—that is, the constituency that keeps the elites in power. This is an important argument for this research because, as we will see, the political leadership

---

[7] Robert A. Dahl, *Polyarchy: Participation and opposition* (New Haven: Yale University Press, 1971).

[8] Barry R. Weingast, "The Political Foundations of Democracy and the Rule of Law," *American Political Science Review*, Vol. 91, No. 2 (June, 1997), pp. 245–263.

[9] The problem of collective action, also called the coordination dilemma, is based on the fact that coercion or specific benefits must be present in order for a group to act collectively for the common interest. For public goods, for example democracy, we need groups, but it is difficult to get everybody to collaborate and pay the costs as individuals prefer to free ride, which is why we need organizations, like a bureaucratic state, to make individuals do their part, like paying taxes, for example. See Mancur Olson, *The logic of collective action: public goods and the theory of groups* (Cambridge: Harvard University Press, 1965).

[10] Bruce Bueno de Mesquita, *The logic of political survival* (Cambridge: MIT Press, 2003).

in Turkey changed strategies toward the Kurdish minority precisely because of the risk of losing the winning coalition.

To conclude about this concept of costs of toleration and repression, this approach can also be applied to minorities: when the cost of giving some autonomy to the minorities (cost of toleration) is lower than the cost of maintaining the status quo by means of securitization or repression, then the state may allow some policies of autonomy (as could be the case with Indonesia). Conversely, securitization as a form of repression could be maintained or restarted (as occurred in Turkey). Elite power and rational choice are, then, the first hypothesis.

THEORIES APPLIED TO CASE STUDIES

Scholars of ethno-nationalist theories[11] affirm that elites often promote exclusive nationalist policies once they fear the loss of power, and so it is the elite interest that could determine a state's approach to ethnic minorities. Snyder in particular argued that the transition to democracy often brings with it ethnic conflict because of nationalism supported by the elites to gain in the popular ballot, especially when there are no preconditions like an adaptable ruling elite or institutions such as the rule of law and a free press. Again, the hypothesis emerging from this theory is that new elites in power, and by extension the shift of power among elites during a democratic transition, could change the state's approach to minorities based on the power calculation among new elites.

Therefore, to understand elites' fear of accommodating minorities or oppositions, it is also important to analyze the democratization processes in addition to the new democracy itself. Following the argument of Cesari,[12] there are three main ways to deal with old elites during a transition to democracy: make a tabula rasa of the old regime and start from scratch, marginalize the actors of the former regime, or erode the former regime from within. Among Muslim-majority countries, the first path was followed by the Islamic revolution in Iran and the post-Saddam Hussein era in Iraq. While the first resulted in a theocracy, the second failed completely in its democratization, precisely because of a lack of inclusiveness of the old regime and system (besides the disasters of the American war). The

---

[11] See Chap. 2.
[12] Jocelyn Cesari, *The awakening of Muslim democracies* (New York: Cambridge University Press, 2014), pp. 229–233.

second path was followed by Turkey, with the AKP in power since 2002, building alliances among the excluded forces in order to marginalize the old regime and gradually excluding the old Kemalist–military elites. This path seemed to bear more democratic fruit, at least regarding the stability of Turkish democracy, until the failed coup of July 2016. However, the internal problems of a sizeable liberal democracy and of the relationship with the Kurdish minority reveal the limits of this marginalization of the old regime. This could indicate that these forces reacted to their loss of power by revitalizing strong nationalist sentiments, something very much related to the terrorist attacks and repression of the Kurdish minority in the Eastern region. Finally, the third type seems to be the model followed by Indonesia following democratization in 1998, with a gradualism that democratized the structures but retained the old political cadres for a while, gradually excluding them from political and economic power, until finally the transition was completed with the first new president not belonging to the old establishment, Joko Widodo, being elected in 2014. This path seemed to work better in the long term regarding the inclusion of minorities, at least judging from Indonesia today.

Rather than examining established elites, other scholars attach importance to the actions of the leadership for the solution of separatist conflicts. Regarding the Indonesian case, for example, Miller argues that "agency, or political will, was the most crucial factor in the resolution of the Aceh conflict, supported by structural preconditions and circumstances."[13] In particular, the structural constraints after the 1997 financial crisis and the 2004 tsunami reduced the Indonesian state's capacity, and this contributed to the final settlement. As Miller recalls, the Indonesian government went through different approaches to the Acehnese issue following democratization in 1998, including military repression, offers of autonomy, peace talks, and a combination of these, and when both parties understood that they could not defeat the other, they were pushed to resolve the conflict by some type of self-government. We could argue that in the Turkish case, the new AKP leadership, in particular Recep Tayyip Erdogan as prime minister and later as president, has had an important impact on the treatment of the Kurdish minority. Structural preconditions, such as the impressive economic growth Turkey saw under the AKP regime, and specific circumstances such as the Syrian

---

[13] Michelle Ann Miller, *Rebellion and reform in Indonesia: Jakarta's security and autonomy policies in Aceh* (London, New York: Routledge, 2009), p. 2.

civil war affected the securitization of the Kurds. But the structural elements are related to other variables that will be treated in subsequent chapters, while the importance of the agency of the leadership, supported by Miller, is not analyzed in this study, leaving it as a topic for future research.

Finally, we need to remember that elites' power is often treated at a deeper level, behind the scenes, not in a transparent way but in a hidden and covert way, that often causes analysts and scholars to talk of a "deep state" or "guardian state," in a manner not too different from a conspiracy theory. In this case, there can be some relationship with elite theory and in particular with the "shadow elite" as one scholar has defined them.[14] In Turkey, for example, it is common to speak about the deep state as an antidemocratic, nationalist coalition among government representatives, bureaucrats, security personnel, intelligence agents, and armed forces.[15] These elite coalitions may be involved in organized crime, corruption, and human rights violations in order to defend their power and the status quo. Others speak about a guardian state, slightly different from the deep state, as a reincarnation of the Kemalist one-party state ideals among the current elites. To retain power, the guardian state elites use the "divide and rule" strategy, fueling ethnic, religious, and political conflicts to marginalize, or repress with military power, whomever the state considers its enemies.[16] When this guardian state feels like its control is slipping away, the elites may foment some new chaos in order to retain control over the situation. Following the Ergenekon allegations, as explained in the previous chapter, this deep state could have felt beaten and reacted as a consequence. By contrast, in Indonesia the concept of the deep state is not as common in the democratization phase, apart from some scholars speaking about it under the Yudhoyono presidency.[17] Therefore, elites seem more transparent about revealing what might affect their decisions. Only during the time of mass killings of Communists and alleged leftists in Indonesia (sometimes referred to as the Indonesian genocide) following the 30 September Movement failed coup in 1965 did some form of deep state

[14] Janine R. Wedel, *Shadow elite* (Basic Books, 2009).
[15] Söyler, Mehtap, *The Turkish Deep State: State Consolidation, Civil-Military Relations and Democracy* (Hoboken: Taylor and Francis, 2015).
[16] Kerem Öktem, *Turkey since 1989: angry nation* (London: Zed Books, 2011).
[17] Marcus Mietzner, "The president, the 'deep state' and policy making in post-Suharto Indonesia: a case study of the deliberation of the civil service act," Report for the Partnership on Governance Reform (Jakarta: Kemitraan, 2014).

begin to play a role in maintaining the status quo at a high cost, but following democratization this no longer seems to be the case.

In conclusion, all of these approaches attach importance to elite power struggles based on rational and utilitarian reasons, the first hypothesis of this study. The following sections, therefore, look for evidence in the two case studies that may support this hypothesis.

Evidence for Turkey: From Autonomization to Securitization

Turkish policy moved from securitization to autonomization when the AKP came to power and then back to resecuritization when Erdogan and the AKP elites felt blocked in attaining absolute power in recent years. To understand these changes in policies over time, we need to analyze the declining influence of military and Kemalist elites, the ascendancy of the AKP elites, and the fluid coalitions with Gulenist elites who later were excluded from power. We should therefore analyze the role of at least three types of state elites and one nonstate elite group that became a state elite for a period: (1) moderate Islamist elites at the base of the AKP, which has been the ruling party since 2002 that accompanied the last democratic transition of Turkey; (2) Kemalist elites, present in the state and bureaucracy of Turkey since its foundation; (3) moderate Islamist elites belonging to the Gulen movement or *Hizmet* ("service," the term that the movement uses to refer to itself)[18] that became part of the state supporting the AKP government during the AKP's early years; and (4) military elites who also have been powerful, in collaboration with the Kemalist elites, since the foundation of Turkish state. There is no evidence that another important nonstate elite, the business class, has had a decisive impact on decision-making regarding minorities in Turkey.[19]

---

[18] The Gulen movement is as an Islamic transnational civil society movement that seeks a balance between Islamic and modern values, considering Islam a "way of life" in the Sufi spiritual tradition. Unlike other Islamic movements like Wahhabism, its goal is not to proselytize but to serve in a kind of "missionary" spirit, so instead of building mosques or *madrasas* it builds schools and hospitals and is active in interfaith dialogue. It is guided by a Turkish preacher, an ex-imam, Fethullah Gulen, who has been living in exile in the USA since 1999. See http://fgulen.com/en/.

[19] With the lack of freedom of press and transparency in Turkey, little information is available on the relationship between the Turkish economic elites and business class and the government. There are only allegations that Erdogan is enriching his family and the business elite close to

The story that emerges from this study's analysis of elites is that three pivotal changes led to the outcome of autonomization attempts and later the outcome of the resumption of the securitization of the Kurdish minority. The first event is the growing marginalization of military elites in Turkey during the period of democratization. The second is a similar gradual exclusion of the old Kemalist elites from the decision-making and bureaucratic power of the state. Finally, the third, and probably most important, event is the end of the alliance between the Islamist elites of the AKP and those of the Gulenists. This third marginalization is quite important because it represents the final step in the attainment of absolute power of the current elites in power. The exclusion of the Gulenists started in 2011 but grew in intensity in 2013, following the corruption scandal with investigations against the AKP (for which Erdogan accused the Gulen movement) and became an open conflict in December 2015; since that time the Gulen movement has been accused of building a "parallel state" inside Turkey and been classified as a terrorist organization.[20] The showdown occurred following the last failed military coup in Turkey, in July 2016, after which Erdogan launched a crackdown on thousands of people from all parts of society, both in Turkey and abroad, accused of being Gulenists. Tens of thousands of military personnel, journalists, teachers, public officials, judges, jail staff, and ordinary people were suspended from their jobs and arrested in the months following the attempted coup.[21]

Therefore, this marginalization represents an important story of two traditional Islamists groups gradually fighting for power in a competition

---

him, as in December 2015 when Russia accused the Erdogan family of profiting from the illegal smuggling of oil from territory held by ISIS. See Reuters, "Turkish leader's son denies Russian allegations of Islamic State trade," December 8, 2015, accessed September 30, 2017, http://www.reuters.com/article/us-mideast-crisis-turkey-russia-idUSKBN0TR15I20151208.

[20] Raziye Akkoc, "A parallel state within Turkey? How the country's democracy came under attack from two men's rivalry," *The Daily Telegraph*, February 24, 2015, accessed September 30, 2017, http://www.telegraph.co.uk/news/worldnews/europe/turkey/11397876/A-parallel-state-within-Turkey-How-the-countrys-democracy-came-underattack-from-two-mens-rivalry.html.

[21] See, among many, BBC News, "Turkey coup: Purge widens to education sector," accessed September 30, 2017, http://www.bbc.com/news/world-europe-36838347.

The National, "Turkey arrests 32,000 people in coup probe," September 28, 2016, accessed September 30, 2017, http://www.thenational.ae/world/europe/turkey-arrests-32000-people-in-coup-probe.

between rising elites: the Gulenists and the "Erdoganist" Islamist elites.[22] This story interacts with the electoral ascendancy of the AKP and Erdogan, which played a fundamental role in the strategy chosen by the AKP with respect to the Kurdish minority. The Islamist elites represented by the AKP and the Erdoganist group, thanks to the growth in their electoral and political power, were able to exclude the other Islamist elites, more related to institutional and social position than political ones (from judicial and security powers to media, businesses, and schools). This also allowed the AKP to support the process of autonomization for the Kurdish minority, which was opposed by the Gulenist movement, without concern for its power. But when the AKP lost the elections in June 2015, these elites took the opportunity to change strategy with respect to the Kurds in order to regain electoral power. The AKP therefore favored autonomization as a viable strategy initially, to win electoral support from the Kurds as well, but then switched to securitization to regain the electoral support from most of the population that it had lost when the strategy of autonomization did not work. The Gulenist elites, who had joined the new AKP administration as a partner, represented a more liberal professional class of Turkey, also with some ability to influence the masses given their concentration in the education sector. However, Gulenists were excluded by the power aims of Erdogan out of fear of the emergence of "another state" inside the state, leaving the AKP elites as the only ones able to set policy regarding the Kurds and so channelizing it at the beginning toward autonomization and later toward securitization.

Before analyzing the different goals and strategies of the elites, we need to remember that both the military and the Kemalist elites (and later also the Islamist elites of the Gulenists) had a conception of the Turkish nation based on an ethno-cultural understanding of who Turks are.[23] This conception in turn affected their understanding of the Kurdish problem during the history of the republic. By contrast, the Islamist elites of the AKP had a more religious conception of the Turkish nation based on Muslim identity. Both of those conceptions remained quite constant over time while policies changed, that is, from securitization they switched to

---

[22] Erdoganism has been compared by several analysts with Kemalism, given the attitude of Erdogan as a "new sultan" or "new Ataturk" wanting to monopolize power to create a new Islamist, even if moderate, Turkey.

[23] Senem Aslan, "Different faces of Turkish Islamic nationalism," in *Rethinking Nation and Nationalism,* Project on the Middle East and Political Science, POMPES studies n. 14, June 2, 2015, p. 10.

autonomization and back to securitization. This variation in policy toward the Kurds suggests elites used these conceptions tactically to negotiate the autonomization versus the securitization strategies to maintain or regain power.

In fact, traditionally the Turkish secular-nationalist elites of the military and the Kemalists approached the Kurdish issue either within the security paradigm or the modernization paradigm. According to the first one, the Kurdish problem was a question of order and security, of violence and terrorism, which required a military solution. The second paradigm looked at the development solution, as the problem was the economic and social backwardness of the Kurdish region. Both approaches excluded political solutions, seeing the solution as not involving recognition of Kurdish rights but instead as a security or economic solution. The new Islamist elites who came to power in 2002 with the AKP instead had a different approach, based as stated earlier on a religious view of commonality between Turks and Kurds. This perspective suggests that the Kurdish problem arose from a lack of recognition of Kurdish diversity, one of the two identities denied with the founding of the Turkish Republic, together with the Islamist one. Owing to this common history of marginalization, the AKP and its elites felt in some way morally and historically obligated to include Kurds in the new polity of Turkey and started with a new approach based on a recognition of and support for Kurdish rights. However, this obligation aligned closely with the goal of these elites—as for all elites: getting and retaining power. When the policy of inclusion no longer served this goal, the strategy changed.

Since winning the elections of 2002, the AKP of Erdogan has increased gradually but consistently its power—and with it its plan to build a new and powerful Turkey, one with a strong presidential system and a moderate conservative Islamist approach to politics and social life. Besides the exclusion of the old elites and the alliance with the more liberal forces to dismantle the old authoritarian nationalistic system, the fundamental strategy of the AKP was to seek the electoral support of a majority of the population, including the Kurds. Kurds of the Turkish Eastern regions generally had voted for pro-Kurdish parties, even if they failed to reach the 10 percent threshold needed to win seats in parliament (from the People's Democracy Party/HADEP in 1999 to the Democratic People's Party/DEHAP in 2002). Because of competition among political parties competing for the Kurdish votes, the "democratic deepening" that started since 2002 therefore made the state, the AKP ruling party, and the elites behind it reflect on the approach to ethnic minorities. As examined in Chap. 4, the need for Kurdish votes made the Islamist elites in the AKP choose—in contrast to Kemalist, military, and later also Gulen elites—an accommodative approach toward the Kurdish minority. This could be done because the AKP was gradually excluding the other elites from the political decision-making process, and this lasted until this strategy of inclusion and accommodation toward Kurdish demands bore electoral fruits. When it started to become a strategy that failed to give the AKP the political support it needed, starting in 2011 but particularly since the summer of 2015, the AKP changed the strategy and went in the opposite direction of securitization. This was consistent with the already authoritarian drift that Erdogan had undertaken since 2011.

Also, before analyzing in detail the different goals and strategies of the elites, we need to remember that Erdogan's path to absolute power has played a decisive role in pushing the AKP toward extreme positions on the Kurdish question. The internal fighting over control of the AKP would be another study altogether. Here it is sufficient to say that positions taken on domestic and foreign policies have played an important role in the power struggle also inside the AKP: Erdogan made sure to exclude from this struggle the most moderate and liberal figures. He had disagreements, for example, with his former deputy prime minister and cofounder of the AKP, Bulent Arinc, when he was still supporting peace with the PKK in early 2015.[24] This is one of the reasons why he chose Ahmet Davutoglu, when he became president in 2014, to replace him as prime minister and not Arinc or Abdullah Gül. Gül was the third founder of the AKP, together with Erdogan and Arinc, who served as president of Turkey before Erdogan between 2007 and 2014, but Erdogan did not like him because he opposed the proposal for a presidential system.[25] Finally, when Davutoglu also engaged in actions of which Erdogan, now president, disapproved—such as reaching an agreement with the EU on the Syrian refugee crisis—he asked Davutoglu to step down and chose

---

[24] "Turkish gov't criticizes Erdogan over Kurdish process," *Daily News*, March 21, 2015, accessed September 30, 2017, http://www.hurriyetdailynews.com/turkish-govt-criticizes-erdogan-over-kurdish-process.aspx?pageID=238&nID=79989&NewsCatID=338.

[25] Erdogan Albay, "Turkey's President Erdogan Shows Machiavellian Instincts Yet Again," *Foreign Policy Journal*, May 13, 2016, accessed September 30, 2017, http://www.foreignpolicyjournal.com/2016/05/13/turkeys-president-erdogan-shows-machiavellian-instincts-yet-again/.

another prime minister on his path toward (what seems clear now) the creation of his absolute power.[26]

Thus, going back to the elites, regarding the Kemalist ones, the nationalist-secularist elites who founded the modern Turkish nation state in 1923, we must say that they marginalized the Islamist elites in the early days of the republic, as they did with the Kurdish or other minority elites.[27] Eighty years later, when the Islamist elites came back to power, the AKP and Erdogan did not sideline the Kemalist elites in the same way, at least initially. As Bechev argues, Erdogan "re-legitimised power by replacing the tutelage of the Kemalist elites with top-down rule backed by an electoral majority."[28] Nevertheless, as other scholars recall, the AKP, with the support of the Gulen movement, as soon as it rose to power started to reduce the power of the military and secularist judiciary.[29] Obviously, the nationalist-secularist Kemalist elites have never been in favor of an accommodative attitude toward the Kurds, and the AKP's new approach to the Kurds therefore may have threatened not only their power but also the values and beliefs of the Kemalist elites. But the Kemalists no longer had much power to influence the AKP's policies toward minorities after being gradually replaced by the new Islamist elites of the AKP, not only in the parliament and government but also in the bureaucracy and state positions, during the so-called AKP's decade-long political tsunami.[30]

Regarding the Gulenist elites, as stated earlier, they started to conflict with the AKP elites in 2011, and with greater intensity starting in 2013, with the scandal of corruption allegations against President Erdogan and the AKP supposedly made by followers of the *Hizmet*. They had played an important role in gradually reducing the power of military and secularist judicial elites, and, sharing the idea of "Muslim nationalism" with the

---

[26] Tim Arando and Ceylan Yeginsumay, "How Erdogan Moved to Solidify Power by Ousting a Pivotal Ally," *New York Times,* MAY 5, 2016, accessed September 30, 2017, http://www.nytimes.com/2016/05/06/world/europe/ahmet-davutoglu-turkey-prime-minister.html?_r=0.

[27] Carter Findley, *Turkey, Islam, nationalism, and modernity: A history, 1789–2007* (New Haven: Yale University Press, 2010).

[28] Dimitar Bechev, "The Travails of Democracy in Turkey," in Valeria Talbot, *The Uncertain Path of the 'New Turkey'* (Milan: ISPI, 2015) p. 11.

[29] Senem Aslan, "Different faces of Turkish Islamic nationalism," 2015.

[30] Soner Cagaptay, "From Ataturk to Erdogan: Reshaping Turkey," *Washington Post,* August 14, 2011, accessed September 30, 2017, https://www.washingtonpost.com/opinions/from-ataturk-to-erdogan-reshaping-turkey/2011/08/11/gIQA5lKjFJ_story.html. See also Senem Aslan, "Different faces of Turkish Islamic nationalism," 2015.

AKP, they blamed the Kemalist nationalists for the loss of Turkey's place in the international community in recent decades. Nevertheless, the Gulen movement supported an ethno-cultural understanding of Turkishness, while the AKP attached more importance to the religious understanding. This played a role in the conflict between AKP and the *Hizmet*, with important consequences for the resecuritization of the Kurdish minority by the AKP. Actually, the AKP had a more pragmatic approach to Kurdish conflict, less related to Turkish identity. By contrast, the *Hizmet* never supported negotiations with the PKK and actually was for a military solution to the insurgency in the Southeastern region, ironically the strategy that has been followed by the AKP since 2015. However, after 2013 the *Hizmet* elites had no role in political decisions, and today the movement is considered a terrorist group, responsible for the attempted coup in 2016. At the same time, while the *Hizmet* has been supporting the small ethnic groups of Greek, Armenians, and Jews, the AKP has been very exclusive toward them. This would confirm that the accommodative approach to the Kurds was based on a political calculus, besides the religious commonality, more than on the "inclusion of ethnic diversity" by the AKP. The Gulen elites therefore were not decisive in the decision-making on the Kurdish issue, as their strategy was not used until they had been excluded from the decision-making process.

Finally, we need to analyze the military elite, one of the most important groups in Turkey, the bastion of the Kemalist identity of Turkey that defends its national security against external and internal enemies. This elite also has been gradually excluded from political power by the AKP since 2002, helped in part by the EU accession process that shifted the balance of power more toward civilian institutions and away from the military. The Turkish armed forces have considered themselves as the protector of the values of the Turkish Republic since its founding, which is why they have staged coups when the party in charge did not adhere to those values, especially when the party claimed an Islamist or socialist identity. This was true at least until 2002, when for the first time, even though the new ruling party was a moderate Islamist one, the military did not intervene. This happened also because the AKP and Erdogan emphasized the secular nature of their government and did not try to alienate military elites, at least initially. However, this changed over the years, in particular starting in 2007. Before the May 2007 elections, the military tried again to intervene in politics as it had in the past, declaring its role as guardian of secularism and their opposition to Islamist candidates. Nevertheless, the Turkish government, as well as the EU and the USA, declared that the military should not have gotten involved in political matters, and so the new democratization of Turkey went on. Moreover, in 2007, a court case known as "Ergenekon" started, accusing the army of a plot against the AKP regime. This was the beginning of the end of the military's power and its recognition as the country's most trusted institution. In 2010, changes approved by referendum amended the 1982 constitution, reducing the power of the military in Turkish political life. Finally, the military's power was reduced economically, too, as its budget increased over the years in absolute value but reduced as a percentage of GDP, going from USD 9 billion (3.9 percent of GDP) in 2002 to USD 12 billion (2.5 percent) in 2005 and USD 15 billion (2.1 percent) in 2015.[31]

Regarding the Kurdish issue, the armed forces had, after 2007 and 2010, a reduced role in decisions about domestic politics, which helped the AKP to take an accommodative approach to the Kurdish minority. Obviously, this did not please military elites. With the final strategic shift of the AKP toward resecuritization, however, there seemed to be a new realignment, at least in goals and interests, between the AKP elites and the military elites. Also, we need to remember that the Turkish armed forces are the second largest standing military force in NATO, after those of the USA (600,000 personnel in 2015, ranked eighth in the world in terms of military strength),[32] and this obviously still gives some kind of power to the nationalist armed forces. Therefore, the Turkish army, even without political power, remains a strong actor and influential institution in Turkey. In some ways, it represents a limit on the resolution of the Kurdish issue,[33] because the primary domestic threats to the military in Turkey are considered to be fundamentalism, leftist extremism, and separatism.[34] Nevertheless, following the attempted coup in 2016, many in the military have been dismissed (or arrested), and this weakened the military's power

---

[31] SIPRI Military Expenditure Database, Stockholm International Peace Research Institute, accessed September 30, 2017, http://www.sipri.org/research/armaments/milex/milex_database.

[32] Global Fire Power, online database, accessed September 30, 2017, http://www.globalfirepower.com/countries-listing.asp.

[33] Sumanto Al Qurtuby, "Interethnic Violence, Separatism and Political Reconciliation in Turkey and Indonesia," *India Quarterly* 71(2) (6/2015): 126–145.

[34] CIA Factbook, *Turkey*, 2016, accessed September 30, 2017, https://www.cia.gov/library/publications/the-world-factbook/geos/tu.html.

since the military as an institution has lost many officials and personnel educated and trained in recent decades.

Let us now examine the evidence testing the hypothesis that AKP elites chose accommodation and even negotiation in the first years of transition, and securitization later, not only because of the elites' power and identity struggle but also because of specific electoral benefits.

According to Romano, "the logic of electoral politics can dictate greater accommodation to win votes, particularly where an ethnic minority commands sufficient numbers to influence electoral outcomes."[35] The AKP was on the right path in subsequent elections in 2007 and 2011, when it won and increased its share of votes, including in the Kurdish region. Also, fewer people voted for the pro-Kurdish candidates who won seats in parliament.[36] These results showed that the AKP strategy worked well.

Regarding the peace process in particular, there are alternative arguments and explanations for this renewal of the AKP's accommodative approach not only to the Kurdish minority but even to the PKK. According to Tekdemir and Goksel, for example, the peace process started because both parties understood that the conflict could not be resolved by securitization.[37] But the recent resecuritization exposes the flaw of this argument, as the AKP seems to believe now that the conflict can actually be resolved by a conventional military approach. Other scholars, such as Serhun Al, speaking about the accommodative approach to the Kurdish minority, argue that this had primarily a security goal for the state (as did the exclusionary policies approach).[38] This is because when the Kemalist worldview of one language, one nation, one state—which was the *raison d'état* throughout the twentieth century—was replaced by a new narrative of

---

[35] David Romano, "The long road toward Kurdish accommodation in Turkey: the role of elections and international pressures," Ch. 9 in Jacques Bertrand and Oded Haklai (eds.) *Democratization and Ethnic Minorities: Conflict or Compromise?* (Abingdon: Routledge, 2014): 165.

[36] This was possible because the candidates presented themselves as independents in an alliance with left-wing parties, the Thousand Hope Candidates in 2007 and the Labour, Democracy, and Freedom Bloc in 2011.

[37] Omer Tekdemir and Oghuzan Goksel, "A turbulent Turkey in a region in turmoil," *Open Democracy*, September 17, 2015, accessed September 30, 2017, https://www.opendemocracy.net/arab-awakening/omer-tekdemir-o%C4%9Fuzhan-g%C3%B6ksel/turbulent-turkey-in-region-in-turmoil.

[38] Al Serhun, "Kurds, state elites, and patterns of nationhood in Iraq and Turkey," in *Rethinking Nation and Nationalism,* Project on the Middle East and Political Science, POMPES studies n. 14, June 2, 2015, p. 6.

nationhood with the new century (a neo-Ottoman identity with an overarching Muslim identity), the AKP started to recognize the Kurdish identity because the status quo of conflict had become a threat to the security of the state. However, this concept of the lack of security because of exclusion clashed with the high level of ontological security that Turkey finally felt with the new century, not only because of its application to the EU but also because of finally having included the Islamist identity in Turkey.

One might argue, therefore, that Erdogan and the rest of the Islamist elites inside the AKP initiated a peace process with the PKK for the same reason that an accommodative approach to the Kurdish minority started at the beginning of the democratic transition. That is, when they saw it as being beneficial to the regime—when the political costs of toleration, accepting an accommodative approach, were calculated as being lower than the costs of repression—they supported a negotiated solution. Because the AKP needed votes from the Kurds to obtain an absolute majority, to go on with repression and avoid the peace process with a negotiation would have carried great political costs. When Öcalan said that the PKK was no longer interested in independence or even "democratic autonomy" but just cultural rights,[39] the costs of toleration were suddenly reduced since they were no longer related to an independent Kurdistan but just to some form of cultural autonomy.

The main reasons for the peace process seem therefore to have been a political calculus of the AKP Islamist elites, to meet political goals, because the strategy changed when this calculus appeared to be wrong in the middle of 2015, when resecuritization started. Actually, the AKP, reversing its growing trend, lost almost 10 percent of the votes in the June 2015 election, and with it its dream to attain a two-thirds (or at least three-fifths) majority in parliament for the plan of changing the constitution.[40] The plan had to be postponed because of the surprising success of the pro-Kurdish HDP party. The AKP strategy of granting cultural rights, at least at the individual level, to Kurds and even try to engage in dialogue with

---

[39] Tulin Daloglu, "Talks with Öcalan Offer Slim Hope for Turkey-PKK Deal," *Al Monitor*, January 2013, accessed September 30, 2017, http://www.al-monitor.com/pulse/ar/originals/2013/01/kurds-pkk-ocalan.html.

[40] Constitutional amendments in Turkey require a three-fifths majority to be put to referendum and a two-thirds majority to be ratified directly. The AKP reached an agreement to be presented in a referendum in January 2017, thanks to the help of the right Nationalist Movement Party (MHP), which has supported the AKP since the end of peace negotiations with the PKK and the resecuritization of the Kurdish issue.

the PKK had not worked: what seemed to be an opportunistic approach of Erdogan and the AKP to the peace process with the PKK did not bear the expected fruits. Some analysts speculate that Erdogan actually had already suspended the peace process shortly before the June elections, when he saw it no longer fit with its strategy and was not attracting more popular or electoral support.[41] Previously, the AKP had curtailed policies of accommodation toward the Kurdish minority to fuel nationalist passions for electoral purposes, in particular in the 2007 and 2011 elections.[42] However, according to other analysts,[43] the AKP would have agreed to advance the peace process if the PKK and HDP had supported Erdogan's executive presidency wishes.

Whatever the case, one thing is evident: to regain the votes of the moderate Kurds lost in June 2015, Erdogan and the AKP Islamist elites decided to stop the peace process as it represented a strategy that did not bear political fruits. The political costs of toleration had become suddenly too high, higher than the costs of repression, and therefore the strategy changed. All this confirms that the change of strategy of the AKP was caused by the need for the AKP ruling Islamist elites to recapture the political power lost in earlier elections, to guarantee not only its political survival and power for a long time to come but also to carry on the program of transformation of Turkey toward a presidential republic. For these reasons, we can conclude that there is enough evidence to support the hypothesis that the shift in power from the old military-Kemalist secular elites to the new moderate Islamist elites provoked the phase of accommodation and autonomization toward the Kurds. But the obstacle to obtaining absolute power by Erdogan, the AKP, and its corresponding moderate Islamist elites, posed by the same strategy of autonomization that gave the Kurds the desire to bring a Kurdish party to parliament, caused the AKP to shift its strategy in the direction of resecuritization.

---

[41] Desmond Butler and Suzan Fraser, "Erdogan slams brakes on Kurdish peace process ahead of polls," *Salon*, April 8, 2015, accessed September 30, 2017, http://www.salon.com/2015/04/08/erdogan_slams_brakes_on_kurdish_peace_process_ahead_of_polls/.

[42] Ofra Bengio, "The 'Kurdish Spring' in Turkey and Its Impact on Turkish Foreign Relations in the Middle East," *Turkish Studies* 12(4) (2011): 623.

[43] Mustafa Akyol, "Who Killed the Turkey-PKK Peace Process?," *Al Monitor*, August 4, 2015, accessed September 30, 2017, http://www.al-monitor.com/pulse/originals/2015/08/turkey-syria-iraq-pkk-peace-process-who-killed-kurds.html.

Amberin Zaman, "A Bombing in Ankara and Erdogan's Political War for Total Power," *Foreign Policy*, October 15, 2015, accessed September 30, 2017, http://foreignpolicy.com/2015/10/15/a-bombing-in-ankara-and-erdogans-political-war-for-total-power/.

Evidence for Indonesia: From Securitization to Autonomization

In contrast to the Turkish case, Indonesia experienced an increase in securitization at the beginning of its democratic transition, but after a few years the state engaged in the autonomization of the Aceh region. As with Turkey, to understand these changes in policies over time in Indonesia, we need to analyze the shift in the elite power balance and in particular the declining influence of the military in the country. Actually, early securitization corresponded to when the military still had power but felt it slipping away, while the later autonomization period happens when that power started to become less effective.

The slow and gradual exclusion of the armed forces from politics in Indonesia was also accompanied by a decentralization of the government. These processes contributed as well to changes in policies toward minorities. By devolving authority to the regional level, the problem of minorities, in particular the Acehnese, was no longer a problem for Jakarta but for the region. For this reason, one important group of elites (the armed forces) no longer had the institutional, material, and bureaucratic benefits of securitization: decentralization made the costs of repression much higher as it would have required a dual system with a centralized security apparatus and at the same time authority devolved to the provinces.

To analyze the Indonesian case, we first need to explore some background elements regarding the elites' power and their perception of national sovereignty. First of all, we need to say that Indonesian political elites had less fear than their corresponding Turkish ones of losing political power to ethnic minorities during the democratization process. This is due to several reasons, among which is the fact that ethnic minorities, including Acehnese, are geographically concentrated on peripheral islands, without the possibility of having a real impact on the central state's power once having achieved autonomy. In addition, ethnic minorities cannot aspire to a national voice in the parliament and even less so in government, not having political parties that can represent them at the national level. Therefore, we could say that during the democratization transition the costs of toleration for Indonesian elites to accommodate minorities, with a decentralization or autonomization process, have been much lower than the costs of repression.

Nevertheless, at the beginning of its democratization process, Indonesia engaged in the repression of its ethnic minorities, even more than during the last period of the authoritarian regime, especially with the minority that had waged an armed guerrilla rebellion for decades: the Acehnese. This is because of another background element regarding the elites' perception of national sovereignty: that at the beginning of the democratization process Indonesia's political and military elites feared the risk of dismemberment of the national territory, with centrifugal forces that would have fought for ethnic and territorial independence. For this reason, initially, the strategy toward Aceh, as explained in Chap. 4, was based on balancing between some ceasefires and concessions, but also military repression. The national strategy shifted from repression to accommodation only some years after 1998, particularly around 2003/2004. This section of the chapter explains why this shift to autonomization occurred, using the rational choice theory of calculation of political benefits for the Indonesian political and state elites.

For the Indonesian case and the state's relationship with the Acehnese minority, this study analyzes the role of two types of state elites and one nonstate elite: (1) military elites, (2) nationalist political elites, and (3) Islamist elites (mostly from civil society). Nonstate elites such as the business class did not have a decisive impact on decisions made regarding minorities in Indonesia, either.[44]

Regarding the military elites, first of all we must say that Indonesia is a unique country (but in this sense similar to Turkey) that without a military dictatorship was able to build a strong military, with political power, and a so-called dual function, known in Bahasa as *Dwi Fungsi*. The military was considered during the Sukarno and Suharto era as a sociopolitical actor as well as the defender of national security, allowing it to occupy a position of power (with guaranteed seats in parliament and top positions in public service) and at the same time to control civilian population in a legitimate way.[45] This is also because in countries with contentious politics based on regional rebellions, the militarization of the state, as occurred in Turkey and Indonesia, is quite common. This is the reason for the other peculiar element of the Indonesian armed forces: the fact that they have always been based on territorial considerations to ensure they were prepared to

---

[44] This book does not analyze the possibly deep but hidden relationship between business and political elites, apart from a few obvious elements like President Yudhoyono choosing businessman Yusuf Kalla as his vice president in 2004, as well as efforts to bring business elites within the government sphere.

[45] Harold Crouch, *The Army and Politics in Indonesia* (Jakarta: Equinox, 2007).

fight both external and, above all, internal enemies, which was the main focus of the army, with the islands of the archipelago having experienced several insurgencies.[46]

The hypothesis relating to this elite is that the military pushed for securitization before and in anticipation of losing power. By contrast, when later the military started to lose power, other elites were able to put in practice policies of autonomy. The military, therefore, was not excluded suddenly at the beginning of democratization.[47] On the contrary, its reformation and marginalization from the politics of the state was gradual,[48] and even the military elites experienced internally a smooth and organized transition, with a very slow replacement of its leaders.[49] Nevertheless, the elites started to feel somewhat abandoned and unheard by the massive democratic changes accompanying decentralization, as the Indonesian army always saw themselves as a defender of the "unitary state of Indonesia." Both the retention of power and the fear of losing it contributed to the repression and securitization toward Aceh at the beginning of democratization.

But how did the military's gradual reformation and marginalization from security issues and public policies happen? First of all, the *Tentera Nasional Indonesia* (TNI) (Indonesian National Armed Forces) had itself already adopted a new doctrine in August 1998, a few months after the fall of Suharto, the so-called New Paradigm. This doctrine, formulated by a group of senior officers headed by General Susilo Bambang Yudhoyono, proposed to move the traditional focus of the military from internal security to external defense, transferring internal security functions to the national police.[50] Nevertheless, the declarations and the facts on the ground were quite different as police functions were separated from military ones only gradually, because only the army had the capability to guar-

---

[46] Dan Slater, *Ordering power: Contentious politics and authoritarian leviathans in Southeast Asia* (Cambridge: Cambridge University Press, 2010).

[47] Aleksisu Jemadu, "Democratization, the Indonesian Armed Forces and the Resolving of the Aceh Conflict," in *Verandah of violence*, edited by Anthony Reid, Singapore: Singapore University Press, pp. 272–292.

[48] Angel Rabasa and John Haseman, *The military and democracy in Indonesia. Challenges, politics and power*, RAND, National Security Research Division, 2002.

[49] Indonesia, Current Data on the Indonesian Military Elite, April 2008–September 2013, Southeast Asia Program Publications at Cornell University, No. 98 (October 2014), pp. 91–139.

[50] Rabasa and Haseman, *The military and democracy in Indonesia*, p. 26.

antee public order and fight armed separatist movements. Indonesia's parliament, for example, passed legislation in 2001 that still assigned four internal security goals to the TNI: operations against separatists, insurgent forces, drug trafficking, and smuggling.[51]

However, the so-called dual function was revoked gradually, making the military a strictly defensive agency and no longer a political actor, along with the civilianization of the public administration and the end of the armed forces in parliament (the military still had 38 seats for the 1999–2004 period of transition). Individuals with military backgrounds continued to serve in the government and other public positions, but active-duty officers had to retire before serving in public positions (even though the ex-general Yudhoyono served as president for a decade, from 2004 to 2014).[52] Even if gradual, these changes were important because they made it less likely for presidents to co-opt the TNI for personal political gain. Finally, military-controlled businesses were gradually limited from the beginning of the transition until 2009, when all military businesses were handed over to a civilian institution, significantly reducing the economic power of the military.[53] This was accompanied by a reduction in military expenditures in the country. Similar to the Turkish case, military spending was quite high during the period of dictatorship but passed from 1.5 percent of GDP in 1997 for a total of USD 3.2 billion (in current prices) to 0.7 percent of GDP in 2002, for a total of USD 2.2 billion, to increase again in 2003/2004 up to 0.9 percent and USD 3.4 billion in 2004.[54]

All these processes during the transition may have contributed to an attempt by the army to retain some of its power, or at least to have the "permission" of the new political elites to use its power in peripheral territorial disputes, crushing minority movements and even fueling more religious and ethnic conflict in which it would need to intervene (as in the case of the Maluku and Sulawesi sectarian conflicts between 1998 and 2002). In this way, the army could retain its institutional structure for at least the first few years, blocking reform of its territorial command structure and so maintain control over the territory and potential problems

[51] Ibid., p. 27.
[52] Ibid., p. 49.
[53] Indonesian National Armed Forces, US database, accessed September 30, 2017, http://datab.us/i/Indonesian%20military.
[54] SIPRI Military Expenditure Database, Stockholm International Peace Research Institute, accessed September 30, 2017, http://www.sipri.org/research/armaments/milex/milex_database.

with minorities.[55] Nevertheless, the result of the armed forces' initial repression of the centrifugal forces of independent movements was either the opposite of the intended outcome, at least in a region like East Timor, which won its independence in 2002, or the failure to crush completely the independence movement (as in Aceh or even Papua). This also could have played a role in the subsequent accommodationist approach by the political civilian elites in Indonesia, which saw that repression and securitization were not helpful in reaching the goals established. The costs of toleration for the military were higher than the costs of repression because the army already had in place the apparatus to keep repressing and securitizing the Acehnese guerrillas, who had been rebelling during the recent preceding decades. To tolerate some form of autonomy or even independence would have been too much for a military that saw itself as the guarantor and keeper of territorial integrity and state sovereignty. Nevertheless, at some point the Army likely understood, as did the national political elites, that neither of the two parties could win. After the tsunami in December 2004, a struggle inside the army seems to have pushed toward a more accommodative leadership. While the chief of the army, Lt. General Riyacudu, openly rejected negotiations with GAM in 2005, resulting in his sudden decision to take "early retirement," his superior, the commander-in-chief of the armed forces, General Sutarto, declared his full support for the Helsinki peace negotiations, declaring: "Enough of the war, the armed forces also lost their men in the battle."[56]

In conclusion, one can argue that the relative retention of power by the military elites at the beginning of the democratic transition, together with the threat of losing that power, allowed them to push the Indonesian state to repress ethnic minorities, and specifically Acehnese, for the first few years. Later, when the armed forces started to lose power and because increased political decentralization reduced the cost of toleration, the new political elites could engage more in processes of autonomization, also because they had seen the failure of the securitization process to end separatist conflicts.

Moving on to the traditional nationalist-secular political elites, before anything else we must say that these elites have been very much interre-

---

[55] Marcus Mietzner, *The Politics of Military Reform in Post-Suharto Indonesia: Elite Conflict, Nationalism, and Institutional Resistance* (Washington: East-West Center, 2006).

[56] Hamid Awaluddin, "Why is peace in Aceh successful?" *Conciliation Resources*, Accord issue: 20, 2008, p. 25.

lated with military elites throughout Indonesian history, much like Turkey. However, whereas in Turkey the new AKP regime started to remove from power the old military-Kemalist elites as soon as it came to power in 2002, in Indonesia the change happened more gradually, leaving to the army and the old nationalist-secular elites more power to decide the strategy toward independence movements, at least early on in the transition. These elites in Indonesia, supported by oligarchs and influential families, were guided by Suharto and his family, as in many similar cases of dictatorships around the world. According to some scholars,[57] with the democratic transition, elites that had belonged to the new order's system of patronage received political benefits from the new reforms, while actors marginalized under the new order, such as organized labor, remained excluded. Others, like Slater,[58] confirm that, with the transition, the "party cartels" formed by new political parties and old military elites cooperated more than they competed, sharing power and money in cabinet positions. This confirms that political nationalist-secular elites and military elites were not marginalized during the democratic transition and influenced the early repression and securitization of minorities. In 2004, however, Indonesia introduced direct presidential elections and, in 2005, direct elections also for local government executives and the national parliament. This process started to reduce the system of corruption and clientelism and hindered the power of old political and economic elites. We can therefore argue that the political and military old elites were excluded only gradually from the power positions.[59] This gradual process contributed both to the initial securitization and to the later policies of autonomy implemented by Indonesia, especially in Aceh.

Finally, regarding Islamist elites in Indonesia, we can say that they are composed of two types of elites: nonstate ones, represented by the influential Islamic civil organizations Muhammadiyah and Nahdatul Ulama (NU), and state ones, represented by small but important Islamist parties. The Islamic civil associations, with tens of millions of members, have been important in social and educational activities, either as reformist associations (like the NU) or more traditionalist but still progressive and pluralist ones (like Muhammadiyah). They indirectly influenced politics in

---

[57] Vedi Hadiz, "Reorganizing political power in Indonesia: A reconsideration of so-called 'democratic transitions,'" *The Pacific Review*, Volume 16, Issue 4 (2003).

[58] Dan Slater, "Indonesia's Accountability Trap: Party Cartels and Presidential Power after Democratic Transition," *Indonesia*, Volume 78 (October 2004), 61–92.

[59] As Jocelyn Cesari argued for the Indonesian case, see: Cesari, 2014, pp. 229–233.

Indonesia. NU even tried to create some Islamist parties between the 1950s and 1980s, but it failed to achieve a national majority and so decided to go back to religious and social activities. Nevertheless, these elites did not have a large influence on decisions made with respect to ethnic minorities; additionally, they represented an inspirational elite out to improve society, more so than the other elites. This is very different from the Turkish case in which an Islamist elite finally attained power with the AKP beginning its rule.

Nevertheless, these parties and their elites played an important role in supporting and strengthening the democratization process, as some scholars argue.[60] These parties have existed since Indonesian independence, but during the dictatorship Islam was repressed as a political ideology, even if a "political Islam" was not considered an enemy of the secular elites, as occurred in Turkey. With the *Reformasi* process, several Islamist parties were recreated, some of them won some seats in parliament and four Islamic parties (in particular the most influential one, the *Partai Keadilan Sejahtera*/Prosperous Justice Party, PKS) were even represented in the six-party coalition of the government of President Susilo Bambang Yudhoyono between 2009 and 2014. As Woischnik and Müller say, these parties have been quite influential in occupying important posts in the institutions of the Indonesian state,[61] but this does not mean that they could influence the decision-making regarding the treatment of ethnic minorities in the country, as their power is still small with respect to other elites and big parties. The PKS, for example, which is the strongest, won only around 8 percent of the popular vote in the 2009 elections, when it ascended to government posts (though today it stands in opposition to rather than in the government). Therefore, we can conclude that these nonstate and state Islamist elites did not play a decisive role in formulating policy toward minorities, and specifically toward the Acehnese in Indonesia.

Conclusions

From this analysis of elites' interest, one can identify two similarities and two differences between Turkey and Indonesia. Regarding the similarities, we see that in both cases the armed forces lost authority, even if in Turkey

---

[60] Jan Woischnik and Philipp Müller, *Islamic parties and democracy in Indonesia*, Konrad-Adenauer-Stiftung International Reports, n. 10, 2013.

[61] Ibid., p. 61.

the military lost it quicker than in Indonesia, and in both cases the reduction in military power seems to be the decisive element for policy shifts. But to explain the different outcomes—the initial autonomization and the later resecuritization in Turkey, and the intensified securitization and the later autonomization in Indonesia—at least two main differences seem to have affected elites' decisions.

First, the old elites who dealt with the transition in Indonesia, for reasons unrelated to Aceh, pursued a policy of decentralization. By contrast, Turkey, even with new Islamist elites in power, remained a centralized state. Administrative devolution in Indonesia contributed to changing the power backdrop (unlike in the Turkish case). This made the costs of repression higher and the costs of toleration lower for elites who decided to engage in autonomization after the failure of securitization.

Second, the fact that old Indonesian secular elites had no need for Acehnese support for their political power made those elites uninterested in accommodation with the minority initially. This was different from the Turkish case, in which new Islamist elites in the AKP needed minority support, first of all to reach its goal of power so it could transform Turkish society, and second because for the first time policies regarding the Kurds were formulated on a religious-integrative basis, more than an ethnic-differentialist one. In Turkey, the search for accommodation was also a way to find common ground at the religious level, based on the ultimate inclusion of Islamist reality, both majoritarian and in the minority.

All of this demonstrates that changes in elites' interests affected the different treatments of minorities in the two countries. Because of the need for Kurdish support, the new Turkish Islamist elites started with autonomization, but when they saw that the strategy failed to produce the benefits they desired, they changed policies. Still having a very centralized state, the costs of repression in Turkey were lower than the costs of toleration. In contrast, in the absence of a need for Acehnese support, the Indonesian old secular elites started initially to increase securitization of this minority, hoping to resolve the issue by military means. However, Indonesian elites then accepted autonomization thanks also to decentralization policies that made the costs of repression higher and costs of toleration lower.

REFERENCES

Akkoc, Raziye. 2015. A Parallel State Within Turkey? How the Country's Democracy Came Under Attack from Two Men's Rivalry". *The Daily Telegraph*, February 24, 2015. http://www.telegraph.co.uk/news/worldnews/europe/turkey/11397876/A-parallel-state-within-Turkey-How-the-countrys-democracy-came-underattack-from-two-mens-rivalry.html. Accessed 16 Apr 2016.

Akyol, Mustafa. 2015. Who Killed the Turkey-PKK Peace Process? *Al Monitor*, August 4, 2015. http://www.al-monitor.com/pulse/originals/2015/08/turkey-syria-iraq-pkk-peace-process-who-killed-kurds.html. Accessed 9 Apr 2016.

Al Qurtuby, Sumanto. 2015. Interethnic Violence, Separatism and Political Reconciliation in Turkey and Indonesia. *India Quarterly* 71 (2): 126–145.

Albay, Erdogan. 2016. Turkey's President Erdogan Shows Machiavellian Instincts Yet Again. *Foreign Policy Journal,* May 13, 2016. http://www.foreignpolicyjournal.com/2016/05/13/turkeys-president-erdogan-shows-machiavellian-instincts-yet-again/. Accessed 30 Sept 2017.

Amberin, Zaman. 2015. A Bombing in Ankara and Erdogan's Political War for Total Power. *Foreign Policy*, October 15, 2015. http://foreignpolicy.com/2015/10/15/a-bombing-in-ankara-and-erdogans-political-war-for-total-power/. Accessed 30 Sept 2017.

Arando, Tim, and Ceylan Yeginsumay. 2016. How Erdogan Moved to Solidify Power by Ousting a Pivotal Ally. *New York Times*, May 5, 2016. http://www.nytimes.com/2016/05/06/world/europe/ahmet-davutoglu-turkey-prime-minister.html?_r=0. Accessed 30 Sept 2017.

Aslan, Senem. 2015. Different Faces of Turkish Islamic Nationalism. In *Rethinking Nation and Nationalism,* Project on the Middle East and Political Science, POMPES Studies n. 14, June 2, 2015, p. 10.

Awaluddin, Hamid. 2008. Why Is Peace in Aceh Successful?. *Conciliation Resources*. Accord Issue: 20: 25.

BBC News. 2017. *Turkey Coup: Purge Widens to Education Sector*. http://www.bbc.com/news/world-europe-36838347. Accessed 30 Sept 2017.

Bechev, Dimitar. 2015. The Travails of Democracy in Turkey. In *The Uncertain Path of the 'New Turkey'*, ed. Valeria Talbot. Milan: ISPI.

Bengio, Ofra. 2011. The 'Kurdish Spring' in Turkey and Its Impact on Turkish Foreign Relations in the Middle East. *Turkish Studies* 12 (4): 623.

Bruce Bueno de Mesquita. 2003. *The Logic of Political Survival*. Cambridge: MIT Press.

Burton, Michael, Richard Gunther, and John Higley. 1992. Introduction: Elite Transformations and Democratic Regimes. In *Elites and Democratic Consolidation in Latin America and Southern Europe*, ed. John Higley and Richard Gunther. London: Cambridge University Press.

Butler, Desmond and Suzan Fraser. 2015. Erdogan Slams Brakes on Kurdish Peace Process Ahead of Polls. *Salon*, April 8, 2015. http://www.salon.com/2015/04/08/erdogan_slams_brakes_on_kurdish_peace_process_ahead_of_polls/. Accessed 30 Sept 2017.

Cagaptay, Soner. 2011. From Ataturk to Erdogan: Reshaping Turkey. *Washington Post*, August 14, 2011. https://www.washingtonpost.com/opinions/from-ataturk-to-erdogan-reshaping-turkey/2011/08/11/gIQA5lKjFJ_story.html. Accessed 30 Sept 2017.

Cesari, Jocelyn. 2014. *The Awakening of Muslim Democracies*. New York: Cambridge University Press.

CIA Factbook. 2016. *Turkey*. https://www.cia.gov/library/publications/the-world-factbook/geos/tu.html. Accessed 30 Sept 2017.

Collier, Ruth. 1999. *Paths Toward Democracy. The Working Class and Elites in Western Europe and South America*. New York: Cambridge University Press.

Crouch, Harold. 2007. *The Army and Politics in Indonesia*. Jakarta: Equinox.

Dahl, Robert A. 1971. *Polyarchy. Participation and Opposition*. New Haven: Yale University Press.

Daily News. 2015. *Turkish Gov't Criticizes Erdogan Over Kurdish Process*. March 21, 2015. http://www.hurriyetdailynews.com/turkish-govt-criticizes-erdogan-over-kurdish-process.aspx?pageID=238&nID=79989&NewsCatID=338. Accessed 30 Sept 2017.

Daloglu, Tulin. 2013. Talks With Öcalan Offer Slim Hope for Turkey-PKK Deal. *Al Monitor*, January 2013. http://www.al-monitor.com/pulse/ar/originals/2013/01/kurds-pkk-ocalan.html. Accessed 15 May 2016.

Dunleavy, Patrick. 1991. *Democracy, Bureaucracy and Public Choice: Economic Models in Political Science*. London: Pearson.

Findley, Carter. 2010. *Turkey, Islam, Nationalism, and Modernity: A History, 1789–2007*. New Haven: Yale University Press.

Geddes, Barbara. 1999. What Do We Know About Democratization After Twenty Years? *Annual Review of Political Science* 2 (115–44): 129.

Global Fire Power. *Database Online Resource*. http://www.globalfirepower.com/countries-listing.asp. Accessed 30 Sept 2017.

Green, Donald P., and Ian Shapiro. 1994. *Pathologies of Rational Choice Theory: A Critique of Applications in Political Science*. New Haven: Yale University Press.

Hadiz, Vedi. 2003. Reorganizing Political Power in Indonesia: A Reconsideration of So-called 'Democratic Transitions'. *The Pacific Review* 16 (4): 591–611.

Indonesia. Current Data on the Indonesian Military Elite. April 2008–September 2013. Southeast Asia Program Publications at Cornell University, No. 98 (October 2014): 91–139.

Indonesian National Armed Forces. *US Data Base*. http://datab.us/i/Indonesian%20military. Accessed 27 Apr 2016.

Jemadu, Aleksisu. 2006. Democratization, the Indonesian Armed Forces and the Resolving of the Aceh Conflict. In *Verandah of Violence*, ed. Anthony Reid, 272–292. Singapore: Singapore University Press.

Mietzner, Marcus. 2006. *The Politics of Military Reform in Post-Suharto Indonesia: Elite Conflict, Nationalism, and Institutional Resistance*. Washington: East-West Center.

———. 2014. *The President, the 'Deep State' and Policy Making in Post-Suharto Indonesia: A Case Study of the Deliberation of the Civil Service Act*. Report for the Partnership on Governance Reform. Jakarta: Kemitraan.

Miller, Michelle Ann. 2009. *Rebellion and Reform in Indonesia. Jakarta's Security and Autonomy Policies in Aceh*. London/New York: Routledge.

Öktem, Kerem. 2011. *Turkey Since 1989: Angry Nation*. London: Zed Books.

Olson, Mancur. 1965. *The Logic of Collective Action: Public Goods and the Theory of Groups*. Cambridge: Harvard University Press.

Rabasa, Angel, and John Haseman. *The Military and Democracy in Indonesia. Challenges, Politics and Power*. RAND, National Security Research Division, 2002.

Reuters. 2015. *Turkish Leader's Son Denies Russian Allegations of Islamic State Trade*. December 8, 2015. http://www.reuters.com/article/us-mideast-crisis-turkey-russia-idUSKBN0TR15I20151208. Accessed 15 May 2016.

Romano, David. 2014. The Long Road Toward Kurdish Accommodation in Turkey: The Role of Elections and International Pressures. In *Democratization and Ethnic Minorities: Conflict or Compromise?* ed. Jacques Bertrand and Oded Haklai. Abingdon: Routledge.

Serhun Al. 2015. Kurds, State Elites, and Patterns of Nationhood in Iraq and Turkey. In *Rethinking Nation and Nationalism*, Project on the Middle East and Political Science, POMPES studies n. 14, June 2, 2015, p. 6.

SIPRI Military Expenditure Database. Stockholm International Peace Research Institute, http://www.sipri.org/research/armaments/milex/milex_database. Accessed 30 Sept 2017.

Slater, Dan. 2004. Indonesia's Accountability Trap: Party Cartels and Presidential Power after Democratic Transition. *Indonesia* 78: 61–92.

———. 2010. *Ordering Power. Contentious Politics and Authoritarian Leviathans in Southeast Asia*. Cambridge: Cambridge University Press.

Söyler, Mehtap. 2015. *The Turkish Deep State: State Consolidation, Civil-Military Relations and Democracy*. Hoboken: Taylor and Francis.

Tekdemir, Omer, and Oghuzan Goksel. 2015. A Turbulent Turkey in a Region in Turmoil. *Open Democracy*, September 17, 2015. https://www.opendemocracy.net/arab-awakening/omer-tekdemir-o%C4%9Fuzhan-g%C3%B6ksel/turbulent-turkey-in-region-in-turmoil. Accessed 15 May 2016.

The National. 2016. *Turkey Arrests 32,000 People in Coup Probe*. September 28, 2016. http://www.thenational.ae/world/europe/turkey-arrests-32000-people-in-coup-probe. Accessed 30 Sept 2017.
Wedel, Janine R. 2009. *Shadow Elite*. New York: Basic Books.
Weingast, Barry R. 1997. The Political Foundations of Democracy and the Rule of Law. *The American Political Science Review* 91 (2): 245–263.
Woischnik, Jan, and Philipp Müller. 2013. Islamic Parties and Democracy in Indonesia. *Konrad-Adenauer-Stiftung International Reports* (10): 59–79.

CHAPTER 6

International Factors: Geopolitical Issues, International Community, and Diaspora

Introduction

With respect to the second variable and the three subhypotheses we can say that regarding the geopolitical issues in the Turkish case, it seems that the Syrian–Iraqi crisis, with the Kurdish kinship and Kurdish regional autonomy issues in both countries, had an important impact in shifting the strategy from autonomization to securitization of Turkey's Kurdish minority. In the Indonesian case, it seems that the lack of regional spillover was a key factor; the case of East Timor, which involved repression, ended in independence; and finally, the 2004 tsunami disaster, where international aid was urgently needed, was decisive in putting an end to the separatist conflict and, thus, in bringing to the fore policies of autonomy by the Indonesian state. Both the Syrian–Iraqi chaos and the tsunami disaster can be considered so-called black swan events (a famous terms coined by Nassim Nicholas Taleb[1]): highly improbable events that have massive consequences. But while the tsunami, even if indirectly, accelerated the solution of the Acehnese conflict, the Syrian–Iraqi crisis exacerbated the Kurdish conflict. The puzzle is to explain the different outcomes with these similar black swan events.

---

[1] Nassim Nicholas Taleb, *The black swan: The impact of the highly improbable* (New York: Random House, 2007).

Regarding the importance of the international community, we can say that in both cases these actors played an important role. In the Indonesian case, some international organizations, in particular NGOs, were decisive for the autonomization of Aceh. By contrast, in the Turkish case the only really important international player—the EU—had some influence at the beginning of Turkish democratization in Turkey's relationship with the Kurds. However, the lack of progress in EU membership, in particular because of the Cyprus veto and the Syrian refugee crisis in Western Europe, gradually eroded the EU's influence on Turkey. While we would expect that a strong actor like the EU would have been able to seriously influence the solution of the Kurdish conflict, and that a weak actor like the international civil society would not have had much of an influence on the Acehnese conflict, the results were the opposite. This shows, first of all, that the "persuasive" power of international NGOs has been stronger or more efficient than both the "hard" and "soft" powers of the EU. It also illustrates that a smaller involvement of great powers in a strategically less important area like Sumatra Island has been more conducive to the resolution of the conflict. Furthermore, the case studies show that the ontological security of a country (as analyzed in Chap. 8), in the sense also of its acceptance of external interventions without fear of invasion, had an influence too. Finally, the consensus decision-making in the EU weakened the ability of the EU itself to demand a resolution of the Kurdish issue because of different priorities.

Regarding the diaspora, the evidence shows that while the Turkish diaspora has not been decisive in the alternation between policies of securitization and autonomization and for the final solution of the conflict, Acehnese civil society, through international networks and the diaspora, has actively participated in lobbying for negotiations and, thus, contributed considerably to the final autonomization of the minority.

Theoretical Background Applied to Case Studies

Regional geopolitical issues may play a fundamental role in the decision-making of domestic actors who deal with the treatment of ethnic minorities. The hypothesis for this variable is that when the regional geopolitical situation is unstable and shows a risk of spillover (because of minority kinship, diaspora, or migration in transborder regions), the domestic outcome for ethnic minorities will go more toward securitization. By contrast, in cases where regional geopolitics are more stable and there is no risk of spillover, the treatment of minorities will lean more toward policies of autonomy.

Regarding the literature on the topic, there are scholars who have studied similar arguments for the Turkish case. Bozarslan, for example, argues that the regional dimension of the Kurdish issue played a big part in the foreign policies of Turkey, Iran, Iraq, and Syria, which always treated the Kurdish demands for autonomy as a potential threat to their national security and territorial integrity, so they implemented policies of regional security against Kurdish separatism.[2] Another scholar, comparing cases of transition to democracy in Europe, the Middle East, and Asia, showed that in the transition to democracy, the presence of transborder ethnic groups (like Kurds in Turkey, Albanians in Macedonia, or Russians in Latvia and Estonia) causes tensions to increase and conflicts to intensify.[3] These arguments serve as an important backdrop for our hypothesis as they illustrate that the regional geopolitical situation may impact the domestic treatment of ethnic minorities in the Turkish case. Regarding Indonesia instead, there is little research on Aceh because ethnic minorities in Indonesia live on islands separated from each other, not in regions with borders that have been drawn dividing ethnic or religious communities as in the Middle East. Hence, Indonesia does not worry about transborder spillover of ethnic conflicts.

The second theoretical background relates to the role of the international community, in particular the EU for Turkey and some INGOs, but also the USA and European governments for Indonesia. The hypothesis here is that when the international community has a strong interest in and an effective ability to influence the actions of a state, the treatment of ethnic minorities will be more toward accommodation and autonomization. By contrast, where the international community is not interested or decisive in impacting another state's policies, the state is more likely to emphasize securitization.

Some scholars argue that the EU had an impact on communal rights in postcommunist countries, while others claim that local variables have been more important. For example, Kelley shows how, in the 1990s, European organizations helped to resolve ethnic tensions, related to language, edu-

---

[2] Hamit Bozarslan, "Kurds and the Turkish State," in *The Cambridge History of Turkey, Volume 4: Turkey in the Modern World*, Reşat Kasaba (ed.) (Cambridge: Cambridge University Press, 2008).

[3] Oded Haklai, "Regime transition and the emergence of ethnic democracies," Ch. 2 in Jacques Bertrand and Oded Haklai (eds.) *Democratization and Ethnic Minorities: Conflict or Compromise?* (Abingdon: Routledge, 2014).

cation, and citizenship issues, in Latvia, Estonia, Slovakia, and Romania.[4] Csergo, on the other hand, studying some of the same countries, argues that the improvement in the treatment of minorities was not based on simple compliance with international requests from the EU but instead on the role of domestic political actors who guided the democratization process.[5] These arguments are important because they show that the EU had some role even if at the end of the day domestic institutions of the candidate states, or the new member states, are the final makers of domestic policies. The same discourse would be valid for the international community in general, as the Indonesian case was impacted positively by pressure especially from the international nongovernmental community.

Finally, the third theoretical background is related to the minority abroad, the diaspora composed of immigrants and refugees. The hypothesis is that when the diaspora has an organized voice to support its cause, to advocate for its kinship inside the country, and to lobby the international community to intervene, the state is pushed to move in the direction of accommodation, which could end in a process of autonomization of the minority.

On the diaspora there are scholars who examined both our case studies. Regarding Turkey, Grojean argues, for example, that thanks to the work of Kurdish activists in Europe, with their transnationalization and skills at organization, identity production, and political engagement, the Kurdish question has been kept constantly on the agenda of Turkey's membership in the EU.[6] Regarding Indonesia, the Acehnese diaspora has been important, too. Misbach, for example, argues that Acehnese immigrants in Scandinavia, the USA, Malaysia, and Australia played an important role in the resolution of the Aceh conflict, with exchanges of people, financial resources, and ideas.[7] The importance of the minority

[4] Judith Kelley, *Ethnic politics in Europe* (Princeton: Princeton University Press, 2004). See also "EU enlargements and minority rights." *JEMIE: Journal on Ethnopolitics and Minority Issues in Europe* n. 1 (2003).
[5] Zsuzsa Csergo, *Talk of the nation: Language and conflict in Romania and Slovakia* (Ithaca: Cornell University Press, 2007).
[6] Olivier Grojean, "Bringing the organization back in: Pro-Kurdish protest in Europe," in Marlies Casier and Joost Jongerden (ed.) *Nationalism and politics in* Turkey (London: Routledge, 2011).
[7] Antje Missbach, *Separatist Conflict in Indonesia: The Long Distance Politics of the Acehnese in Diaspora* (New York: Routledge, 2012).

diaspora allows us to understand that the international community is complex and not only based on nation-states but also on actors coming from civil society.

As we can see there is a literature on the matter that validates the importance of studying these issues; for this reason, we now turn to the evidence with which to test the main hypotheses regarding the influence of international actors in the treatment of ethnic minorities.

International Factors for Turkey

Geopolitical and Security Issues

In the Turkish case, it is impossible to understand the current Kurdish problem without first understanding the three regional security challenges related to the Syrian and Iraqi civil wars. First of all is the Kurdish autonomy in both Syria and Iraq. Second is the terrorist group ISIS, with its attacks and infiltration in Turkey. Third is the issue related to the refugees fleeing the wars in these countries. These three phenomena contributed recently to create a police state in Turkey, a permanent state of emergency that, as explained in Chap. 4, can be defined also as a "state of exception," to the detriment of democracy and the treatment of minorities, particularly Kurds. Regarding the importance of the geopolitical situation, Turkey therefore looks at its domestic issues very much in the context of regional issues. Let us review these three security challenges.

First, the territorial and political gains in the Kurdish areas of Syria by the PYD (*Partiya Yekîtiya Demokrat*, or the Democratic Union Party movement), in some way an offshoot of the PKK, caused Turkey to fear a similar situation at home. The Kurdish population of Syria has created three autonomous cantons since 2013 in Jazira, Kobane, and Afrin (collectively known as *Rojava*, or Western Kurdistan), which Turkey fears might be a step toward full statehood for the Kurdish people.[8] This Syrian reality, together with the Kurdistan Regional Government (KRG) that exist in the Kurdistan Autonomous Region of Iraq since 2005, caused Turkey to fear it may be encircled in the future by a Kurdish state or

---

[8] Tol Gönül, "Syria's Kurdish Challenge to Turkey," *Middle East Institute*, August 29, 2012, accessed September 30, 2017, http://www.mei.edu/content/syrias-kurdish-challenge-turkey.

suprastate entity.[9] For these reasons, regional events have had a significant influence on the changing attitude of Turkey's relations with its Kurdish population, starting in 2013 and more so since 2015. This has pushed Turkey toward a resecuritization of the Kurdish minority in the Eastern Turkish region. Also, the successful fight of the YPG (*Yekîneyên Parastina Gel*, or People's Protection Forces, the military wing of the PYD) against ISIS has worried Turkey about a similar strong military force in the PKK.

The evidence shows that Turkey cannot accept the presence of a Kurdish autonomous region on its borders with Syria, much less a Kurdish state.[10] This situation influenced the resecuritization of the Kurdish issue in Turkey, going back to the old Kemalist and military philosophy of viewing domestic minority groups through the lens of regional security issues. The Turkish government, but especially Erdogan, again became suspicious that the demands for decentralization and legal reforms for cultural rights represented a thinly veiled separatist agenda. Erdogan made a strong shift in the narrative since the Siege of Kobane,[11] starting with equating the PKK with ISIS even as Turkey was still negotiating with the PKK up to 2015. Erdogan also insisted on unconditional PKK disarmament, without offering any concessions such as allowing Kurds who were displaced in Turkish military operations to return to their native villages.[12] The attitude of the Turkish president became even more authoritarian after the YPG fighters captured from ISIS the northern Syrian border town of Tal Abyad in June 2015. The conquest of this town increased Turkish fears of future

---

[9] Michael Gunter, "Unrecognized De Facto States in World Politics: The Kurds," *Brown Journal of World Affairs* 20(2) (2014): 161–178.

[10] After the KRG referendum on independence in September 2017, Turkey even threatened a military invasion, or at least economic sanctions and border closure if the independence threatened Turkish security. "The Latest: UN says Kurdish vote could be 'destabilizing,'" *Washington Post*, September 25, 2017, accessed September 30, 2017, https://www.washingtonpost.com/world/middle_east/the-latest-turkey-says-it-rejects-iraqi-kurds-referendum/2017/09/25/d8d37a46-a1bc-11e7-b573-8ec86cdfe1ed_story.html?utm_term=.4905960da7e2.

At the time of this book's editing, things are still moving.

[11] Kareem Fahim and Karam Shoumali, "Turkey to let Iraqi Kurds Cross to Syria to Fight ISIS," *New York Times*, October 20, 2014, accessed September 30, 2017, http://www.nytimes.com/2014/10/21/world/middleeast/kobani-turkey-kurdish-fighters-syria.html.

[12] "Turkey and the PKK: Saving the Peace Process," *International Crisis Group Europe Report No. 234*, November 6, 2014, accessed September 30, 2017, http://www.crisisgroup.org/en/regions/europe/turkey-cyprus/turkey/234-turkey-and-the-pkk-saving-the-peace-process.aspx.

invasions and dismemberments, first of all because it connected the two cantons of Kobane and Jazira, making a ministate in Northern Syria[13]; second, there were accusations of ethnic cleansing of Arabs and Turkmen[14]; and finally, the US air support to the YPG exacerbated Turkey's concerns about future risks of dismemberment.[15] This, in the mind of Erdogan, showed that the USA was supporting the PYD's territorial demands and that the Kurds of Syria were not interested in a coexistence with the Turks. As some scholars like Yavuz and Ozcan state, this created "the realization that the Kurdish issue cannot be resolved within the borders of Turkey alone; it has become part of a larger regional problem."[16]

After the events of Tal Abyad, together with the June 2015 elections when the pro-Kurdish People's Democratic Party (HDP) won an amazing 13 percent of the vote, the securitization of the Kurdish issue restarted. With the ISIS attacks in Suruç in July, the breakdown between the Turkish government and the PKK accelerated the securitization of the Kurdish issue. The elections were very important for pluralism because they created one of the most representative parliaments in Turkish history, since besides the pro-Kurdish party many Alevis were elected in the Republican People's Party (CHP) and the HDP, and representatives of religious minorities—Armenians, Assyrians, and Yazidis—were also elected.[17] However, Erdogan lost the elections and with it his desire to reach an absolute majority to transform Turkey in a presidential system. This, as stated in the preceding chapter, also contributed to his strategic shift, accompanied by a regional shift in the Syrian situation with the YPG empowerment concerning the Turkish government and president.

Regarding the impact of ISIS attacks on the worsening of the relationship between Turkey and the Kurds, it must be said that ISIS attacks in Turkey concentrated mostly on tourists and on left-wing Kurdish groups.

---

[13] Ben Hubbard and Maher Samaan, "Kurds and Syrian Rebels Storm ISIS-Held Border Town," *New York Times*, June 16, 2015, accessed September 30, 2017, http://www.nytimes.com/2015/06/16/world/middleeast/kurds-and-syrian-rebels-push-to-evict-isis-from-border-town.html.

[14] M. Hakan Yavuz and Nihat Ali Özcan, "Turkish Democracy and the Kurdish Question," *Middle East Policy*, Volume 22, Issue 4 (Winter 2015) 73–87.

[15] Jamie Dettmer, "Turkey Warns US About Kurdish Advances in Syria," *Voice of America*, June 22, 2015, accessed September 30, 2017, http://www.voanews.com/content/turkey-warns-us-about-kurdish-advances-in-syria/2832298.html.

[16] Yavuz and Özcan, *Turkish Democracy and the Kurdish Question*, p. 80.

[17] Ibid., p. 73.

Starting in mid-2015, ISIS began claiming responsibility for attacks made on the HDP party, before those on its Adana and Mersin offices, in June on its Diyarbakır rally, and finally in July the massacre of Suruç at a youth-socialist gathering, killing 34 people. These attacks exacerbated the conflict between the Turkish government and Kurdish rebellion and contributed to the resecuritization of the Kurdish issue as Turkey also accused the PKK of being behind the attacks. Of the 1300 people arrested by Turkey following the bombings, 847 were accused of being connected to the PKK and only 137 to ISIS.[18] Many Kurds in Turkey started to suspect that the Turkish discourse of fighting ISIS was in reality an attempt to hide a fight against the Kurdish nationalist movement. The Turkish government and president increasingly blurred the distinction between ISIS and the PKK and conflated peaceful and violent elements of Kurdish activism. These, as we see, are important indicators of resecuritization. In fact, securitization requires treating an issue only as a security issue, without any possibility of political engagement using a narrative defined as a "speech act" by securitization theory (see Chap. 4 on this). But as Unver recalls, this approach did not bear and is not bearing any fruit, either in terms of garnering international support or securing domestic social peace, as "the open-ended nature of security operations also serves to significantly alienate Kurdish public opinion within Turkey, creating another long-term radicalization problem."[19]

Finally, regarding refugees, Turkey is by far the country with the most Syrian refugees, increasing from a few hundred thousand in 2013 to more than three million refugees registered in 2017 (out of a total of five million).[20] The presence of Syrian refugees obviously raises the possibility of many Syrian Kurdish and ISIS-affiliated people in Turkey, with a sure increase in security issues for Turkey. The EU actually was obliged to draw up an agreement with Turkey, signed in March 2016, to block illegal immigration from Turkey to Europe, specifically agreeing to send back to Turkey all irregular migrants crossing over into Greece before March 2016 in exchange for €3 billion (and an additional €3 billion at the end of

---

[18] Sarah Almuhtar and Tim Wallice, "Why Turkey is Fighting the Kurds Who Are Fighting ISIS," *New York Times*, August 12, 2015, accessed September 30, 2017, http://www.nytimes.com/interactive/2015/08/12/world/middleeast/turkey-kurds isis.html.

[19] Akin Unver, *Turkey's policy towards ISIS*, Wikistrat Crowdsourced Consulting, April, 2016.

[20] "UNHCR Syria Regional Refugee Response—Turkey," data from UNHCR, accessed September 30, 2017, http://data.unhcr.org/syrianrefugees/country.php?id=224.

2018) and the lifting of visa requirements for Turkish citizens.[21] This also impacted the Kurdish issue, as this chapter will explain later in a section on the EU impact on Turkish domestic politics.

For these reasons, all three regional security challenges related to the Syrian and Iraqi civil war represented a big challenge in terms of resolving the Kurdish question in Turkey, contributed to the end of the peace process and the resecuritization of the Kurdish issue, and in the future will make the treatment of the Kurdish minority in Turkey even more difficult and complex.

The International Community and European Union

If we cannot understand the contemporary Kurdish issue without considering regional security challenges for Turkey, neither can we understand it without considering the role played by the international community. Specifically, the EU has for long been the international-supranational organization to which Turkey would like to belong. Since the Copenhagen meeting in 1993, the EU started to commit itself to ensuring the protection of minorities in its candidate states. Did this commitment have a fundamental impact on the domestic politics of Turkey, or was it just a carrot without a stick? And from the Turkish perspective, has the respect for the Copenhagen criteria been a real engagement for the future of its republic or just another bus to ride until it reaches its destination and then step off, as Erdogan allegedly said about democracy?[22] It seems that up until recently the EU could have had an impact in helping Turkey on its path to democratization and that Turkey was interested in taking that path. This is no longer so. After almost twenty years of unfruitful negotiations, after the chaos of Syrian civil war, with its security consequences for both Turkey and the EU itself, and after the democratic reversal of Turkey in the last few years, the two actors no longer seem able to affect each other or even seem interested in helping each other along a democratic and pluralist path. Therefore, let us briefly review the timeline of the Turkish EU membership process to illustrate how the prospect for membership historically impacted Turkish domestic politics toward the Kurdish issue.

---

[21] "EU-Turkey Agreement: Questions and Answers," European Commission, March 19, 2016, accessed September 30, 2017, http://europa.eu/rapid/press-release_MEMO-16-963_en.htm.

[22] *BBC*, "Jordan's King Abdullah criticizes regional leaders," March 19, 2013, accessed September 30, 2017, http://www.bbc.com/news/world-middle-east-21844349.

Turkey first applied for associate membership in the European Economic Community (EEC) in 1959, and in 1963 it signed the Ankara Agreement for a customs union with the EEC but also acknowledging the idea of future membership. When the EEC became the EU in 1992, Turkey considered the moment right for applying again, and so in 1995 it signed another customs union agreement. It was officially recognized as a candidate for EU membership in 1999. Since then, negotiations have been blocked many times, owing to political and economic problems, both domestic and external, in particular because of the Cyprus issue.

The slow pace of the Turkish membership process became a topic of hot debate among European and Turkish politicians and people. On the one hand, historical supporters of Turkish admission have been few, mostly Poland, the UK, and, outside the EU, the USA, while opponents—preferring instead a "privileged partnership" that recognizes economic, political, cultural, and geographical differences—traditionally have been most EU members, guided by France, Austria, Germany, and the European Commission. Nevertheless, to fulfill the Copenhagen criteria rules that since 1993 have defined whether a country is eligible to join the EU, Turkey tried to improve its treatment of the Kurdish minority. First of all, the Turkish parliament started to passed some constitutional amendments starting in October 2001, and new legislation allowed broadcasting and publishing in Kurdish, Arabic, Zaza, and other minority languages.[23] In October 2002, to meet the Copenhagen criteria, the parliament even abolished capital punishment, commuting Öcalan's death sentence to life imprisonment.[24] With the AKP regime, in power since 2002, matters improved for the Kurdish minority even more. In December 2002, the Copenhagen European Council decided that the EU would open negotiations with Turkey if the European Council of December 2004 decided that Turkey was trying to satisfy the Copenhagen criteria. This was an important moment for the AKP because it showed that the new regime could do what Turkish governments for decades could not do: finally start negotiations to join the EU. At the same time, this process was also important for the Kurdish minority, who benefited from these negotiations as

---

[23] Sener Akturk, 2012, *Regimes of Ethnicity and Nationhood in Germany, Russia, and Turkey* (New York: Cambridge University Press): 175–92.

Kemal Kirişci, The Kurdish Question and Turkish Foreign Policy, in Lenore G. Martin and Dimitris Keridis, eds., *The Future of Turkish Foreign Policy* (Cambridge: MIT Press, 2004): 277–314.

[24] Kirişci, p. 279.

the AKP had to show greater inclusion of minorities. Erdogan himself pushed some EU harmonization policies in the parliament between 2003 and 2004, including a ban on torture, expansion of the freedom of association, restoration of Kurdish names to Kurdish villages, and broadcasting in the Kurdish language. The parliament also approved a partial amnesty for PKK militants and a program for the repatriation of internally displaced Kurds to return to the Southeast region.[25] As reported by BBC, then Interior Minister Abdulkadir Aksu "thanked the deputies for choosing the path to peace and reconciliation […] he said Turkey had to learn the lessons of the past and it has to embrace all of its people, including some of its terrorists."[26] Quite a different approach from today's Turkish policies toward the PKK and Kurds in general. This was also because, according to some scholars like Romano, EU membership requirements on human rights and respect for minorities pushed the AKP government to become an ally of some part of Kurdish population, both to obtain political benefits and to marginalize the armed insurgency.[27]

Official negotiations with the EU finally started in October 2005, and again both the AKP and the Kurdish minority believed that they could benefit from it. Nevertheless, because of the issue of Cyprus, things started to deteriorate and the negotiations came to a halt in December 2006, with the EU freezing talks in 8 of the 35 key areas, over Turkey's rejection of a proposal to open its ports and airports to traffic from Cyprus. This did not discourage Turkey, as the country believed that EU accession would happen sooner or later. Again according to Romano, playing the card of EU accession, the AKP could even gain protection from the Kemalists and military elites who tried to attack the AKP, including in a judicial accusation in 2008, for violating the constitutional prohibition of "religious politics."[28] For the AKP the European card was an important one also with respect to internal politics.

---

[25] Özlem Pusane, "Turkey's Kurdish Opening: Long Awaited Achievements and Failed Expectations," *Turkish Studies* 15(1): 81–99, 2014, p. 85.

[26] *BBC*, "Turkey approves amnesty for Kurds," July 29, 2003, accessed September 30, 2017, http://news.bbc.co.uk/2/hi/europe/3108539.stm.

[27] David Romano, "The long road toward Kurdish accommodation in Turkey: The role of elections and international pressures," Ch. 9 in Jacques Bertrand and Oded Haklai (eds.) *Democratization and Ethnic Minorities: Conflict or Compromise?* (Abingdon: Routledge, 2014): 175–176.

[28] Ibid., pp. 176–177.

Therefore, in 2009, with the so-called Democratic initiative process, Turkey resumed democratic progress, in particular with respect to the Kurdish minority, in order to show respect for the Copenhagen criteria. However, the steps toward minority cultural rights were unclear. The country granted a license to a public satellite television channel offering programming exclusively in Kurdish, for example, and reduced restrictions on the use of Kurdish in election campaigns, prisons, and universities. Nevertheless, the language was still not allowed in public primary or secondary schools or in official public services, even in cities where a majority of the population spoke Kurdish. Nor was the constitution changed to recognize the status of Kurdish to that of a second national official language.

Regarding the resolution of the conflict, the AKP tried to show good intentions. First, it prepared a partial amnesty law aimed at PKK militants and then introduced the Return to Village and Rehabilitation Project for the repatriation of internally displaced Kurds.[29] At the same time, however, in 2009, thousands of Kurdish activists started to be arrested on terrorism charges.[30] Therefore, both these actions of cultural rights and peaceful resolution of conflict, which seemed to go demonstrate respect for the Copenhagen criteria, in reality were neither answering basic Kurdish demands nor creating a peaceful environment in the Kurdish region. Actually, in its annual reports on Turkey, as the EU had been saying all those years since the start of negotiations, the Kurdish issue saw some improvements but still fell short of the complete inclusion of the minority and resolution of the conflict.

Besides this problem, the Cyprus one remained ever present. In December 2009, Cyprus blocked 6 out of 35 EU negotiation chapters, arguing that Turkey needed first to normalize relations with Cyprus itself. Since then, the negotiations have stalled. Again, the Cyprus–Turkey conflict proved to be one of the main issues in Turkish accession, and actually, since 2009, the Kurdish conflict has gradually progressed toward more securitization by the Turkish side. At this point, one could argue that Cyprus' accession to the EU could have represented even a limit to the solution of the Kurdish issue in Turkey. Actually Cyprus applied for mem-

---

[29] Özlem Pusane, "Turkey's Kurdish Opening: Long Awaited Achievements and Failed Expectations," *Turkish Studies* 15(1) (2014): 81–99.

[30] Tol Gönül, "Kurdish Consensus at Home Can Serve Turkey Abroad," *Middle East Institute*, February 9, 2012, accessed September 30, 2017, http://www.mei.edu/content/kurdish-consensus-home-can-serve-ankara-abroad.

bership in 1990, and EU accession started to be seen on one side, by the Greek Cypriots, as a protection against possible Turkish aggression and on the other side, by the EU, as possible motivation for a future resolution of the Turkish–Cypriot conflict given also the interest of Turkey in joining the EU.[31] Unfortunately, when Cyprus joined the EU in May 2004, it became a member not as a single United Republic of Cyprus, as the Annan Plan for Cyprus had hoped,[32] but as Republic of Cyprus (with a part of the island that the Greek Cypriot government cannot control) because the Greek Cypriots rejected the plan in a referendum one week before.[33] So the separate Turkish Cypriot state—recognized only by Turkey and established in 1983 almost ten years after the Turkish invasion of 1974 (after the Cypriot military coup ordered by the military junta in Greece)—is still considered by the EU as an illegal occupation of European territory.

As discussed, Cyprus has blocked the accession of Turkey to the EU since 2009 and will continue to do so until Turkey's domestic issues are resolved. Cyprus, among others, has been one of the major advocates for not accelerating Turkish negotiations even regarding the recent Syrian migrant deal, threatening to use its veto power to block it if Turkey does not recognize the Greek Cypriot government.[34] This evidence indicates that because EU accession and external agreements are consensual and unanimous, Cyprus has used its veto power to block Turkish accession. One could say that the Greek population in Cyprus has asserted its rights in a strong way toward Turkish membership, while the Kurds have not had the same power of advocacy, as they cannot have a voice in the process of accession. This shows first of all the power of even small states in a consensus-based decision-making process, which has always been a concern for the EU. It is also evidence that the Cyprus issue may even have

---

[31] George Kyris, "The European Union and Cyprus: The Awkward Partnership," EurActiv, accessed September 30, 2017, http://www.euractiv.com/section/euro-finance/opinion/the-european-union-and-cyprus-the-awkward-partnership/.

[32] The Annan Plan for Cyprus was a UN proposal to resolve the Cyprus issue with a federation of two states. Turkish Cypriot accepted it with 65 percent of votes in the referendum, but 76 percent of Greek Cypriots rejected it.

[33] Actually the EU-safeguarded accession was one of the reasons why Greek Cypriots rejected the UN plan. Thus, the earlier good intentions of the EU had an opposite effect to the intended one. See again Kyris, "The European Union and Cyprus: The Awkward Partnership".

[34] Barbara Tasch, "One of the smallest countries in Europe is standing in the way of a massive migrant deal between the EU and Turkey—here's why," March 17, 2016, accessed September 30, 2017, http://www.businessinsider.com/eu-turkey-deal-could-fail-because-of-cyprus-2016-3?r=UK&IR=T.

reduced the power of the EU with respect to the Kurdish issue. The Cyprus problem had to be a top priority for the EU because of the presence of Greece as a member of the EU, and that meant that as important as the Kurdish concern was, it was a secondary element in the negotiations with Turkey. To put it succinctly, the EU could not credibly offer membership to Turkey as long as Cyprus demonstrated its willingness to veto agreements. This may have given Turkey some margin and flexibility in its respect for other Copenhagen criteria and, consequently, some discretion on how to deal with Kurds.

Turkey, to give a new boost to the process of EU accession, in June 2011 even created the Ministry of EU Affairs, to reinforce the role of the Chief Negotiator for Turkish Accession to the EU (a position that has existed since January 2005), who since then has been appointed to serve concurrently also as Minister of EU Affairs. These formal changes were not accompanied, however, by substantive democratic improvements. Therefore, as we can see, geopolitical issues related to Turkey's past, administrative issues related to the consensual process of EU admission, and the relationship of the EU itself with its minorities, like the Turkish minority in Cyprus (regarding which Turkey also often speaks about double standards in the EU), have represented some of the major causes of the blocking of Turkey's admission to the EU, besides the slow pace of the process as a result of Turkey's political and economic limits.

Today only 15 out of 33 chapters are open for negotiation, 17 are frozen, and only one is provisionally closed (the one on science and research).[35] A positive conclusion of the Turkish membership in the EU seems unlikely (as of late 2017 it remained unrealized and appeared uncertain at the time as German Chancellor Merkel had stated that she even wanted to end talks over Turkey's membership in the EU).[36]

The problem will come following the eventual conclusion of the process of membership (and this could be one of the reasons to keep it alive) because the manipulative attitude of the Turkish state, to the point of blackmail, and the superior attitude of the European side will not be conducive to a better future relationship between the two sides.

[35] "European Neighborhood Policy and enlargement negotiations—Turkey," *European Commission*, Membership Status, accessed September 30, 2017, http://ec.europa.eu/enlargement/countries/detailed-country-information/turkey/index_en.htm.
[36] "In shift, Merkel backs end to EU-Turkey membership talks," *Reuters,* September 3, 2017, accessed September 30, 2017, https://www.reuters.com/article/us-germany-turkey-merkel/in-shift-merkel-backs-end-to-eu-turkey-membership-talks-idUSKCN1BE15B.

In conclusion, the evidence suggests that the presence of Cyprus in the EU has been important in reducing EU pressure on the Kurdish issue because the Cyprus issue takes precedence over the Kurdish one. Second, the reduced pressure, but also openness, of the EU toward Turkey's membership—in the sense of the diminished use of the "stick" of the Copenhagen criteria because of more urgent priorities and the diminished use of the "carrot" of membership owing to Turkish political regression—contributed to the resecuritization of the Kurdish minority, which occurred in 2015. From the Turkish perspective, the difficulty of attaining EU membership has also played a role in Turkey's bold attitude toward the EU, reducing its cooperative stance with respect to satisfying the Copenhagen criteria.

The Diaspora

Finally, regarding the diaspora, the last of the international factors analyzed in this chapter, we must say that the Kurdish diaspora did not have much of an impact in shaping Turkish domestic policies. Kurds from Turkey represent 85 percent of Kurds in Europe. They went in particular to Germany and France during the 1960s and 1970s as immigrant workers and as political refugees since the 1980s, mostly to Northern Europe (fewer Kurds from Turkey went to the USA as refugees).[37] Some authors argue that the diaspora played some role in the EU's support of the Kurdish cause,[38] while others claim that the "Europeanization" of the Kurdish minority in Europe, with the growing importance of European institutions, represents both a good and bad thing for the lobbying of the transnational diaspora.[39] Obviously the Kurdish diaspora cannot be ignored today[40] because the Kurds in Europe have economic and political associations, newspapers, and television stations, are elected to the European Parliament, and are capable of bringing tens of thousands of people into the streets for demonstrations against Turkey. But it is one

---

[37] The Kurdish Diaspora, *Foundation Institute Kurd de Paris*, accessed September 30, 2017, http://www.institutkurde.org/en/kurdorama/.

[38] Grojean, *Bringing the Organization back in: Pro-Kurdish Protest in Europe*, 2011.

[39] Lenka Berkowitz and Liza M. Mügge, Transnational Diaspora Lobbying: Europeanization and the Kurdish Question, *Journal of Intercultural Studies*, Volume 35, Issue 1 (2014): 74–90.

[40] Ihsan Kurt, "Kurdish Diaspora Cannot Be Ignored," *Al Monitor*, March 25, 2013, accessed September 30, 2017, http://www.al-monitor.com/pulse/politics/2013/03/kurdish-diaspora-cannot-be-ignored.html.

thing to affirm the strong presence of a diaspora and quite another to have an impact on the domestic politics of a country, and the Kurdish diaspora is not listened to by the Turkish government and is not interested in being listened to either. As Kurt says, the Kurdish diaspora "is not only radical, but also has no confidence in Ankara."[41]

Therefore, the effectiveness of this diaspora is different from that of other ethnic minorities, above all the Acehnese. The fact is that the Kurdish diaspora, connected as it is to Kurdish civil society in Turkey, even if strong and organized, has been unable until now, as its Acehnese counterpart did, to get powerful actors such as governments, international organizations like the UN, or INGOs take the lead in the negotiations, or at least to convene international conferences in which the two sides could meet to discuss the possibility of holding negotiations (as Acehnese international civilian organizations were able to do). The conferences organized by the diaspora on the Kurdish issue usually are quite confrontational with regard to the Turkish government, which is not conducive to a peaceful resolution of the conflict. This does not mean that the diaspora failed to play a role in lobbying the EU or raise consciousness in the international community. Such efforts were not enough, however, or did not reflect the correct approach to have a decisive impact on the resolution of the conflict.

The conclusion for Turkey is that, besides regional geopolitical factors and in relation to them, international actors—especially the EU—had a clear influence on both the early autonomization and the late resecuritization of the Kurdish issue during the democratization of Turkey. Today, in late 2017 and early 2018, the European impact is less important because of the refugee crisis on the one hand and the evident Turkish political reversal on the other.

INTERNATIONAL FACTORS FOR INDONESIA

Geopolitical and Security Issues

Indonesian geopolitics is very different from that of Turkey. Indonesia is an archipelago of 17,000 islands, with no neighboring countries that share land borders apart from Malaysia on Borneo Island and New Guinea on Papua Island. Unlike Kurds, Acehnese are located entirely within the national borders of Indonesia (as Aceh is at one tip of Sumatra Island sur-

[41] Ibid.

rounded by ocean). The lack of regional spillover, therefore, is an important element in understanding the fact that the Indonesia autonomization of Aceh did not risk regional destabilization with transborder effects in neighboring states.

Regarding security, apart from some sporadic problem of piracy, illegal fishing, arms smuggling, or Rohingya refugees from Myanmar, the Malacca Strait and the Indian Ocean surrounding Aceh do not compare with the chaos of the Middle East. Some foreign military vessels, especially American, often crisscross the Malacca Strait, but Indonesia does not object, protesting only if planes from US carriers sometimes enter Indonesian air space. There is nothing parallel to the Middle East situation of Turkey, with regional powers mistrusting each other and reacting to even small provocations or mistakes, as we saw in 2016 with Turkey's shooting down of a Russian plane.

From the ethnic movement perspective, geographic isolation also played a role in its identity and goals. Being surrounded by water obviously weakens a self-determination movement, offering less opportunity to have close external support, and so is more conducive to possible accommodation. For Acehnese belonging to the GAM guerrilla, to flee the country across the sea meant living abroad as refugees, not as retreating fighters ready to regroup and return to fight again, as for the PKK forces escaping to Syria or Iraq. Therefore, the first element to analyze in the international arena, the regional geopolitical situation, has always been for Indonesia a quite safe environment that was more conducive to autonomization. Consequently, we can assert that the first subhypothesis is confirmed by the Indonesian case too: when the regional geopolitical situation is stable, the environment is more conducive to autonomization policies.

Nevertheless, like Turkey with the Syrian civil war, Indonesia also experienced an unexpected regional crisis: the Indian Ocean earthquake and tsunami of December 2004 that killed an estimated 170,000 people and left homeless about half a million people (out of a population of 4 million people). This recalls the concept of the black swan, improbable events that have massive consequences. Even if not a perfect parallel, there are deep similarities between the two humanitarian crises, notwithstanding the fact that one is a chronic manmade crisis and the other an acute natural disaster. Both required a strong international aid response and forced the international community to make a pronouncement on the treatment of the two ethnic minorities. Both seem to have had an impact on the minority conflict, one toward autonomization and one toward resecuritization.

Actually, according to several politicians, journalists, and activists, the tsunami was one, if not the, crucial cause that ended the conflict and started the process of autonomization for Aceh,[42] mostly because of the need to allow international help to arrive in the region. The International Crisis Group declared, for example, that the tsunami "made it politically desirable for both sides to work toward a settlement, offered ways of linking the reconstruction effort and peace process, and ensured the availability of major donor funding outside the government budget."[43] But in reality, even if this event might have had a role in facilitating the final solution to the conflict, it cannot be considered the fundamental factor in the solution of the conflict, representing more a contingent fact that just accelerated a process that had already started (like the black swan for the securitization of Kurds in Turkey that worsened a situation already under way). As some scholars argue, comparing the similar cases of ethnic conflict in Aceh and Sri Lanka, the tsunami was not a real decisive factor but rather an important event that reinforced preexisting political trends. According to Stokke, Törnquist, and Syndre, for example, the tsunami that hit Sri Lanka as well as Aceh was used by elites and different actors for strategic reasons. Consequently, it brought autonomization to Aceh on one side and instead restarted the repression in Sri Lanka, after the attempts of joint efforts between the government and the Liberation Tigers of Tamil Eelam rebels for the post-tsunami reconstruction failed. This is because in Sri Lanka the competition over post-tsunami resources produced a form of ethnic and religious chauvinism that sustained the conflict.[44]

Edward Aspinal also remembers how a few months after the tsunami the progress toward peace in Aceh was still difficult because of oppression, exploitation, and violence framed by two rival national identities.[45] Therefore, we can conclude that among the international factors the one related to post-tsunami reconstruction was probably the less impactful

---

[42] Olle Törnquist, "Dynamics of peace and democratization. The Aceh lessons," *Democratization*, 18(3), s 823–846.

[43] International Crisis Group. *Aceh: A New Chance for Peace*, Asia Briefing 40, Jakarta and Brussels: ICG, August 15, 2005, p. 1.

[44] Kristian Stokke, Olle Törnquist, Gyda Marås Syndre, "Conflict Resolution and Democratization in the aftermath of the 2004 Tsunami: A Comparative Analysis of Aceh and Sri Lanka," *Power, Conflict and Democracy in South & Southeast Asia*, 1(1–2), (2009): 129–149.

[45] Edward Aspinall, "The Helsinki Agreement: A More Promising Basis for Peace in Aceh?," *Policy Studies* 20, Washington, DC: East-West Center, 2005.

one, even if the Indonesian state used the crisis differently from Turkey and accelerated the autonomization process in Aceh. Instead, the geopolitical regional situation itself—the fact that Acehnese are an intrastate community concentrated at a tip of an island while Kurds are a transboundary community in the process of creating independent states in two Turkish neighboring failing states—played a crucial role in the different outcomes.

Regarding geopolitical and regional security factors, there could be another international element, or better yet a domestic element, that became international—that is, the East Timor case, which could have played a role in the final solution of the conflict with Indonesian policies of autonomy toward Aceh. In other words, did the experience with East Timor's independence shape how Indonesia negotiated the end of the Aceh conflict? In reality we need to say that the two cases are not exactly the same because East Timor was not, like the rest of Indonesia, part of the Dutch colony that formed Indonesia in 1949. Instead, it was a Portuguese colony, with a different language, story, and institutions, annexed by Jakarta in 1975 when Portuguese left, and so the situation was different from Aceh. Besides this, following East Timor's independence in 2002, Aceh's situation was still in troubling waters, with a strong military offensive of the Indonesian army in 2003–2004 during the Megawati presidency. Actually, we could argue that the East Timor precedent, the fact that one of the Indonesian islands had already been fragmented with the creation of a new state, may have had an opposite effect by blocking the strategy of accommodation and autonomization that was already in process in Aceh. President Megawati, after seeing East Timor's independence in 2002, may have been worried again about the possible centrifugal forces of Indonesian democratization and so may have thought it better to allow another strong offensive of the Indonesian army in Aceh rather than risk another secession. The role of national leadership actually is an important area for future research and could clarify the relationship between the systemic impact of international factors and Indonesian domestic agency in Aceh autonomization and in general in the treatment of ethnic minorities in democratizing Muslim majority countries.[46] Finally, the international intervention in East Timor (the International Force for

---

[46] For the Yudhoyono presidency, for example, scholars argue that he was famous for his lack of resolution, even if the Aceh autonomy arrived exactly under his presidency. See on this Greg Fealy, "The politics of Yudhoyono, majoritarian democracy, insecurity and vanity," in

East Timor, a multinational non-United Nations peacekeeping taskforce) was not well received by Indonesia. As a consequence, the country may have opposed a possible similar international intervention in Aceh.[47] But in reality this is more related to a cost–benefit analysis, as fTimor independence the risk was to repeat a similar thing in Aceh, so the state may have chosen the final dialogue instead of continuing the repression because it was beneficial and rational to do that, as explained in Chap. 5.

The International Community

With respect to the second hypothesis, the interest and impact of international actors, again the Indonesian situation is quite different from the Turkish one. The interest and efficiency of the international community (both governmental and nongovernmental) during the democratization process, but a smaller involvement of "great powers" in a strategically less important area, had a positive impact and affected the final Indonesian policies of autonomy with respect to Aceh. The EU, some of its member states, and European NGOs contributed in lobbying the Indonesian government and bringing the parties to the negotiating table for solutions to the separatist conflict.[48] The EU intervention with its soft power of financial, political, and moral support (for example, for the Aceh Monitoring Mission) helped to assure the success of the Helsinki peace negotiations. But the most important actors to arrive at those negotiations were not governmental actors: the Henri Dunant Centre (or Centre for Humanitarian Dialogue/HDC), a Swiss-based NGO, and later the former president of Finland, Martti Ahtisaari, with his NGO Crisis Management Initiative (CMI).

By contrast, the corresponding regional authority in Southeast Asia, the Association of Southeast Asian Nations (ASEAN), did not seem to play a crucial role in the peace process and autonomy for Aceh. Some scholars argue that the funding principles of ASEAN, with guidance for ASEAN countries' foreign policy, opened to door to the involvement of these countries in domestic issues of other members. This has been the

---

The Yudhoyono presidency: Indonesia's decade of stability and stagnation, ed. Edward Aspinall (Singapore: Institute of Southeast Asian studies, 2015), 35–54.

[47] "Aceh initiative. Internal Review," *Center for Humanitarian Dialogue*, Geneva, November 2003, p. 37.

[48] Sumanto Al Qurtuby, "Interethnic Violence, Separatism and Political Reconciliation in Turkey and Indonesia," *India Quarterly* 71(2) (6/2015): 126–145.

case, for example, with the Aceh Monitoring Mission (AMM) for the Aceh peace process, established by the EU with contributions from five ASEAN countries.[49] Still, the AMM was established by the EU rather than ASEAN, and the small contribution of ASEAN came after the peace process, not during it. ASEAN offered, therefore, only peripheral support to Aceh but had no active role in the resolution of the Aceh conflict. Instead the non-governmental international actors played a stronger role in the autonomization of the Acehnese minority in Indonesia.

Until the end of twentieth century, the Acehnese case was quite isolated from international interests. There was practically no international intervention beyond regular reports and protests from human rights NGOs such as Human Rights Watch, Amnesty International, Forum Asia, and others. Since the launch of Indonesian democratization, however, this started to change. First, given the importance of a stable and strong Indonesia in the new geopolitical reality, especially following the economic and financial crisis of Southeast Asia in 1997/1998, Western governments realized that the conflict in Aceh was limiting the growth of the Indonesian economy. Added to this, there was a surge of protests and pressure from civil society, human rights movements, and humanitarian organizations in Europe and the USA for their governments to end military support for Indonesia. The free press and free speech accompanying democracy allowed open discussions organized by several international human rights organizations in the country. Cultural visas to visit Aceh were granted to some foreign researchers, and well-known journalists were coming to Aceh somewhat "illegally" (arriving in the country with tourist visas and continuing to Aceh without obtaining the special permit that was still required). In brief, the isolation of Aceh had started to end, unlike the isolation of the Southeastern part of Turkey, which was perceived as very unsafe by the international community and so was quite isolated from the rest of the world.

At that point, starting with the mediation of the HDC since 2000, there were several stages of ceasefire and peace talks known as the Geneva Peace Process, culminating in the Cessation of Hostilities Agreement

---

[49] Nara Rakhmatia, *ASEAN as Regional Mechanism in Aceh Peace Process: Constructivist View on the Norm of 'ASEAN Way'*, Academia.edu, open access source, accessed September 30, 2017, https://www.academia.edu/3263062/ASEAN_as_Regional_Mechanism_in_Aceh_Peace_Process_Constructivist_View_on_the_Norm_of_ASEAN_Way_.

(CoHA) in December 2002.[50] In addition to this agreement, Japan, the USA, the EU, and the World Bank hosted a "Preparatory Conference on Peace and Reconstruction for Aceh" in December 2002 in Tokyo, Japan, to raise funds for initiatives in the province.[51] Nevertheless, in May 2003, after last-minute talks in Tokyo with representatives of the Government of the Republic of Indonesia and GAM collapsed, martial law was declared in Aceh once more. Indonesia carried out the largest military operation in the country since 1975, again with many dead and human rights violations.

However, after the tsunami, another international actor, former Finnish president Martti Ahtisaari (and future Nobel Peace Prize recipient in 2008) and his CMI restarted the talks; this time they succeeded. The memorandum of understanding (MoU) was signed in 2005, and this international mediator had a crucial role in the final agreement. According to several scholars, Ahtisaari's approach was much better than previous ones, first of all because the proposition included a comprehensive political settlement, allowing, for example, GAM to become a political party.[52] As Törnquist argues, the assertiveness of Ahtisaari in proposing possible and feasible solutions was accompanied also by a "constitutionally-democratic approach towards a comprehensive agreement, to which were added the issues of justice and the reintegration of victims and combatants (but unfortunately not the Sharia law and the role of women)."[53] It was therefore the democratic process that accompanied the negotiations, with the transformation of the GAM into a political party since October 2005, that led to a successful outcome to the negotiations. Again, Törnquist explains also how GAM received from Ahtisaari the definition of "self-government" that was not used in the final agreement but allowed both GAM and Indonesia to accept something different from "independence" and "special autonomy." This created the eventual successful path to the autonomization of Aceh.

---

[50] Suryadinata, Leo, *The making of Southeast Asian Nations. State, ethnicity, indigenism and citizenship* (Singapore: World Scientific, 2015) p. 147/150.

[51] "Aceh initiative. Internal Review," *Center for Humanitarian Dialogue*, Geneva, November 2003, p. 37.

[52] Konrad Huber, "Reconfiguring politics: The Indonesia-Aceh peace process," *Conciliation Resources*, Accord issue: 20, 2008, accesses May 21, 2016, http://www.c-r.org/accord/aceh-indonesia/acehs-arduous-journey-peace.

[53] Olle Törnquist, "Dynamics of peace and democratization. The Aceh lessons," 2010, p. 834.

All this should represent important lessons learned also for the Turkish case: negotiations that would include elements of democratization of Turkey, for example transforming the PKK into a political party, or elements of "self-government," instead of speaking of autonomy, could have a higher probability of success. But this does not seem to be the case for the Kurdish minority in Turkey. Therefore, regarding the role of the international community, we can see how third-party mediators played an important role in Aceh, in contrast to Turkey, where there has not been a respected and trusted third party to negotiate between the government and the PKK.[54]

The Diaspora

Finally, the last international factor to analyze is the Acehnese civil society abroad, the diaspora. The Acehnese diaspora has also been very influential in lobbying the international community to defend human rights and help in the resolution of the conflict at home. One of most important Acehnese international NGOs for this has been the International Forum for Aceh (IFA), established in 1998 in New York to build networks with Amnesty International and Human Rights Watch and to start lobbying the American government. In July 1999, they organized a conference in Bangkok, in which the Support Committee for Human Rights in Aceh (SCHRA) was created and the first meeting ever between an Indonesian government official delegation and leadership of GAM, starting to "agree to disagree" in a very friendly atmosphere.[55] Two years later, in September 2001, the IFA held another conference in Bangkok, the Aceh Brotherly Dialogue, where the Acehnese Civil Society Task Force was formed and started collaborating with the SCHRA to increase lobbying in the USA against Indonesian military and police violations of human rights in Aceh. By this time, Megawati Sukarnoputri was the new president of Indonesia (since July) and had already signed special autonomy legislation for Aceh (Chap. 4). The December 2002 Cessation of Hostilities Agreement (CoHA) suggests the international awareness fostered by IFA

---

[54] This was also because the Turkish government does not accept any external comment on its domestic affairs. National leadership and the role of agency therefore should be analyzed, too, in future research, to understand the systemic impact of international factors.

[55] Eva-Lotta E. Hedman, "Aceh Under Martial Law: Conflict, Violence and Displacement," *RSC Working Paper*, No. 24, July 2005, Oxford: University of Oxford Refugee Studies Centre, p. 48.

also contributed to the path to this agreement. Then, with the Helsinki Agreement, the Acehnese civil society, both in the diaspora and locally, played an important role. Because the agreements were based on a "democratic roadmap," old Acehnese civil and political associations became important for the processes of peace building and democratization.[56]

As we can see, civil society activity and the "social capital" of this ethnic minority, with its international diaspora, exerted considerable influence in pushing the state toward accommodation with the Acehnese minority and finally negotiations for its autonomization. This could be another area of future research: the study of the role of the civil society of ethnic minorities, taking a more cultural and civic approach to explain different outcomes.

To conclude regarding the Indonesian case, all three international factors analyzed—the geopolitical situation, the international community, and the diaspora—seem to have impacted the outcome of the process of autonomization, with the most important factors being the international actors that took the lead in negotiations, above all ex-Finnish President Ahtisaari and his NGO.

Conclusions

Geopolitical factors and the international community of governments were the external factors that had the greatest impact for Turkey. By contrast, for Indonesia the nongovernmental international community was the most decisive factor in the state's decisions to switch from securitization to autonomization. The catastrophes that happened in both countries—the tsunami in Indonesia and the Syrian war in Turkey—led to opposite outcomes because the two states had already embarked upon different paths.

For Turkey, the geopolitical situation based on Kurdish transborder kinship, the Kurdish autonomous region born in Syria in 2014, and the relationship between the PKK and the YPG have increased security concerns for the country, with a threat to national security and national sovereignty. This contributed strongly to the resecuritization of the Kurdish minority. For Indonesia, the geopolitical situation was never quite so unstable because the country is an archipelago with no transborder kinship for the Acehnese and no eventual autonomous regions in border states.

[56] Olle Törnquist, "Dynamics of peace and democratization. The Aceh lessons," 2011.

But this can be said with respect to other independence movements in Indonesia, such as in Papua, that had different results. The sudden tsunami of 2004 accelerated a trend toward decentralization already in place and so enhanced the processes of conflict resolution and autonomization.

Regarding the international community, while for Turkey the most important international actor has been a governmental one, the EU, for Indonesia it has been a nongovernmental one, the ex-Finnish president's association, the CMI. Therefore, the second track of diplomacy, based on INGO efforts, had more influence than the supranational diplomacy of the EU, in helping the state resolve the ethnic conflict and start policies of autonomy instead of securitization. Because of the limits to the power of the EU—specifically, a system of consensus—political priorities like the Cyprus case, the Syrian refugee crisis, and Turkey's general skepticism toward external influence led to a breakdown on the path toward satisfying the Copenhagen criteria.

This seems to be the most important factor impacting the Turkish case at the international level. As we can see, a paradox stemming from the EU's consensual rule weakened the bargaining position of the EU with respect to that of Turkey. According to the logic of two-level games,[57] domestic ratification procedures can affect bargaining at the international level, increasing bargaining leverage. In this case, paradoxically, the rule of unanimous ratification of a new application for membership weakened the EU's bargaining position. The EU was offering Turkey benefits with membership, but the opportunity to join the EU was not a credible offer, as it was based on empty promises until the Cyprus situation was resolved. The EU therefore could not offer dependable incentives to Turkey; in the absence of those, Turkey felt free to resecuritize the Kurdish issue. Finally, with respect to the diasporas, for Indonesia this has been a quite decisive factor, with its effective international advocacy work, while for Turkey it has been a wrong approach, and again the disinterest by the Turkish state prevented the Kurdish diaspora from playing an important role in coming up a resolution to the conflict.

In conclusion, it may be asserted that the second independent variable of the international factors (and corresponding black swan events) played a role in the treatment of ethnic minorities. The three subhypotheses are valid for both countries: when facing an external security threat, states are

---

[57] Robert Putnam, "Diplomacy and Domestic Politics: The Logic of Two-Level Games," *International Organization*, 42 (1988): 427–460.

more likely to securitize minority demands; when external actors intervene in minority issues, states are more likely to grant autonomy to minorities; and when the diaspora has an organized voice to support its cause, the state is impelled in the direction of accommodation.

Nevertheless, these factors (as with the first variable, elites' power) built upon trends already in place based on different levels of self-security established by the two countries and on different histories of institutions and territorial structures. The next two chapters will analyze these elements.

REFERENCES

Akturk, Sener. 2012. *Regimes of Ethnicity and Nationhood in Germany, Russia, and Turkey*. New York: Cambridge University Press.

Al Qurtuby, Sumanto. 2015. Interethnic Violence, Separatism and Political Reconciliation in Turkey and Indonesia. *India Quarterly* 71 (2): 126–145.

Almukhtar, Sarah, and Tim Wallice. 2015. Why Turkey Is Fighting the Kurds Who Are Fighting ISIS. *New York Times*, August 12. http://www.nytimes.com/interactive/2015/08/12/world/middleeast/turkey-kurds isis.html. Accessed 10 Apr 2016.

Aspinall, Edward. 2005. The Helsinki Agreement: A More Promising Basis for Peace in Aceh? *Policy Studies* 20, Washington, DC: East-West Center.

BBC. 2003. *Turkey Approves Amnesty for Kurds*. July 29. http://news.bbc.co.uk/2/hi/europe/3108539.stm. Accessed 30 Sept 2017.

———. 2013. *Jordan's King Abdullah Criticizes Regional Leaders*. March 19. http://www.bbc.com/news/world-middle-east-21844349. Accessed 30 Sept 2017.

Berkowitz, Lenka, and Liza M. Mügge. 2014. Transnational Diaspora Lobbying: Europeanization and the Kurdish Question. *Journal of Intercultural Studies* 35 (1): 74–90.

Bozarslan, Hamit. 2008. Kurds and the Turkish State. In *The Cambridge History of Turkey, Volume 4: Turkey in the Modern World*, ed. Reşat Kasaba. Cambridge: Cambridge University Press.

Center for Humanitarian Dialogue. 2003. *Aceh Initiative. Internal Review*. Geneva, November.

Csergo, Zsuzsa. 2007. *Talk of the Nation: Language and Conflict in Romania and Slovakia*. Ithaca: Cornell University Press.

Dettmer, Jamie. 2015. Turkey Warns US About Kurdish Advances in Syria. *Voice of America*, June 22. http://www.voanews.com/content/turkey-warns-us-about-kurdish-advances-in-syria/2832298.html. Accessed 9 Apr 2016.

European Commission. 2016. *EU-Turkey Agreement: Questions and Answers*, Press Release, 19 March. http://europa.eu/rapid/press-release_MEMO-16-963_en.htm. Accessed 25 May 2016.

European Neighborhood Policy and Enlargement Negotiations—Turkey, European Commission, Membership Status. http://ec.europa.eu/enlargement/countries/detailed-country-information/turkey/index_en.htm. Accessed 30 Sept 2017.

Fahim, Kareem, and Karam Shoumali. 2014. Turkey to Let Iraqi Kurds Cross to Syria to Fight ISIS. *New York Times*, October 20. http://www.nytimes.com/2014/10/21/world/middleeast/kobani-turkey-kurdish-fighters-syria.html. Accessed 18 May 2016.

Fealy, Greg. 2015. The Politics of Yudhoyono, Majoritarian Democracy, Insecurity and Vanity. In *The Yudhoyono Presidency: Indonesia's Decade of Stability and Stagnation*, ed. Edward Aspinall, 35–54. Singapore: Institute of Southeast Asian Studies.

Gönül, Tol. 2012a. Kurdish Consensus at Home Can Serve Turkey Abroad. *Middle East Institute*, February 9. http://www.mei.edu/content/kurdish-consensus-home-can-serve-ankara-abroad. Accessed 30 Sept 2017.

———. 2012b. Syria's Kurdish Challenge to Turkey. *Middle East Institute*, August 29. http://www.mei.edu/content/syrias-kurdish-challenge-turkey. Accessed 18 May 2016.

Grojean, Olivier. 2011. Bringing the Organization Back in pro-Kurdish Protest in Europe. In *Nationalism and Politics in Turkey*, ed. Marlies Casier and Joost Jongerden. London: Routledge.

Gunter, Michael. 2014. Unrecognized De Facto States in World Politics: the Kurds. *Brown Journal of World Affairs* 20 (2): 161–178.

Haklai, Oded. 2014. Regime Transition and the Emergence of Ethnic Democracies. In *Democratization and Ethnic Minorities: Conflict or Compromise?* ed. Jacques Bertrand and Oded Haklai. Abingdon: Routledge.

Hedman, Eva-Lotta. 2005. *Aceh Under Martial Law: Conflict, Violence and Displacement*. RSC Working Paper, No. 24, July, University of Oxford Refugee Center, Oxford.

Hubbard, Ben, and Maher Samaan. 2015. Kurds and Syrian Rebels Storm ISIS-Held Border Town. *New York Times*, June 16. http://www.nytimes.com/2015/06/16/world/middleeast/kurds-and-syrian-rebels-push-to-evict-isis-from-border-town.html. Accessed 9 Apr 2016.

Huber, Konrad. 2008. Reconfiguring Politics: The Indonesia-Aceh Peace Process. *Conciliation Resources*, Accord Issue: 20. http://www.c-r.org/accord/aceh-indonesia/acehs-arduous-journey-peace. Accessed 21 May 2016.

International Crisis Group. 2005. *Aceh: A New Chance for Peace*. Asia Briefing 40, Jakarta and Brussels: ICG, August 15.

———. 2014. *Turkey and the PKK: Saving the Peace Process*. ICG Europe Report No. 234, November 6. http://www.crisisgroup.org/en/regions/europe/turkey-cyprus/turkey/234-turkey-and-the-pkk-saving-the-peace-process.aspx. Accessed 18 May 2016.

Kelley, Judith. 2004. *Ethnic Politics in Europe*. Princeton: Princeton University Press. See also: EU Enlargements and Minority Rights. *JEMIE: Journal on Ethnopolitics and Minority Issues in Europe* n. 1 (2003).

Kirişci, Kemal. 2004. The Kurdish Question and Turkish Foreign Policy. In *The Future of Turkish Foreign Policy*, ed. Lenore G. Martin and Dimitris Keridis, 277–314. Cambridge: MIT Press.

Kurt, Ihsan. 2013. Kurdish Diaspora Cannot Be Ignored. *Al Monitor*, March 25. http://www.al-monitor.com/pulse/politics/2013/03/kurdish-diaspora-cannot-be-ignored.html. Accessed 27 May 2016.

Kyris, George. The European Union and Cyprus: The Awkward Partnership. *EurActiv*. http://www.euractiv.com/section/euro-finance/opinion/the-european-union-and-cyprus-the-awkward-partnership/. Accessed 1 June 2016.

Missbach, Antje. 2012. *Separatist Conflict in Indonesia: The Long Distance Politics of the Acehnese in Diaspora*. New York: Routledge.

Pusane, Özlem. 2014. Turkey's Kurdish Opening: Long Awaited Achievements and Failed Expectations. *Turkish Studies* 15 (1): 81–99.

Putnam, Robert. 1988. Diplomacy and Domestic Politics: The Logic of Two-Level Games. *International Organization* 42: 427–460.

Rakhmatia, Nara. *ASEAN as Regional Mechanism in Aceh Peace Process: Constructivist View on the Norm of 'ASEAN Way'*. Academia.edu, Open Access Source. https://www.academia.edu/3263062/ASEAN_as_Regional_Mechanism_in_Aceh_Peace_Process_Constructivist_View_on_the_Norm_of_ASEAN_Way_. Accessed 27 May 2016.

Reuters. 2017. In Shift, Merkel Backs End to EU-Turkey Membership Talks, September 3. https://www.reuters.com/article/us-germany-turkey-merkel/in-shift-merkel-backs-end-to-eu-turkey-membership-talks-idUSKCN1BE15B. Accessed 30 Sept 2017.

Romano, David. 2014. The Long Road Toward Kurdish Accommodation in Turkey: The Role of Elections and International Pressures. In *Democratization and Ethnic Minorities: Conflict or Compromise?* ed. Jacques Bertrand and Oded Haklai. Abingdon: Routledge.

Stokke, Kristian, Olle Törnquist, and Gyda Marås Syndre. 2009. Conflict Resolution and Democratization in the Aftermath of the 2004 Tsunami: A Comparative Analysis of Aceh and Sri Lanka. *Power, Conflict and Democracy in South & Southeast Asia* 1 (1–2): 129–149.

Suryadinata, Leo. 2015. *The Making of Southeast Asian Nations. State, Ethnicity, Indigenism and Citizenship*. Singapore: World Scientific.

Taleb, Nassim Nicholas. 2007. *The Black Swan: The Impact of the Highly Improbable*. New York: Random House.

Tasch, Barbara. 2016. *One of the Smallest Countries in Europe Is Standing in the Way of a Massive Migrant Deal Between the EU and Turkey—Here's Why*, March 17.

http://www.businessinsider.com/eu-turkey-deal-could-fail-because-of-cyprus-2016-3?r=UK&IR=T. Accessed 1 June 2016.

The Kurdish Diaspora. Foundation Institute Kurd de Paris. http://www.institut-kurde.org/en/kurdorama/. Accessed 30 Sept 2017.

The Washington Post. 2017. The Latest: UN Says Kurdish Vote Could Be 'Destabilizing', September 25. https://www.washingtonpost.com/world/middle_east/the-latest-turkey-says-it-rejects-iraqi-kurds-referendum/2017/09/25/d8d37a46-a1bc-11e7-b573-8ec86cdfe1ed_story.html?utm_term=.4905960da7e2. Accessed 30 Sept 2017.

Törnquist, Olle. 2011. Dynamics of Peace and Democratization. The Aceh Lessons. *Democratization* 18 (3): 823–846.

UNHCR Syria Regional Refugee Response—Turkey, Data from UNHCR. http://data.unhcr.org/syrianrefugees/country.php?id=224. Accessed 25 May 2016.

Unver, Akin. 2016. *Turkey's Policy Towards ISIS*, Wikistrat Crowdsourced Consulting, April.

Yavuz, Hakan, and Nihat Ali Özcan. 2015. Turkish Democracy and the Kurdish Question. *Middle East Policy* 22 (4) (Winter): 73–87.

CHAPTER 7

Historical Institutionalism: Nationalism, Institutions and Citizenship of Ethnic Minorities

INTRODUCTION

Historical institutionalism is one of the major theoretical schools in comparative politics, together with rationalism, culturalism, and structuralism. Historical institutionalism attaches importance, as suggested by the name, to two specific variables in political analysis, history and institutions, more than to structural-systemic elements, cultural elements, or the rational thinking of decision makers. Historical institutionalism seeks to explain political outcomes by evaluating the impact of historical institutions on the policies of today. In the words of Thelen and Steinmo, it evaluates a "range of state and societal institutions that shape how political actors define their interests and that structure their relations of power to other groups."[1] Historical institutionalism speaks about the so-called path dependency of states—meaning the decisions states face are shaped by history and past decisions. But it is also a method of research, in the sense that it relies on case studies, analyzing their institutions and history, to understand trends and countertrends across time.

---

[1] Kathleen Thelen and Sven Steinmo, "Historical institutionalism in comparative politics," in *Structuring politics. Historical Institutionalism in comparative analysis*, ed. by Sven Steinmo, Kathleen Thelen, and Frank Longstreth, Chapter 1, (Cambridge: Cambridge University Press, 1992, p. 1/32): p. 2.

© The Author(s) 2018
M. Geri, *Ethnic Minorities in Democratizing Muslim Countries*, Minorities in West Asia and North Africa,
https://doi.org/10.1007/978-3-319-75574-8_7

So what can we say about our two case studies from the perspective of historical institutionalism? Briefly we can say that there are fundamental differences in the historical path between the Turkish case and the Indonesian one that may have impacted the treatment of ethnic minorities over the long run. Turkish history and institutions can be defined as more exclusive, both before and after democratization, due to the experience of nation-building preceding state-building, an individual-rights model of citizens' rights, a "social engineering" of the Kurdish minority since the foundation of the Republic, and, finally, an "ethnic-based democracy." By contrast, Indonesia had a more inclusive path, both before and after democratization, because state formation preceded nation formation, because it adopted a communitarian-liberal model for the citizenship, and because it did not view itself as an ethnic democracy but, on the contrary, implemented decentralization during the period of democratization.

In particular, while Turkey's founding relied on a very exclusive nationalism based on the Kemalist philosophy of one nation, one language, one secular, centralized, and strong state, Indonesia had at its foundation a pluralist ideology called *Pancasila*, literary "five principles," that aimed for unity, democracy, and social justice. Indonesia's motto, "unity in diversity," expresses the ideal pluralism with respect to ethnic and religious diversity, even if Indonesian law only recognizes six religions and does not recognize nonbelievers. All this played a role in the different final outcomes of the two countries with the securitization of Kurds and the autonomization of Acehnese.

Therefore, looking at the historical configuration of forces at the moment of national formation, we can say that the Turkish sense of the nation as an ethnic community emerged endogenously, in the sense that the model of citizenship emerged within the nation before it formed a state. Many multiethnic empires (from the Austro-Hungarian to the Russian, for example) recognized the differences of their ethnicities, as they acknowledged that they were not homogeneous societies. However, while the European model was founded on nations based on ethnicities, in the Middle Eastern model—in particular in the Caliphate of the Ottoman Empire—nations based on religious identities were more important than ethnic ones (see subsequent discussion about the millet system). Instead, with the formation of the state, a Turkish ethnic identity was institutionalized in a "monoethnic" exclusive nation-state, Western style, which resulted in a de facto multinational country with a juridically mononational state. This coincided with a post-World War I view of nationalism in which every nation should have had a state, but, following this Western model of nation-state building, Turkey opened the door to a Turkish-Kurd conflict because the Kurds were the only ethnic group after the implosion of the Ottoman Empire that was not given a state. This was reinforced also by the Kemalist elite, a secular nationalist elite, who searched for foundations other than religion to create the state and found in ethnicity a cohesive alternative to Muslim identity. Likewise, the military elite that allied with Kemalist elites in the foundation of the Republic, aiming to defend the territorial sovereignty of the Turkish nation, always saw the Kurdish identity—for example, the use of the Kurdish language in public—as a violation of the Turkish constitution and, hence, helped to establish Turkish as the only official language.[2] All this made the path of autonomization of Kurds very difficult and securitization as the most apt strategy and policy for a country like Turkey.

The model of nation-state building in Indonesia instead was more exogenous. The conception of the Indonesian community derived from the Dutch model of communitarianism, which is intrinsically pluralist. While Kurds as a community threatened the identity of Turkishness and the idea of an ethnic state, the claim of the Acehnese was related more to a sovereign right than an identity one, affirming the pluralistic principles of Indonesia, in a way that was consistent with the founding myth. The Acehnese claim, therefore, was less threatening, and so it was easier for the state to autonomize when the moment of democratization arrived.

This does not mean that Indonesia did not have its period of securitization too, as we saw in Chap. 4. That is why this study examines several variables—to try to understand those periods with other explanations. Obviously, each of these variables and frameworks have some limitations, but historical institutionalism in particular has difficulties explaining some nuances and changes over time and can therefore be considered more as a background variable on top of which the first two variables build.

Theories Applied to the Case Studies

The two states analyzed here have different historical institutional experiences, and they can represent four independent subvariables that may have shaped the contemporary securitization and autonomization of ethnic

---

[2] Sumanto Al Qurtuby, "Interethnic Violence, Separatism and Political Reconciliation in Turkey and Indonesia," *India Quarterly* 71(2) (6/2015): p. 129.

minorities. The first is the timing and type of state formation, with consequences for the type of citizenship; the second is the nature of citizen rights (either individual or community rights); the third is the presence of historical discrimination, or at least the "intrusion" of the state inside the life of ethnic minorities; and finally, the fourth subvariable is the institutionalization of ethnicity in the creation of the so-called ethnic democracies. This section analyzes these four elements one by one.

Regarding the first element, Turkey and Indonesia have different histories of state formation that fostered differing approaches to nationalism and citizenship through their institutions. Following Brubaker and Hammar's arguments, explored in the third chapter, one could argue that for Turkey (as for Germany) the nation antedated the state.[3] One consequence of this is that the history of citizenship and institutions has been more exclusive than inclusive, first of all because of the nationalist principles of the state based on "one nation and one language," thereby excluding other native minorities like Kurds. Second, because citizenship was based on *jus sanguinis*, the legal doctrine that citizenship derives from parentage, this is still the way in which one can obtain citizenship in Turkey (as in a majority of European countries), but this excludes new minorities born from migrants' parents, for example.

In Indonesia, on the other hand (as in the case of France), with its history as a Dutch colony, the state predated the nation. This pattern of state formation resulted in citizenship principles and institutions that have been more inclusive, for both autochthonous and immigrant minorities. This greater inclusiveness has existed since the founding, even if Indonesian citizenship today is based on a mix of *jus sanguinis* and *jus soli* principles (to be a citizen one must have one Indonesian parent, besides being born in Indonesia, and dual citizenship is not recognized). These differences in state formation have consequences today for the treatment of minorities, making one (Turkey) more prone to securitize minorities and the other (Indonesia) more apt to autonomize minorities.

Regarding the nature of citizenship rights and the type of citizenship law, if we look at the institutions that created their national law, we see how Turkey resembles the French model, while Indonesia resembles a mix of the French and Dutch models, the latter from its colonizer. Following

---

[3] Rogers Brubaker, *Nationalism reframed: Nationhood and the national question in the New Europe* (New York: Cambridge University Press, 1996). Tomas Hammar, *Democracy and the Nation-State: Aliens, Denizens, and Citizenship in a World of International Migration* (Aldershot: Avebury, 1990).

Stuurman, we can say that the Indonesian case, similar to the Netherlands, built a communitarian-liberal model based more on a conception of rights inhering in communities rather than in individuals.[4] The Turkish case, by contrast, following the French model as early as the Tanzimat reforms (Chap. 4) was more based on a liberal-republican or individual-rights model that rejected the notion of communal rights and, by extension, the recognition of different communities and minorities. Nevertheless, the Indonesian state also has a history of state centralization on the French style because, as Vickers argues,[5] the "colonial multiculturalism" of Indonesia had to cohabit with a strong centralized state power and experienced real multiculturalism only with decentralization following the democratization process in the twentieth century. These observations suggest that the different types of citizenship rights and national laws have facilitated for Turkey an approach of repression and securitization of minorities and for Indonesia their inclusion and autonomization during the country's democratization process.

Regarding the historical discrimination of states against minorities during the era of nation-building, we can take our cue from a scholar who compared Turkey and Morocco. Aslan argues that the reason why some ethno-national groups come into conflict with the state authority while others do not resides in the implementation of specific state policies during the period of nation-building.[6] Sometimes states, in their striving to build a cohesive national identity, demand that minorities change their everyday behaviors, such as what language they speak, how they dress, or what names they give to their children. Minorities may view these requirements as a threat to their own identity. When policies are too intrusive, they may even provoke violent ethnic mobilization, as in the case of Turkey, while when they do not infringe on the values, habits, and lifestyle of minorities, they may lead to state–minority reconciliation, as in Morocco. The reason why states differ in their actions toward minorities, Aslan argues, depends on the type of nation-state building: states follow a radical nation-building strategy, with even a "social-engineering" construction of identity, when they are completely autonomous from other local centers of power. For example, in Turkey, according to Aslan:

---

[4] Stuurman, *Citizenship and cultural differences in France and the Netherlands,* 2004.

[5] Adrian Vickers, *A History of Modern Indonesia* (Cambridge: Cambridge University Press, 2005).

[6] Senem Aslan, *Nation-Building in Turkey and Morocco. Governing Kurdish and Berber Dissent* (New York: Cambridge University Press, 2014).

a military-bureaucratic elite, which inherited a large state apparatus from the Ottoman Empire, founded the Turkish Republic and consolidated the central state at the expense of local authorities, more specifically the tribal leaders and religious sheikhs. In their attempt to create a homogeneous nation, these political elites aimed at an "extreme makeover" of the society and sought a wide range of changes in people's behavior, values, habits, and lifestyles. As the largest minority and living in areas that are hard to control, Kurds became the main targets of this social-engineering project.[7]

Indonesia, one could argue, represents instead a case similar to that of Morocco. As in Indonesia, the state did not intrude too much in the life of minorities, leaving them free to follow their habits and customs. Accordingly, the argument of Aslan could be applied to the Indonesian case, as the elites in Indonesia were not cut off from other centers of power, these centers being very spread out and considered important in the archipelago. The Indonesian state, therefore, unlike the Turkish one, needed the support of the local authorities to consolidate state institutions and so avoided a strategy of invasive and transformative homogenization of society. These local authorities helped also in maintaining stronger security during the democratic transition with decentralization, as explained in the next chapter. Here again we could argue that the differing histories of the approach to minorities by the nation-state created different paths that finally led Turkey to ultimate exclusion and repression and Indonesia to ultimate autonomization.

The fourth and last element, besides the path-dependent consequences of different institutions or historical experiences, to understand the inclusion or exclusion of minorities during the democratization period is the concept of an "ethnic democracy." Scholars of democratic studies like Linz and Stepan, and later Smooha, use this term to refer to regimes that combine democracy with some kind of "ownership" of the state by a dominant ethnic group, creating in this way "exclusive democracies."[8] When a state is a multiethnic state—unlike Japan and South Korea, which are very homogeneous states, but in many cases American states, for example—and is dominated by an ethnic group, as in the Turkish case, it is defined as "ethnic democracy." While Linz and Stepan used this definition for states

---

[7] Ibid., p. 4.

[8] Juan Linz and Alfred Stepan, *Problems of democratic transition and consolidation: Southern Europe, South America and Post-Communist Europe* (Baltimore: John Hopkins University Press, 1996). Sammy Smooha, "The model of ethnic democracy: Israel as a Jewish and democratic state," *Nations and nationalism*, 8 (4) (October 2002): 475–503.

that deny basic citizenship rights to ethnic minorities and hence are less democratic, Smooha treats as an ethnic democracy a state that grants "citizenship to all but institutionalizes superior status for the ethno-national majority."[9] According to another scholar, to define a state as an ethnic democracy we need even a "formal ownership" by the dominant group: Haklai argues that the "ethnic ownership of the state is formalized and the state is *officially* cast as an expression of the ethno-national identity of the dominant group."[10] This formal ownership is demonstrated, according to the scholar, first of all by the name of the country, which reflects the dominant group (like Romania for Romanians, Latvia for Latvians, Italy for Italians, or Turkey for Turks). Likewise, in an ethnic democracy the constitution and laws of a country formalize the ethno-national identity and guarantee the superiority of the predominant group identity while they guarantee the individual rights of a democracy. Because of this, according to Haklai, the Indonesian case would not be an ethnic democracy, while the Turkish case would.[11] Therefore, this distinction between the two case studies is another that could have affected the outcome of this study: Turkey as an ethnic democracy makes it difficult for the country to extend even basic rights to other ethnic groups.

Based on these four subvariables, let us now consider the body of evidence supporting the hypothesis that Turkey and Indonesia had different nationalistic institutions and different histories in their approach to their citizens and minorities and answer the following question: Did these differences in state formation lead to different outcomes of securitization or autonomization of their ethnic minorities?

Evidence from Turkish History

Regarding the state formation and creation of citizenship law, first of all we must say that in the Middle Eastern region, these processes had different histories than in the states of Europe. The caliphates that ruled in suc-

[9] Ibid., p. 499.
[10] Oded Haklai, "Regime transition and the emergence of ethnic democracies," Ch. 2 in Jacques Bertrand and Oded Haklai (eds.) *Democratization and Ethnic Minorities: Conflict or Compromise?* (Abingdon: Routledge, 2014), p. 22.
[11] To notice that ethnic democracies are not a transitional phase between authoritarianism and liberal democracies, as they can endure and even going backwards, if they don't develop sufficient pluralism and substantive advancements of minority or communal rights, as we are seeing today in Turkey.

cession over the course of many centuries had a different kind of nation-building and a different system of citizenship, based on nonterritorial religious identities and "nations," with respect to the territorial ethnic identity of the nations in the European case. Since the twentieth century, under the Ottoman Empire the so-called millet system (from Arabic *millah* for "nation") allowed every confessional community to rule itself under its own system through a separate legal court.[12] This created a system of communal rights instead of individual rights. Later, starting in 1839,[13] the *Tanzimat* reforms influenced by the French Enlightenment aimed to bring Western "modernity" to the Ottoman Empire, making all citizens equal under the law: individual rights started therefore to become important instead of community or religious rights.[14] This precolonization phase of the Ottoman Empire showed that the West already had started to influence the Middle East, precipitating the rise of nationalism, in particular the Arab one, under the Ottoman Empire ruled by Turks. This eventually caused the breakdown of the Ottoman millet concept.

When the Ottoman Empire fell, European colonization imposed this concept of secular nationalisms and "monoethnic" nation-state building with the creation of Iraq, Syria, Lebanon, and Palestine as nation-states, blocking Arab nationalist hopes for a politically united self-determination. Turkey also, as the non-Arab center of the Ottoman Empire, created a state based on a strong nationalism, following the ideology of Kemalism, again influenced by French ideals, to build a strong, united, and secular Turkish centralized state. This seems, therefore, to be strong and compelling evidence that Turkey's history of exclusionary nationalism and individual rights more than communal rights shaped its subsequent policies toward ethnic minorities, particularly its ultimate securitization of the Kurdish community.

However, the relationship between the Turkish model and the European model is not always treated in the literature as so direct. For one thing, Akturk states that because the religious nationalism at the base of the founding of Muslim states differs from the ethnic nationalism of the

---

[12] Bernard Lewis, *The Emergence of Modern Turkey* (New York: Oxford University Press, 2001).

[13] The reforms were executed starting with the Imperial Reform Edict (*hatt-ı hümayun*) in 1856, which promised equality in education, government appointments, and administration of justice to all regardless of creed.

[14] William Cleveland, *A History of the Modern Middle East* (Boulder: Westview Press, 2004).

European states, we need to be careful in using nationalist theories based on European cases for understanding Muslim nation-states.[15] According to the scholar, Turkey (like Pakistan and Algeria) was founded because a multiethnic Muslim population was reunited against non-Muslim opponents in order to create a new state based on a religious war (jihad). Therefore, the idea of opposition to foreign invasions became part of the country's Islamic identity—similar to the current reappropriation of Islamic identity in the Turkish state with the AKP regime—that often feels threatened by external actors. Likewise, in Indonesia, even if the country had a different war of independence, during the Dutch rule the ulama (the scholars of the Islamic religious studies) led the opposition and, as Esposito says, "renewalist, ulama-defined Islam became identified with opposition to foreign rule … giving added strength to the process of Islamization of social life among the peasantry."[16]

Nevertheless, after that religious founding the post-independence government of Turkey founded the state on a secular and monolingual nation-state model that ultimately pushed Islamist or ethnic separatist movements to challenge the state, as the Kurdish community did. It is evident, therefore, that the external example of centralized and exclusive ethnic nationalistic institutions did not conduce to an environment where minorities could have been included. This disjuncture between religious foundation and nationalist creation is useful to understand also the shift in ontological security, as will be explained in Chap. 8, with changes in routines of self-identity, both at the founding of the republic and with the new Islamist AKP party, which tried to recover the past by breaking the Turkish Republic "routines of self-identity" during the democratization phase of the new century.

Also, following the arguments of Brubaker and Hammar, one could argue that Turkey as a state was formed subsequent to its formation as a nation. This sequence created an exclusive citizenship, on the German style, with a nationality law based primarily on *jus sanguinis*,[17] as with the

---

[15] Sener Akturk, "Religion and Nationalism: Contradictions of Islamic Origins and Secular Nation-Building in Turkey, Algeria, and Pakistan," *Social Science Quarterly*, Volume 96, Number 3 (September 2015): 778–806.

[16] Edward Schneier, *Muslim Democracy: Politics, Religion and Society in Indonesia, Turkey and the Islamic World* (New York: Routledge, 2016), p. 25.

[17] *Jus soli* and *jus sanguinis* are two different principles of nationality law, two different ways of obtaining citizenship in a country. In the first case, citizenship is determined by place of birth, in the second by having one or both parents as citizens of that state, which confers

majority of European states. For example, the first article of the first Turkish constitution in 1921 (later Article 3 in the 1924 constitution) states: "sovereignty is vested in the nation without condition,"[18] already demonstrating the presence of a nation, Turkey. This was clearly reiterated later in the constitution of 1961, which states in its preamble: "the Turkish Nation, prompted and inspired by the spirit of Turkish nationalism, which unites all individuals, be it in faith, pride, or distress, in a common bond as an indivisible whole around national consciousness and aspirations."[19] This nationalism was reinforced with the choice of official language, making Turkish the only language taught in public schools and used in the public sphere since the founding of the republic and making it even clearer with the prohibition of the use of other languages in the media after the military coup of 1980. In 1983, Law 2932, "The Law Concerning Publications and Broadcasts in Languages Other Than Turkish," was passed, declaring that "the mother tongue of all Turkish citizens is Turkish"[20] forbidding the use of any language in the media but Turkish.

This nationalist exclusivity concept at the foundation of the Turkish state favored the banishment of threatening ethnic minorities from its territory or national identity, either by an attempt of genocide, as in the Armenian, Assyrian, and Greek cases during the last years of the Ottoman Empire, or with assimilation, as in the Kurdish case in the first years of the Turkish Republic. Recently, Turkey also used a new concept of "Turkishness," introduced in 2005, with the intention of increasing freedom of opinion as part of the reforms adopted for admission into the EU. However, the law was amended in 2008 to change "Turkishness" into "the Turkish nation," to avoid the risk of intending it as a big umbrella under which various identities could find a place, as some scholars like Oran and Kaboglu argued.[21] Thus, we see again the risk of losing national Turkish identity to a plural identity was blocked, excluding the possibility of having Kurdish identity included in the definition of Turkishness.

---

rights to ethnic citizens and their descendants (as in the majority of the states in the world, apart from the Americas, for the obvious reason of being the Western Hemisphere land of immigration).

[18] Accessed September 30, 2017, http://genckaya.bilkent.edu.tr/1921C.html.

[19] Accessed September 30, 2017, http://www.anayasa.gen.tr/1961constitution-text.pdf.

[20] Accessed September 30, 2017, http://usefoundation.org/view/871.

[21] Cited by Marlies Casier and Joost Jongerden, *Nationalisms and politics in Turkey: Political Islam, Kemalism, and the Kurdish issue* (New York: Routledge, 2011): p. 4.

Regarding the history of discrimination against minorities and the intrusion of the state in their daily life, this process of discrimination and assimilation of the Kurds is evident, as explained in Chap. 4, confirming the evidence adduced by Aslan. Not only Kurds but much smaller ethnic groups, Albanians, Pontics, Arabs, Bosniaks, Circassians, and Chechens (many of them coming from the lands lost by the Ottoman Empire), started to be considered Turkish under Turkish law, assimilating into the Turkish identity even if they were still ethnically different from Turks.[22] Since the beginning of the Turkish state, therefore, Kurds started to lose their language and identity in a process of assimilation, or acculturation as some scholars define it, into the Turkish nation, also known as "Turkification."[23] This assimilation always had the same goal: that Kurds would become Turks sooner or later. To do this, the state also implemented small-scale population transfers to reduce concentrations of Kurds in areas where some nationalist uprisings could have happened. When they did happen, nationalist movements were neutralized with deportations and the arrest or execution of leaders, dismemberment of traditional institutions, and finally the support to Kurdish feudal landowning class (ağas) and tribal leaders (şeyhs) to block any nationalist desire in their communities.[24]

Finally, regarding the institutionalization of ethnicity and the creation of an ethnic democracy, we can say that the criteria of Smooha and Haklai—that is, a state that grants citizenship to all but institutionalizes superior status for the ethno-national majority—can be seen first of all as falling under the legal status granted at the founding of the republic only to small non-Muslim minorities, such as Armenians, Greek, and Jews, but not to a large Muslim ethnic minority or nation inside the Turkish state, such as the Kurds. As again explained in Chap. 4, the Kurds were left out as Turkey refused to recognize any ethnic minority within its borders based on the belief that recognition could threaten the unity of the new Turkish state. Today, privileges for the ethno-national majority are in place. Even if some steps recognized the cultural rights of the Kurds, the

---

[22] Stephen Kinzer, *Crescent and Star: Turkey between two worlds* (New York: Farrar, Straus and Giroux, 2008).

[23] Heper for example argues that the theory of acculturation is more suitable than that of assimilation in the Kurdish case in Turkey, given the centuries of amicable relations between the state and the Kurds. See Metin Heper, *State and Kurds in Turkey: The Question of Assimilation* (New York: Palgrave Macmillan, 2007).

[24] Denise Natali, *The Kurds and the State: Evolving National Identity in Iraq, Turkey and Iran* (Syracuse: Syracuse University Press, 2005).

plain recognition of their parity with Turks in the Turkish democracy (for example, by approving of the use of the Kurdish language in public schools) has not yet been realized.

EVIDENCE FROM INDONESIAN HISTORY

Regarding state formation and the creation of citizenship law, Indonesia had a multinational identity that her colonial period, unlike the *divide et impera* of Middle Eastern history, could not destroy. With the formation of the state after World War II—26 years after Turkey and with a different approach than the destruction of the multiethnic empires after World War I—this multinationalism was supported by the *Pancasila* principles of the Indonesian constitution and her "unity in diversity" (*Bhinneka Tunggal Ika*) motto. As stated earlier, one could argue that Indonesia was once "a state in search of a nation," following Brubaker's distinction, and therefore more inclusive in its political foundations, with an emphasis on belonging to the state rather than belonging to the nation. To put it with President Sukarno:

> Gandhi said, "I am a nationalist, but my nationalism is humanity." The nationalism we advocate is not the nationalism of isolation, not chauvinism, as blazoned by people in Europe who say "Deutschland über alles"…do not let us say that the Indonesian nation is the noblest and most perfect, whilst belittling other people. We should aim at the unity and brotherhood of the whole world.[25]

The first constitution of the Republic of Indonesia, the *Undang-Undang Dasar* 1945 (UUD 45), was drawn up by revolutionary leaders, containing 33 chapters, with very strong presidential powers meant to cope with the situation of the Indonesian war of independence that lasted until 1949 and that needed quick and decisive decisions. In 1950, this system was replaced by a parliamentary system called the *Undang-Undang Dasar Sementara* 1950 (UUDS-50) with the 1950 Provisional Constitution. Independent of the system of government, the most important feature of the Indonesian constitutions was the concept of *Pancasila* and the national motto of "unity in diversity." The five principles Sukarno

---

[25] President Sukarno's speech, "The birth of Pancasila" June 1, 1945, in Clive J. Christie, *Southeast Asia in the Twentieth Century* (New York: Tauris, 1998): pp. 135–136.

had listed for *Pancasila* at the beginning were Indonesian nationalism, internationalism (or humanism); consent (or democracy), social prosperity; and belief in God.[26] Finally, the constitutions changed the order: (1) belief in the one and only God; (2) just and civilized humanity; (3) unity of Indonesia; (4) democracy guided by the inner wisdom in the unanimity arising out of deliberations among representatives; and (5) social justice for all the people of Indonesia. As we can see, there is no reference to an ethnic group (Javanese, for example, who were the majority). Instead, what is importance is the notion of a unity of the different groups of the country based on democracy and social justice.

These principles, together with the motto "unity in diversity," brought pluralism to institutions in Indonesia, even if unity and pluralism did not necessarily lead to equality and inclusion. Also, because of the vast difference between the numbers of Javanese and the numbers of small minorities of other ethnic groups from the outer islands, some form of discrimination in practice existed in many sectors of life, from politics to the economy and culture, from development to employment, and from representation to education. However, discrimination was not institutionalized like it was in Turkey, as Indonesia has more than 300 ethnic groups who speak more than 700 languages.[27] It was difficult to exclude specifically some part of the population based on ethnicity, making it an "improbable nation" as some scholars have called it.[28] This does not mean that the Indonesian nation did not exist, but that it had to be built and rebuilt after state formation (following Brubaker's concept). For this reason, one of the keys to the discourse on the treatment of ethnic minorities and on separatist movements has always been the idea of Indonesian national unity, considered natural and final.[29]

Actually, the country's large number of cultures and ethnicities is reflected not only in state institutions but also in the identity of Indonesians, who often consider themselves as first of all belonging to their ethnic

---

[25] Ibid.

[27] See on this Handoyo Puji Widodo and Aan Erlyana Fardhani, "The language rights of indigenous languages: An approach to maintaining Indonesia's linguistic and cultural diversity," in Quynh Lê and Tao Lê (ed.) Ch. 12 in *Linguistic diversity and cultural identity: A global perspective* (New York: Nova Science Publishers, 2011).

[28] Pisani, Elizabeth, *Indonesia, Etc.: Exploring the Improbable Nation* (New York: Norton, 2015).

[29] Dave McRae, "A discourse on separatists," *Indonesia* No. 74 (Oct., 2002) (Ithaca: Southeast Asia Program Publications at Cornell University) pp. 37–58.

group and only secondarily as belonging to the country. This is because Indonesia did not have a clear assimilation policy at its founding as other countries like Turkey had, which included such features as limiting the use of local cultures, traditions, and languages in favor of the Indonesian ones. On the contrary, the state was open to a form of "pluralistic nationalism," allowing the different identities to express their culture and above all not prohibiting local ethnic languages (Acehnese included).[30] Actually, in Indonesia, besides the national lingua franca (Bahasa Indonesia), all people speak either a majority (Javanese) or a minority indigenous language.[31] This is because for its national language, in another action typical of its pluralist identity and in contrast to Turkey, Indonesia chose Malay and not Javanese—even though Javanese was spoken by the majority of the population—because Javanese was concentrated on the island of Java while Malay was spoken across the islands, being the language of traders and ports. Malay, as an Indonesian language, before being formally adopted by the 1945 constitution, was already institutionalized as a national language in 1928, with the "Youth Pledge"[32] of one motherland, one people, and one language, a fundamental step in building Indonesian nationalism but at the same time interethnic solidarity.[33] In addition, the model of Sukarno of "guided democracy," based on the traditional village system of discussion and consensus, allowed for some path of consensus decision-making (though still centralized at the national level), reducing the risk of the "tyranny of the majority" and allowing for inclusiveness in the long run of the Indonesian Republic.[34]

Regarding citizens' rights, therefore, since its founding, Indonesia looked at communal identities more than individual rights, not only in languages but in identities and religions, which led the Indonesian constitution to recognize six religions. Nevertheless, cultural rights did not correspond to a decentralization of the Indonesian state, which on the contrary was quite centralized, out of fear of losing national control, and

---

[30] Sumanto Al Qurtuby, "Interethnic Violence, Separatism and Political Reconciliation in Turkey and Indonesia," *India Quarterly* 71(2) (6/2015): 126–145.

[31] Widodo and Fardhani, 2011, p. 131.

[32] The Youth Pledge was a declaration made on October 28, 1928, by young Indonesian nationalists (among whom was Sukarno) during the "Indonesian national awakening" that culminated in Indonesian independence.

[33] Ibid., p. 132.

[34] Daniel Lev, *The Transition to Guided Democracy: Indonesian Politics 1957–1959* (Sheffield: Equinox Publishing, 2009).

so refraining from granting autonomy to its regions and provinces. Therefore, as explained in Chap. 4, more than their identities, the ethnic groups—above all the Acehnese—were looking for territorial sovereignty, often being heirs of ancient independent "states" before colonial times.

As we can see, the history and institutions of the Indonesian Republic differ from those of Turkey and have made Indonesia an environment in which plurality is the norm, both in the identity of the nation and, in part at least, in its institutions. For this reason, autonomization, even though it was not put into practice until the decentralization of the *Reformasi* era, fell within the spectrum of possibilities thanks to the background of the state's formation as a pluralist one, a communitarian-liberal model of community rights, and a daily life of ethnic minorities that was not changed by the majoritarian ethnic group. Nevertheless, as Bowen, among other scholars, recalls, during the New Order under Suharto in the 1960s things started to change:

> One could only speak in terms of the residents of a geographical region, as in "people of South Sulawesi" and not mention ethnic names, lest one be guilty of exacerbating ethnic tensions. The forbidden categories for public discussion were known by the acronym SARA: suku (ethnicity), agama (religion), ras (race), and antargolongan, literally "intergroup" and applicable to nearly any discussion of group identity.[35]

Therefore, discrimination, even if not institutionalized, became evident under the Suharto regime, and with it the securitization of ethnic separatist movements like GAM. Actually, as Bertrand argues,[36] at the end of the New Order, the narrow and constraining reinterpretation of Indonesia's "national model" created tensions that opened the door to ethnic conflicts with the start of democratization. The process of decentralization during democratization, therefore, was fundamental to addressing the risk of increasing secessionist conflicts and to avoiding the risk of the creation of an "ethnic democracy," as Smooha and Haklai label it.

During the period of democratization, the Indonesian constitution had its first amendments, introducing human rights, the separation of powers,

---

[35] John Bowen, "Normative Pluralism in Indonesia: Regions, Religions, and Ethnicities," in *Multiculturalism in Asia*, edited by Will Kymlicka and Baogang He (Oxford: Oxford University Press, 2005): pp. 152–169.

[36] Jacques Bertrand, *Nationalism and ethnic conflict in Indonesia* (Cambridge: Cambridge University Press, 2004).

and decentralization. The Acehnese rebellion always hoped for the disintegration of the republic because of its internal conflicts and despotic leadership, but this hope vanished with democratization when Indonesia was transformed into a decentralized system, causing the provinces to lose interest in seceding. Nevertheless, there is no consensus in the scholarship about how processes of decentralization allowed for the resolution of ethnic conflict and the autonomization of ethnic minorities. Actually, the fact that substantial decentralization and autonomization of Aceh in reality did not arrive until the Helsinki agreements in 2005 would show how historical institutionalism has not been the only fundamental factor in explaining it: autonomization did not appear until other factors impacted the elites' decision-making.

Stokke, Törnquist, and Syndre, for example, agree that the resolution of the conflict in Aceh and its transition to peace and democracy was influenced by structural evolutions like decentralization.[37] However, it was also shaped by strategies of elites and popular political forces. Törnquist specifically argues that initially, the radical process of decentralization promoted centrifugal forces, motivating the renewed military intervention of Wahid and mostly Megawati, but by 2004 signs indicated that Indonesia was not going to fragment and that a decentralized but unified system was emerging.[38] By contrast Hadiz, comparing the Philippines, Thailand, and Indonesia, argues that the local system of power remained strong and resilient after the democratization and decentralization period.[39] In particular, Hadiz shows how the decentralization of the *Reformasi* period just dispersed corruption and predatory politics, failing to transform power relations on the ground, for which reason local elites hijacked democracy. This means that decentralization was not much of a democratizing process, but that does not change the fact that it could have facilitated some form of autonomization for local authorities, as in the case of Aceh and its region. To reinforce this argument, Miller posits that the three offers of special autonomy made to Aceh in 1959 (Special Region formula), 1999

[37] Kristian Stokke, Olle Törnquist, Gyda Marås Syndre, "Conflict Resolution and Democratization in the aftermath of the 2004 Tsunami: A Comparative Analysis of Aceh and Sri Lanka," *Power, Conflict and Democracy in South & Southeast Asia*, 1(1–2), (2009): 129–149.
[38] Olle Törnquist, "Dynamics of peace and democratization. The Aceh lessons," 2011, p. 829.
[39] Vedi R. Hadiz, *Localising Power in Post-Authoritarian Indonesia: A Southeast Asia Perspective* (Palo Alto: Stanford University Press, 2010).

(Law 44 on Special Status), and 2001 (Law 18 on Special Autonomy) all failed because of the central government's lack of commitment, its failure to address human rights violations, and GAM's rejection of autonomy as a compromise.[40] Finally, according to Bubandt, securitization happened precisely to reassert the state during the phase of decentralization.[41] Therefore, decentralization could have produced even more securitization instead of favoring autonomization. Actually, during the first phase of decentralization, Aceh experienced its highest level of violence, between 1999 and 2003.

Thus, one could argue that during the first phase of decentralization, the outcome for the state was more securitization of the ethnic minorities, with a typical approach of granting some autonomy or cultural rights but clamping down on the independence movement. Later, however, when it was clear that the armed conflict was not going to end, the state resorted to a negotiation of some sort of self-rule. The point is that Indonesia never became an ethnic democracy like Turkey because it never institutionalized the superior status of one ethnic group over others. This is the fundamental difference from Turkey, which came from a different history of nation-state building, citizenship law, and assimilation of ethnic minorities.

Conclusions

In conclusion, we can assert that even if nationalism and institutions assumed different forms in Turkey, there remains the fact that nationalist and exclusive institutions created a path dependency for Turkey. This history led to the emergence of different elites and international factors that have played a role in the shift from securitization to autonomization during the democratic period and back to securitization in recent years. Despite the nuances revealed in the creation of an exclusionary nationalism, one could argue that this feature of Turkey's founding has played an important role in the securitization of the Kurdish minority, in particular during the history of the republic but also with the democratization process starting in 2002. Emblematic of this history of ethno-nationalism is

---

[40] Michelle Ann Miller, "What's special about special autonomy in Aceh?," in *Verandah of violence: the background to the Aceh problem*, ed. by Anthony Reid, Singapore: Singapore University Press, 2006, p. 292–324.

[41] Nils Ole Bubandt, "Vernacular security: Governmentality, traditionality and ontological (in)security in Indonesia," *Danish Institute for International Studies*, Working Paper 24, 2004.

the rejection, during the autonomization phase, of cultural rights such as public education in the Kurdish language or territorial concessions such as decentralization of government allowing for some form of self-rule. By contrast, for Indonesia the more open nationalism and more inclusive institutions dating to the beginning of its independence allowed for more decentralization and autonomization. Even if discrimination against ethnic minorities was evident with respect to the Javanese majority, in particular in the New Order times, political institutions guaranteed a plurality of identities and created the framework necessary for the decentralization put in practice during the democratization period.

Nevertheless, the fact that the securitization process was up and down at different moments of both Turkish and Indonesian history, and in particular during their democratization, shows that historical institutionalist hypotheses should be considered as background factors, attaching importance to the other changing variables, including elites' struggles for power and international factors, and the interacting variable of ontological security. This is the last hypothesis of the study and is treated in the next and last chapter: how different levels of ontological security impacted the treatment of ethnic minorities in Turkey and Indonesia.

References

Akturk, Sener. 2015. Religion and Nationalism: Contradictions of Islamic Origins and Secular Nation-Building in Turkey, Algeria, and Pakistan. *Social Science Quarterly* 96 (3): 778–806.

Al Qurtuby, Sumanto. 2015. *Interethnic Violence, Separatism and Political Reconciliation in Turkey and Indonesia*. India Quarterly 71 (2): 126–145.

Aslan, Senem. 2014. *Nation-Building in Turkey and Morocco. Governing Kurdish and Berber Dissent*. New York: Cambridge University Press.

Bertrand, Jacques. 2004. *Nationalism and Ethnic Conflict in Indonesia*. Cambridge: Cambridge University Press.

Bowen, John. 2005. Normative Pluralism in Indonesia: Regions, Religions, and Ethnicities. In *Multiculturalism in Asia*, ed. Will Kymlicka and Baogang He, 152–169. Oxford: Oxford University Press.

Brubaker, Rogers. 1996. *Nationalism Reframed: Nationhood and the National Question in the New Europe*. New York: Cambridge University Press.

Bubandt, Nils Ole. 2004. Vernacular Security: Governmentality, Traditionality and Ontological (In)security in Indonesia. *Danish Institute for International Studies*, Working Paper No. 24.

Casier, Marlies, and Joost Jongerden. 2011. *Nationalisms and Politics in Turkey: Political Islam, Kemalism, and the Kurdish Issue*. New York: Routledge.

Cleveland, William. 2004. *A History of the Modern Middle East*. Boulder: Westview Press.
Hadiz, Vedi. 2010. *Localising Power in Post-Authoritarian Indonesia: A Southeast Asia Perspective*. Palo Alto: Stanford University Press.
Haklai, Oded. 2014. Regime Transition and the Emergence of Ethnic Democracies. In *Democratization and Ethnic Minorities: Conflict or Compromise?* ed. Jacques Bertrand and Oded Haklai. Abingdon: Routledge.
Hammar, Tomas. 1990. *Democracy and the Nation-State: Aliens, Denizens, and Citizenship in a World of International Migration*. Aldershot: Avebury.
Heper, Metin. 2007. *State and Kurds in Turkey: The Question of Assimilation*. New York: Palgrave Macmillan.
Kinzer, Stephen. 2008. *Crescent and Star: Turkey Between Two Worlds*. New York: Farrar, Straus and Giroux.
Lev, Daniel. 2009. *The Transition to Guided Democracy: Indonesian Politics 1957–1959*. Sheffield: Equinox Publishing.
Lewis, Bernard. 2001. *The Emergence of Modern Turkey*. New York: Oxford University Press.
Linz, Juan, and Alfred Stepan. 1996. *Problems of Democratic Transition and Consolidation: Southern Europe, South America, and Post-Communist Europe*. Baltimore: Johns Hopkins University Press.
McRae, Dave. 2002. A Discourse on Separatists. *Indonesia* No. 74 (October). Ithaca: Southeast Asia Program Publications at Cornell University, pp. 37–58.
Miller, Michelle Ann. 2006. What's Special About Special Autonomy in Aceh? In *Verandah of Violence. The Background to the Aceh Problem*, ed. Anthony Reid. Singapore: Singapore University Press.
Natali, Denise. 2005. *The Kurds and the State: Evolving National Identity in Iraq, Turkey and Iran*. Syracuse: Syracuse University Press.
Pisani, Elizabeth. 2015. *Indonesia, Etc.: Exploring the Improbable Nation*. New York: Norton.
Schneier, Edward. 2016. *Muslim Democracy: Politics, Religion and Society in Indonesia, Turkey and the Islamic World*. New York: Routledge.
Smooha, Sammy. 2002. The Model of Ethnic Democracy: Israel as a Jewish and Democratic State. *Nations and Nationalism* 8 (4): 475–503.
Stokke, Kristian, Olle Törnquist, and Gyda Marås Syndre. 2009. Conflict Resolution and Democratization in the Aftermath of the 2004 Tsunami: A Comparative Analysis of Aceh and Sri Lanka. *Power, Conflict and Democracy in South & Southeast Asia 1* (1–2): 129–149.
Stuurman, Siep. 2004. *Citizenship and Cultural Differences in France and the Netherlands*. In *Lineages of European Citizenship: Rights, Belonging and Participation in Eleven Nation-States*, ed. Richard Bellamy, Dario Castiglione, and Emilio Santoro, 167–186. New York: Palgrave Macmillan.
Sukarno Speech. 1998. The Birth of Pancasila June 1, 1945. *From: Clive J. Christie, Southeast Asia in the Twentieth Century*. New York: Tauris, 135–136.

Thelen, Kathleen, and Sven Steinmo. 1992. Historical Institutionalism in Comparative Politics. In *Structuring Politics. Historical Institutionalism in Comparative Analysis*, ed. Sven Steinmo, Kathleen Thelen, and Frank Longstreth. Cambridge: Cambridge University Press.

Törnquist, Olle. 2011. Dynamics of Peace and Democratization. The Aceh Lessons. *Democratization* 18 (3): 823–846.

Vickers, Adrian. 2005. *A History of Modern Indonesia*. Cambridge: Cambridge University Press.

Widodo, Handoyo Puji, and Aan Erlyana Fardhani. 2011. The Language Rights of Indigenous Languages: An Approach to Maintaining Indonesia's Linguistic and Cultural Diversity. In *Linguistic Diversity and Cultural Identity: A Global Perspective*, ed. Quynh Lê and Tao Lê. New York: Nova Science Publishers.

CHAPTER 8

Interacting Variable: Ontological Security

INTRODUCTION

Being a sociological-ideational explanation, difficult to operationalize in order to understand its impact on outcomes, ontological security cannot really be considered an independent variable of this study like the others. Rather, we can consider it an "interacting variable" that interrelates with the three main independent variables, being influenced by them but at the same time influencing them. This is because all the previously discussed variables—elites' power, international factors, and history and institutions—may impact the level of ontological security of a state, which in turn affects the securitization or autonomization of ethnic minorities. For example, a state may have a history of strength and trust or a history of insecurity with strong or weak institutions; a state may have military elites allied with political ones, either secular or Islamist, or elites that struggle among them; and a state may dwell in a stable and safe region or in a chaotic and conflict-ridden region. All these elements affect the ontological security of a state, how the state feels about itself, either secure or insecure, with trust or with anxieties. These in turn impact the final outcome of treatment of ethnic minorities. In this respect, ontological security should be considered an intervening variable.

At the same time, though, all the scholarly works share the idea that ontological security is a concept that can be defined in a relational sense. There are processes of identity that states exercise in relation to other actors;

for this reason, ontological security does not occur in isolation. Because it is a relational concept, if something happens at the international level (in particular at the geopolitical and regional level), a country can begin to feel ontologically insecure, and this in itself can shape how the elites' power struggle impacts the final outcome. For example, we could argue that elites do not directly create but in reality exploit the ontological insecurity already present among the masses to perpetuate a conflict or the securitization of a minority group.[1] In this case, ontological security precedes the independent variables and so is a "background variable," one could say.

For these reasons, ontological security should be considered an interacting variable, more than an intervening one, as it may have recursive effects on and with the study's other independent variables. We should add here that as a relational process, the interaction can happen at the domestic level, with different and new relations among the actors and parts of a society and a state, but also at the international level, as the relationship of the state with its neighbors and the international community can affect the level of ontological security of a state, as we will see in the cases of Turkey and Indonesia. Therefore, the concept of ontological security for a state is used in this study both for international interactions and domestic ones.

As explained in Chap. 2, which contained a literature review, "ontological security" is a psychological concept applied to states. In international relations theory, ontological security refers to the needs of a state to feel safe and secure, not only physically in the sense that its survival is guaranteed, its national security maintained, and its borders protected (following the realist approach), but also "ontologically" (following the constructivist and critical approaches) in the sense of its being—that is, its national self-identity feels safe and not threatened by external or internal challenges. We can say that forms of uncertainty sometimes threaten this identity security, with a state feeling "ontologically insecure." This could explain irrational actions of states like protracted conflicts caused by security dilemmas,[2] but also, as in the case of this study, the treatment of minorities, specifically in democratizing countries.

Because this study is about comparative politics rather than international relations, it analyzes this concept for its consequences at the internal

---

[1] See on this Bahar Rumelili, *Peace Anxieties: Ontological Security and Conflict Resolution*, Seminar at Koç University, May 2, 2014, accessed September 30, 2017, https://www.youtube.com/watch?v=wkQUbYN7BH4.

[2] See Jennifer Mitzen, "Ontological Security in World Politics: State Identity and the Security Dilemma", European Journal of International Relations, vol. 12 no. 3 (2006).

rather than international level. Nonetheless, it is still based on the ontological security of the state, considering the state as the main level of decision making.[3] Thus, the state is the main actor impacting policies, more so than other actors like the population, elites, or civil society organizations, so higher than the individual level of the agents. This does not mean that an abstract concept such as the state or its institutions may feel emotions—it is still the individuals, leaders, and elites inside the states that feel a low or high ontological security—but it is the state that represents these aggregate feelings and act as a consequence.[4]

As background to this factor, and as a premise to the following literature review that will try to operationalize this variable, we need to say that every state has different ontological interpretations of its "self-security" depending on the environment in which the state lives, meaning its geography, culture, and geopolitical situation. Besides these differences in space, ontological security may also change over time, depending on the domestic and international conjuncture that the state itself experiences. For example, in some periods a state may feel safer, given its geopolitical and international situation, and so exhibit a high level of ontological security. At other times it may feel threatened and so manifest a low level of ontological security. The important thing to understand about the ontological security of a state threatened by the insurrection of an ethnic group is that when the violent actions of the armed group rise in scale, with broad attacks on militaries, state institutions, or even civilians, they start to become not only a problem of security but also an existential threat to the state. Actually, this is one of the reasons for the state labeling a rebel group a terrorist group, not only to delegitimize the requests of the group but also to make sure that the group is framed as an existential threat to the self-identity of the state. By this logic, the state must take specific measures that range from repression to securitization. Besides these case studies, there are many cases of in-state armed groups that have been considered an existential threat and labeled as terrorist groups: from the FARC in Colombia to Northern Ireland's IRA and Spain's ETA in its Basque region.

[3] Regarding the problem of passing a psychological concept from individual to state level, see the literature on the role of emotion and biases in international relations, for example, Steve Yetiv, *National Security through a Cockeyed Lens: How Cognitive Bias Impacts U.S. Foreign Policy* (Baltimore: John Hopkins University Press, 2013).

[4] See on this Bahar Rumelili, *Conflict resolution and ontological security: peace anxieties* (New York: Routledge, 2015), p. 17.

The hypothesis for this variable therefore is that when the ontological security of a country is low, the state tends to resort to repression and securitization of internal issues and challenges. In particular, the state will securitize minorities considered enemies specifically of the national identity or the sovereign territory and in general a risk to social peace and internal stability. Conversely, when the ontological security of a country is at a high stage, the country tends to engage more in accommodation of the internal social conflicts and issues, including ethnic minority requests regarding autonomization.

As a historical introduction, we can say that regarding the two case studies, the Turkish case has historically experienced a low level of ontological security arising from at least four elements: a delicate geopolitical position between Europe, Russia, and the Middle East, often under risk of instability and tensions with bordering countries; a history of implosion of an old empire contrasted with a proud resistance to external invasion, but also with a top-down imposition of a secular and centralized state structure; a complicated and complex identity since the foundation of the republic dwelling in a bridging world, having a Western model to follow and an Eastern identity to avoid, having been Eastern for centuries (actually Turkey has been in part a Western enclave in the Eastern world, a NATO member that resided for a century between the Islamist and the communist threats, with a stressful role of a bastion against both); and finally values of unity and homogeneity that, even if in theory should have facilitated a higher ontological security, in reality created an exclusion for values of tolerance of diversity and a disruption of the preceding acceptance of pluralistic society that favored a low ontological security.

Indonesia, on the other hand, has historically experienced a higher level of ontological security, with a geographic structure of an archipelago, impossible to be conquered completely even if dismembered, in a relative stable area; a history of trade and exchange between the Indian and Pacific Oceans that brought more openness toward different cultures; a pluralistic identity coming from hundreds of languages and ethnic groups; and finally Asian (and in particular Southeast Asian) values of acceptance and tolerance. These experiences and values increased the trust and the pluralism among the populations, language communities, and religions of the country. Such pluralism was conducive to the autonomization that Indonesia adopted in Aceh.

Ontological Security as a Concept

The concept of ontological security was first developed by Anthony Giddens, as a sense of continuity and order in events of an individual's life, in order for the person to feel a sense of agency.[5] Later, the work of Jennifer Mitzen and Brent J. Steele adapted Giddens's concept to the study of international relations.[6] But we can also draw the concept of ontological security from securitization theory. Even if Buzan et al. do not speak precisely of ontological security, in their theory there are five different sectors of security: military, environmental, economic, societal, and political. The societal sector of security is defined also as "identity security,"[7] a concept that resembles the concept of ontological security, what they define as the "security of self-identity." This social security, according to the scholars, can be characterized by a horizontal or vertical competition[8]; the first is related to the threat of neighboring cultures, while the second is the threat coming from above or below the state, which is from a wider identity (as in the EU case, for example) or a narrower one (as in the case of a minority, for example). Both the Kurdish and Acehnese cases evidently represent a case of vertical societal securitization, with a narrower identity of an ethnic minority that threatens the national identities.

The point to argue here is that the "security of identity," that is to say ontological security, is low when the state feels an ontological concern for its national identity because of internal or external threats. Actually, the securitization process, according to Bahar Rumelili, a scholar who devoted a recent and interesting deep study to this concept of ontological security, can be considered precisely a means of dealing with ontological insecurity because it transforms the anxieties of self-identity into concrete fears based on threats that can be managed, in particular in the presence of a conflict.[9] Also, according to Rumelili, to contain anxiety and ontological insecurity, the state, besides securitization, may "construct meanings" in order to

---

[5] Anthony Giddens, *Modernity and Self-identity: Self and Society in the Late Modern Age* (Palo Alto: Stanford University Press, 1991).
[6] Jennifer Mitzen, "Ontological Security in World Politics: State Identity and the Security Dilemma", European Journal of International Relations, vol. 12 no. 3 (2006). Brent J. Steele, *Ontological Security in International Relations: Self-Identity and the IR State* (Abingdon: Routledge, 2008).
[7] Buzan et al., 1998, p. 120.
[8] Ibid., p. 121.
[9] See on this also Bahar Rumelili, *Conflict resolution and ontological security: peace anxieties* (New York: Routledge, 2015).

maintain ideational stability: even conflict resolution, therefore, can be referred to as the management of anxiety without securitization.[10] This is important to consider because the narratives behind the ontological security of a state represent exactly the creation of a meaning of stability and security.

However, Rumelili argues that there needs to be a process of coping also with "peace anxieties" because not only conflict but even peace can create anxiety. This process formulates alternative self-narratives that situate the self in relation to others with new conflicts and threats, which become embedded again in habits and routines. For example, the end of the Cold War created anxieties because the international system no longer knew what it was based on, with clear enemies (however, one could argue that with 9/11 a new enemy was created for the USA, and with NATO expansion a new enemy was created for Russia, reducing anxieties and renewing stability). Thus, the peace processes in the Kurdish and Acehnese cases could also have created anxieties and reduce ontological security.

Regarding specifically ethnic minorities, other scholars show, even if without speaking about ontological security explicitly, that states feeling threatened by internal minorities will not incorporate them into the body politic. As Weiner argued with respect to the case of Macedonia,[11] for example, a state will not be inclusive of a minority if it feels that this minority is the "fifth column" of an external enemy against the nation state. Likewise, Kymlicka claims that "minority groups are often seen as a kind of 'fifth column', likely to be working for a neighbouring enemy"[12]; they are therefore stigmatized or repressed. This is an important concept with respect to the Kurdish issue, considered by Turkish leaders sometimes to be a fifth column of international terrorism or external powers.

But the threat can arrive also from the independence of a new state on one's borders, in particular if there is a transborder kinship group as in the cases of Syria and Iraq for Turkey. It is important, therefore, to evaluate how the autonomy of kinship groups in bordering countries may represent a threat not only to the national security but also to the ontological security of a country. It is interesting to consider also the case of Greece,

---

[10] Ibid., pp. 14–15 (Rumelili following Huysmans 1998, Marlow 2002, Kinnvall 2004).

[11] Myron Weiner, "The Macedonian syndrome: An Historical Model of International Relations and Political Development," New Balkan Politics- Journal of Politics, 2, 2001; originally published in World Politics (1971) pp. 665–683.

[12] Kymlicka, 2002, p. 19.

which felt threatened by the autonomy of a neighboring country, Macedonia, a few years ago. As a member of NATO and much stronger than Macedonia, Greece's concerns were not so much a question of national security as they were of identity security. As Kymlicka again reports, for Greece it was a question of ancient foundational myths: Greece claimed that "the use of the name 'Macedonia' by its neighboring state is a threat to Greece's very existence."[13]

Going back to the ontological security theory, how can one operationalize this variable in order to examine the times and cases in which its level changed and possibly affected the outcomes of this study. Mitzen argues that ontological security is achieved with routines that attach importance to social relationships at the individual level as well as to international relationships at the state level. However, she does not operationalize precisely this variable with indicators; she merely posits that "leaving old routines behind generates ontological insecurity."[14]

Also according to Steele, in order for states to be ontologically secure, they must give answers to existential questions, and so they tend to turn their actions into routines for "continuity and order" that is so important to their sense of self.[15] When a critical situation undermines a state's identity, causing anxiety or shame, the state may take actions that seem irrational but are prompted by this reduction of ontological security. Taking a different approach with respect to the realist and neoliberal ones (based on rational self-interest) and the constructivist and English School ones (based on collective identities and principles), Steele argues that state actions can be rational also when they follow the protection of self-identity, which is based on emotions too, in particular feelings of honor and shame.[16]

---

[13] Will Kymlicka, "Justice and security in the accommodation of minority nationalism," in *The politics of belonging: nationalism, liberalism, and pluralism*, by Alain Dieckhoff (Lanham: Lexington Books, 2004): p. 138.

[14] Jennifer Mitzen, "Ontological security in world politics," 2006, p. 353.

[15] Brent J. Steele, *Ontological Security in International Relations*, 2008, pp. 2–3.

[16] Trying to explain why Belgium decided to fight Germany in World War I, Steele argues, for example, that the cause must be found in Belgium's conception of honor: analyzing the statements and speeches of the foreign policy elites, Steele shows how feelings of honor played an important role in the country's decision to fight a stronger adversary. The same holds for shame, analyzing the feeling for the UK and NATO allies with respect to Milosevic's actions, feeling related to a possible ontological insecurity that played a role in the Kosovo war.

He lists four important factors for ontological security seekers that can be useful to better evaluate our variable: material and reflexive capabilities, crisis assessment, biographical narratives, and discursive framing by co-actors.[17] The first factor that impacts ontological security is the fact that stronger states, with more material capabilities, are under more stress with respect to small states as they must influence more outcomes in international politics. Ontological insecurity therefore appears for great powers in specific cases, for example when they do not intervene in humanitarian crises or resolve minority issues. Consequently, this may produce shame based on "reflexive capabilities," that is, how the state feels about itself in the world. The second factor is how a state assesses a crisis. To assess a crisis, there are three related abilities: "(1) discursive abilities, in the sense of constructing a situation as a crisis; (2) plausibly linking that crisis to the national Self; and (3) identifying which policy might effectively terminate the crisis."[18] These abilities are very much related to the third element, which builds a sense of ontological security: the biographical narrative, which is how agents build their self-identity and in turn how states create meanings for their actions. The narrative therefore contributes to the construction of a stable sense of self-identity, to transcend the anxiety of the fragile nature of biography (as Giddens says).[19] A state that is able to have a coherently organized narrative about itself and its routine actions will have a stronger ontological security. This is because if a state realizes that its narrative no longer reflects its actions, then this creates ontological insecurity (one could say almost like cognitive dissonance, in psychological terms) and forces the state to establish new routines to maintain its sense of self and identity. The last element is the "co-actor" discourse strategies, which are the narratives of the international community (Steele calls it "co-actors") to remember one state's past failure, pushing, as Steele says, to "insecuritize" targeted agents, to learn from past mistakes and change their future behaviors. This factor therefore can also contribute to the ontological insecurity of the state.

Thus, given the fact that the literature is not very specific on how to operationalize this concept of ontological security, one could consider in particular the third factor of Steele's framework, the biographical narrative of the state (intended especially as its government and the corresponding

[17] Ibid., pp. 69–75.
[18] Ibid., p. 71.
[19] Ibid., pp. 72–73.

elites and leadership supporting it) as the indicator of ontological security or insecurity. This is sometimes related as well to the fourth factor, the narrative of the international community, at least as the element that reflects and shows the high or low level of the ontological security of the state. This is useful to analyze the Turkish and Indonesian cases.

The idea here is that when the narrative of a state, through its leaders, shows an "identity crisis" and "identity insecurity" based on elements of anxiety, paranoia, fear, shame, anger, and other negative emotions, this type of narrative can be considered indicative of a low level of ontological security. Also, when a narrative feels the need to refer to nationalistic elements or other elements related to self-identity like religion or foundational myths, this can also be considered emblematic of a low level of ontological security. This is because when we, as people, feel lost or in identity crisis, in order to regain ontological security, we resort to the traditional inner nucleus of our identity, which is related to our ethnic, nationalistic, and religious background and heritage.[20] Let us therefore consider the evidence for Turkey and Indonesia with respect to this final interacting factor.

Turkey: Ontological Insecurity and Securitization of Kurds

Before analyzing Turkey's ontological security during its democratization phase and during the recent resecuritization of Kurds, one needs to remember that Turkey has experienced generally a low level of ontological security since the foundation of its republic. This insecurity derives from the fear of dismemberment before the Turkish war of independence—and even before with the secession of many territories from the Ottoman Empire (in some way similar to the implosion of the Soviet Union).[21] This foundational ontological insecurity, because of external or internal threats, has been reinforced for an entire century by conspiracy theories, deep state concepts, and military coups and manifests today as the repression of

---

[20] According to Kinnvall, for example, people feeling ontologically insecure in the increasingly global world look to groups with strong nationalistic and religious characteristics. This can explain also the recent religious revivals and success of radical groups. See Catarina Kinnvall, "Globalization and religious nationalism: self, identity and the search for ontological security," *Political Psychology*, 25, n. 5 (2004): 714–767.

[21] Actually Russia too can be considered as having a low level of ontological security today.

Kurdish minority considered an internal threat. The homogeneous Turkish identity that was imposed with the Kemalist philosophy of one state, one nation, one language, and one ethnic group makes diversity out to be a threat to Turkish identity. To put it along with Kinzer: Something about the concept of diversity frightens Turkey's ruling elite. It triggers the deep insecurity that has gripped Turkish rulers ever since the Republic was founded in 1923, an insecurity that today prevents Turkey from taking its proper place in the modern world."[22]

The process of stigmatization of Kurdish ethnic diversity during Turkish history has accompanied a specific construction of the Kurdish question through the political narrative of the state. Actually, as Akin Unver argues, the Kurdish question in Turkey has divided and often polarized the society on the definition and even existence of this question, often denied or reduced to the accusation of separatism by the political discourse. Therefore, the Kurdish question has not been resolved because it has not been clearly defined (and there is no scholarly analysis on a discourse survey of the Turkish definition of the Kurdish question).[23]

According to another scholar, Ferhat Kentel, the historically based "anxious" feelings of Turkey (feelings of ontological insecurity) are based on the reconstruction of grand narratives of past traumas, representing a constant tension between loyalty and resistance. This anxiety has been intensified recently not only for Turkey but also for many other countries because of the general erosion of the nation-state as an institution and the old boundaries fading in globalization.[24] The past trauma of Turkey was the end of the Ottoman Empire and its dismemberment. Traditionally, the Turkish state narrative is that Turks are the descendants of a great empire and civilization. An important part of this discourse is the belief that the West has always wanted to weaken Turkey, a "siege paranoia" that scholars and historians have labeled the "Sèvres Syndrome."[25] The Sèvres Syndrome

---

[22] Stephen Kinzer, *Crescent and Star: Turkey between two worlds* (New York: Farrar, Straus and Giroux, 2008), p. 10.

[23] Akin Unver. *Turkey's Kurdish question: discourse and politics since 1990*. London: Routledge, 2015.

[24] Ferhat Kentel, "Nationalist reconstructions in the light of disappearing borders," in Marlies Casier and Joost Jongerden, *Nationalisms and politics in Turkey: political Islam, Kemalism, and the Kurdish issue* (New York: Routledge, 2011): pp. 48–64.

[25] See: Dietrich Jung, "The Sèvres Syndrome, Turkish foreign policy and its historical legacies," *American Diplomacy*, August 2003, accessed September 30, 2017, http://www.unc.edu/depts/diplomat/archives_roll/2003_07-09/jung_sevres/jung_sevres.html.

arose in Turkey because at the end of World War I the country feared dismemberment at the hands of external powers, often affiliated with internal enemies, which found expression in the Treaty of Sèvres.[26] The Sèvres Syndrome has impacted the actions of Turkey since then. Acording to Guida: "This paranoia (also) inevitably leads to irrational overreactions and apparently irrational behaviors by the masses and by politicians."[27] Therefore, Turkish ontological security can be evaluated historically as low because Turkish national identity, "Turkishness," has always felt threatened by external or internal challenges.[28] When the PKK started the insurgency in 1984, the ontological security of the country declined even more, considering a possible independence or even autonomy of the Kurdish region as an attack not only on the state's unity but also on the nation's identity as a secular, monoethnic political community.

Mesut Yegen, an expert on the Kurdish issue, explains how the Kurdish question has been constructed by the Turkish state with different identities during the history of the republic.[29] At the beginning, the Kurdish question was seen in terms of a backward, premodern, tribal past of Turkey, in contrast to the progressive and modern present and future of Turkey. In the 1950s and 1960s, it was considered more a problem of a peripheral economy versus the national market, while in the 1970s the Kurdish question was more a question of communist threat (similar to the red terrorism in Italy during the same time). In general, however, Kurds were seen always as "future Turks," people that would sooner or later integrate into Turkish society and the community as new Turks. Since the 1980s, according to Yegen, and increasingly until today, Kurds are no longer seen as such, in part because of their resurgent nationalistic iden-

[26] The Treaty of Sèvres was one of the treaties that the Central Powers had to sign after WWI. It planned the partition of the Ottoman Empire, fragmenting Anatolia into "zones of influence" under the European powers, leaving to Turkey a small part of the peninsula. The treaty was refused by Ataturk, who started the Turkish war of independence.

[27] Michelangelo Guida, "The Sèvres Syndrome and "Komplo" Theories in the Islamist and Secular Press," *Turkish Studies*, 9:1, (March 2008): p. 37.

[28] As examples of policies also prompted by low ontological security, consider many of the recent actions of Erdogan against internal and external enemies, for example, the incarceration, in January 2016, of Turkish academicians who had signed a petition criticizing the government of Turkey in repressing the PKK and the Kurds. These people were defined as terrorists by Erdogan, affiliated with some obscure "international forces." The same was repeated about the Gulenists following the attempted coup in the summer of 2016.

[29] Mesut Yegen, "Turkish nationalism and the Kurdish question," *Ethnic and Racial Studies*, Volume 30, Issue 1 (2007) pp. 119–151.

tity. In some way, then, one could argue that the ontological security of Turkey came to be viewed as more and more threatened precisely because of this resurgence of Turkish identity that eliminated the possibility of a future of "identity fusion." Yegen, in contrast to the literature's assertion that the Kurdish question was considered an issue of tribal backwardness but not an ethnopolitical question,[30] argues also that the Turkish state discourse does not misrepresent the Kurdish question but instead "enunciates the exclusion of Kurdish identity and thus has been the language of that exclusion."[31] Again, one can see how the ontological security of Turkish identity, or Turkishness, has always depended on this juxtaposition and contrast to Kurdish identity.

Nevertheless, in the new century, Turkey started to feel a level of self-confidence rarely felt previously, reducing the Sèvres Syndrome with a new trust in the future and in the world based on a new self-identity. One would expect an improvement in its ontological security. This happened first because Turkey was able to stop temporarily the war with the PKK with the capture of Öcalan in 1999. Second, with the start of the EU membership application in 1999 Turkey opened the door to a new democratic path with a feeling of inclusiveness and so higher ontological security. Finally, with the AKP in power starting in 2002, Turkey enter into a new phase of democratization with the inclusion of a repressed traditional religious identity. All this also brought with it the emergence of a new economic and international status, causing Turkey to aspire to become not only a regional but a world power. Turkey began to engage for the first time with the Kurdish issue in a different way, specifically with an accommodative approach to cultural rights, as explained in Chap. 4. Nevertheless, despite this progress, this seemingly increased level of ontological security would not last for long: ontological insecurity reappeared quite soon. To put it again with Kinzer: "Turkey is finally being shaped by its hopes rather than its fears, but the fears have not disappeared."[32] So why has ontological security reverted again to a lower level in the last few years?

[30] On the Turkish orientalist view of tribal, backward Kurdish group,s see also the study on Iraqi Kurds by Ipek Demira and Welat Zeydanlioğlub, "On the Representation of 'Others' at Europe's Borders: The Case of Iraqi Kurds," *Journal of Contemporary European Studies*, Volume 18, Issue 1, 2010.

[31] Mesut Yegen, "The Kurdish Question in Turkish State Discourse," *Journal of Contemporary History*, Vol. 34, No. 4 (Oct., 1999): p. 555.

[32] Kinzer, *Crescent and star*, xiv.

One scholar, Ayse Betul Çelik, studying specifically the ontological security of Turkey with respect to the Kurdish issue, argues that in reality Turkey still felt secure during the PKK insurgency years. Ontological security started to decline only starting in 2009, specifically because of the "Kurdish opening" in 2009 (a government initiative to address the Kurdish issue) that stoked Turkey's original fears.[33] Çelik shows how after the first phases of escalation (1984–1999) and de-escalation (1999–2005), the conflict between Turkey and the PKK passed through a phase of re-escalation (2005–2009), with physical but not ontological insecurity for Turkey; finally, with the Kurdish opening in 2009, ontological insecurity started to emerge. Celik's argument, based on the work and narratives of some workshops on civil society on the Kurdish issue, showed how the Kurdish minority was more concerned with identity recognition while the Turkish majority was concerned with territorial integrity.[34] Turkish ontological security therefore was reduced because of the anxieties provoked by the peace process, as Rumelili would have argued.

But besides Çelik's and Rumelili's arguments regarding the internal "peace process" that may have affected the people and state anxieties about self-identity, this study also argues that, since 2011, the regional and international situation has not played out in favor of a stronger ontological security for Turkey. The birth of autonomous regions in Iraq in 2008 and especially in Syria in 2013—with the fear of a "Northern Kurdistan" to be created also in Turkey—the challenges of ISIS and the Syrian chaos, international terrorism and the refugee crisis, and the failure of progress on EU membership all contributed to reduce the ontological security of Turkey. At the end of the day, the self-identities that remain at the base of ontological security, and the narratives that reflect them, are often influenced not only by domestic but also by international issues.

Thus, in 2013, Turkey started a phase of resecuritization of the Kurdish issue with the resumption of large-scale hostilities. This escalated especially

---

[33] Following the framework of Rumelili, Çelik explains how the Kurdish conflict in Turkey is an "unstable conflict," that is, a conflict with high levels of both anxiety and fear, with different levels of physical and ontological insecurity because of the asymmetric relationship, and with different levels of conflict (between the Turkish state and the ethnic minority at the cultural and political levels, between the Turkish state and the PKK at the military level, and between Turks and Kurds at the social level). See Ayşe Betül Çelik, "The Kurdish issue and levels of ontological security," in *Conflict Resolution and Ontological Security*, ed. Bahar Rumelili, New security studies, PRIO (Abingdon: Routledge, 2015).

[34] Ibid., p. 57.

during the summer of 2015, following the conclusion of the peace process that had started in 2013. As explained in Chap. 4, resecuritization went hand in hand with an authoritarian drift of the Turkish government caused by several elements, including an overwhelming popular support of the AKP, the events of the Arab Spring that caused the regime to fear internal issues, and the Middle Eastern chaos that instilled in the government to feel a need to become more centralized and stronger even at the expenses of liberal elements of its democracy, such as free speech or the rule of law. Therefore, the year 2013 can be considered the pivotal year in the change in Turkey's strategy toward the Kurds and of the reawakening of the ontological security issue. The threat of the Arab Spring arrived in Turkey, with the events of Gezi Park in May, but the ultimate Arab Spring failure (apart from the Tunisian case) was completed in the summer, with the removal of Egyptian President-elect Mohamed Morsi by the military. This important event left Erdogan and the AKP feeling very much threatened as they became the last representatives, though more moderate than the Muslim Brotherhood, of the political Islam approach to democracy. Therefore, we can affirm that the ontological security of the self-identity of the AKP, and with it of the Turkish state, that had increased ten years before started to diminish after that time.

Also, since 2013, the presence of ISIS in Syria and Iraq threatened not only the AKP government but the Turkish state itself, on at least three levels: the territorial level, the state-identity level, and the ideological level. First of all, the threat was territorial because the Syrian war and ISIS opened up space for a larger Kurdish territory and autonomy (the Rojava region, which into existence in 2013). This facilitated collaboration between the Syrian Kurdish forces of the PYG and the Turkish ones of the PKK, with exchange of people, weapons, and goods (besides the already existing exchange between the PKK and the Kurds in Iraq, which was also a bad thing for Turkey). Second, the threat was also related to the identity of the modern nation-state because suddenly it was possible for a proto-state to arise inside another state, like a type of "cancer" of a state— even Turkey supported this cancer initially as a tool against the Assad regime in Syria. This reinforced the fact that also inside Turkey another proto-state could emerge from scratch, with a new Kurdish nationalism competing with Turkish nationalism (the same thing happened with the Iraqi Kurdistan referendum in September 2017). Finally, the threat was also ideological because, increasingly owing to the chaos in Syria and Iraq, the PKK was organizing new forms of self-autonomy in some areas of

Turkish Kurdistan (the so-called Democratic Autonomy in Northern Kurdistan).[35] These forms of self-autonomy were based on alternative models of the free market and at the same time a moderate Islamist model of the Turkish state, closer to Marxist philosophy and communist views,[36] though somewhat different from them, being based on the Democratic Confederalism concept, also influenced by communalism and libertarian municipalism philosophies.[37] This part has not been studied in depth in connection with the conflict between Turkey and the PKK, but it plays an important role in how Turkey configures the Kurdish issue in its Southeastern regions today.

But the new ontological insecurity of Turkey, which pushed for the resecuritization of the Kurdish issue, came also from domestic political elements, the rational calculation of the Turkish regime, as explained in Chap. 5. The AKP started a peace negotiation process with the PKK in 2013 in an attempt both to secure more political support from the Kurds and to resolve once and for all the Kurdish issue, which was becoming dangerous given the region's geopolitical earthquakes. The negotiations would have resolved—or at least contained—the Kurdish question and avoided a risk of spillover with uncontrollable consequences, as was happening in Syria with the birth of the Rojava Kurdish Autonomous Region. However, when the AKP saw that the peace process was not bearing the expected fruits, reflected by losses in the 2015 elections, and in addition new self-governing municipalities were developing in the Eastern part of the country during the negotiations, the ontological security of the government started to decline and with it that of the state (given also the fact that Turkey became a dominant-party system). This contributed to the AKP's change in strategy, bringing an end to the peace process and reigniting securitization.

[35] Tatort Kurdistan (Author) and Janet Biehl (Translator), *Democratic autonomy in north Kurdistan: the council movement, gender liberation, and ecology–in practice : a reconnaissance into southeastern Turkey* (Porsgrunn: New Compass Press, 2013).
[36] See on this Sener Akturk, "The PKK and PYD's Kurdish Soviet Experiment in Syria and Turkey," *Daily Sabah,* January 27, 2016, accessed September 30, 2017, http://www.daily-sabah.com/op-ed/2016/01/27/the-pkk-and-pyds-kurdish-soviet-experiment-in-syria-and-turkey#.
[37] Communalism is a libertarian socialist political philosophy created by American activist Murray Bookchin. Communalism proposes that markets and money be abolished and that land and enterprises, i.e., private property, be placed increasingly in the custody of the community, with the custody of citizens in free assemblies and their delegates in confederal councils. See: http://www.communalismpamphlet.net/.

Another element that changed the political costs of the peace process, and with it the ontological security of Turkey, was the ascendancy of the HDP, the pro-Kurdish party, to the parliament for the first time in the summer of 2015. This represented a significant threat again both to the political power of the AKP and the Turkish state's identity, which was coming to be increasingly identified with the AKP's. This is because the pro-Kurdish HDP, which held views that were close to communalism concepts, challenged the basic foundations of the new Turkey that had been built starting in the Erdogan era, with a stronger Islamist approach and presidential system that Erdogan and the AKP wanted to create. Among other things, for example, the HDP has a copresidential system of leadership, with one chairman and one chairwoman, a guarantee of a 50 percent quota to women and 10 percent to the LGBT community, and a modern progressive platform very different—indeed, practically the opposite—from the Islamist conservative identity of the AKP. Therefore, to block this "biographical narrative" (in Steele's terms) of the HDP that threatened the "biographical narrative" of the AKP, and so its identity, President Erdogan and the AKP started to delegitimize and stigmatize the pro-Kurdish party when it won seats in parliament. This process included passing a law to remove parliamentary immunity from MPs under criminal investigation for terrorism[38] (see again Chap. 4 on this). Thus, as we can see, both international and domestic issues contributed to reducing the state's ontological security and with it to push for policies of resecuritization.

Erdogan's Narratives Expressing Ontological Insecurity

Returning to the main indicator that identifies the level of ontological security of a state—that is, narratives of leaders in charge of political decision-making—we can say that in the first decade of democratization, the narratives regarding the Kurdish issue showed ontological security (besides rational political interests) based on a safe "self-identity" and trust in the future for the resolution of the Kurdish issue. However, in the period since 2013 and particularly since the summer of 2015, the narra-

---

[38] Kadri Gursel, "Ouster of Kurdish MPs threatens to fuel separatism in Turkey," Turkey Pulse, Al Monitor, The pulse of the Middle East, May 23, 2016, accessed September 30, 2017, http://www.al-monitor.com/pulse/originals/2016/05/turkey-kurdish-hdp-lawmakers-lifts-immunities-arrest.html.

tives mostly of President Erdogan and the AKP indicate increasing fears of terrorism, sometimes expressed as a "siege or invasion" paranoia, recalling the old Sèvres Syndrome, which, as stated earlier, was understandable because of the geopolitical facts in the region.

Erdogan's perspective and narrative on the Kurdish issue date back to the early 1990s, when he was chairman of Istanbul district networks of the Welfare Party. It is surprising to read what Erdogan wrote in a report for the party about the Kurdish question:

> What is termed the "Eastern problem" or "southeastern problem" is in fact the "Kurdish problem" [...] What is today defined as "the east" or "southeast" are in fact parts of what is historically known as Kurdistan. Kurdish is irrelevant to Turkish and is a language spoken exclusively by the Kurds. [...] Due to PKK attacks that began in 1985 [sic] the region is squeezed between state terror and PKK terror. The region's people are put under sustained pressure and torture citing their alleged help to the PKK. The special forces' activities in the region are almost non-legal.[39]

The report goes on to suggest a revision of state policy toward the PKK, proposing a comprehensive approach based on "complete democracy and cultural plurality." And this is actually what the AKP tried to do when it assumed power at the beginning of the new century. However, starting in 2011 and particularly 2013, international and domestic events changed the attitude of the government toward the Kurdish question, and with that the narrative about it. This does not mean that Erdogan's narrative did not change during the first ten years, because it actually changed a lot depending on the audience, contingent situations, and electoral calculus, among other factors.[40] However, the narrative did not seem to demonstrate a low level of ontological security for the first decade of the AKP regime, thanks also to its increasing electoral success, the relative stability of the Middle East until the Arab Spring, the growing Turkish economy, and finally the restrained Kurdish separatist movement.

However, by 2013 Erdogan, who by that time had been prime minister for ten years already (and in 2014 became president), was clearly developing a harsher narrative, mistrustful and almost paranoid, often delegitimiz-

---

[39] Akin Unver, *Turkey's Kurdish question*, 2015, p. 153.
[40] Tulin Daloglu, "Erdogan's Many Positions on the Kurdish Issue," *Al Monitor*, April 23, 2013, accessed September 30, 2017, http://www.al-monitor.com/pulse/originals/2013/04/erdogan-kurdish-issue-flip-flop-turkey-peace.html.

ing the Kurdish issue, increasingly associating Kurdish demands with violent actions. His narrative also delegitimized Kurdish politicians, treating them as being close to known rebel fighters, and asserted their connection to external enemies. Even during the peace process Erdogan declared: "Turkey should continue to conduct operations against those groups that shed blood in the interests of foreign countries. Indeed, when the PKK lays down its arms, operations will automatically stop."[41]

It got worse in 2015, with the growing number of terrorist attacks in Turkey from ISIS, often mixed up with the Kurdish issue, either accusing the two parties of plotting together against the Turkish state or denying the fact that there was still a Kurdish issue in Turkey. Erdogan started to assert that there was no Kurdish issue in Turkey, just terrorism:

> … in Turkey, there are those who have one-track minds: "Kurdish problem and Kurdish problem, Kurdish problem and Kurdish problem." You cannot get anyone to buy it….We closed this matter in my Diyarbakır speech in 2005.[42] We said then, "There is no such problem in Turkey anymore, you cannot explain this to anybody. There is a terror problem in Turkey."[43] And again: "What Kurdish question? There is no such thing anymore! What are you [Kurds] lacking? Have you been President in this country? You have! … What do you want? For God's sake, what's the difference between you and [the Turks]? You have it all!"[44]

Again, the problem of low ontological security and a power threat is associated in the narrative with the problem of a clear definition of the Kurdish question. This in turn raises the question of the precise identity of Turkey and Turkishness in a new globalized and mobile world in which all national identities are "under threat." But this represents a different level

---

[41] Johanna Nykanen, "Identity, Narrative and Frames: Assessing Turkey's Kurdish Initiatives," *Insight Turkey,* Vol. 15, No. 2 (Spring 2013): pp. 85–101.

[42] In a 2005 rally in Diyarbakır, Erdogan made a famous declaration that the answer to the Kurds' long-running grievances was not repression but democracy. Unfortunately, the democracy that Erdogan meant was the bus to step down from when they arrived at their last stop, as in 2011 and 2013 things have changed dramatically for Turkish democracy and the Kurdish issue.

[43] *Hurriyet Daily News,* "There's no Kurdish issue in Turkey, just terrorism: Erdogan," January 6, 2016, accessed September 30, 2017, http://www.hurriyetdailynews.com/theres-no-kurdish-issue-in-turkey-just-terrorism-erdogan.aspx?pageID=238&nID=93511&NewsCatID=338.

[44] Unver, *Turkey's Kurdish question,* p. 166.

of discourse. Nevertheless, the clear tendency in Erdogan's recent narrative is to paint all who support the Kurdish issue against securitization as terrorists. For example, in early 2016, academics who signed a petition titled "Academics for Peace" to protest the military intervention against the PKK and civilians in the Eastern region were harassed and arrested. The day after the Ankara terrorist attack of March 2016 Erdogan declared that "there was no difference between 'a terrorist holding a gun or a bomb and those who use their position and pen to serve the aims' of terrorists."[45]

Also after the failed military coup in July 2016, Erdogan's public pronouncements again illustrated relatively low ontological security. He accused external and internal enemies of plotting against him and Turkey, accusing the Gulenist movement of being behind the coup and arresting thousands of people accused of being affiliated with it. In his speech following the attempted coup he said, "We will not hand this country over to a few terrorists. We will fight this parallel state structure with our principle of a single state....The operation of getting rid of them, of cleansing our system, is under way."[46] Actually, the state of emergency lasted for one year and practically became permanent in the Kurdish region after the resecuritization phase.

Also, nationalist and right-wing parties (like the far-right Nationalist Movement Party/MHP) have taken up their historical role of fueling fear of a threat to Turkish identity and nation, having every interest in increasing ontological insecurity, following the typical nationalist right-wing strategy of attracting votes for more authoritarian and repressive policies. In 2015, for example, the leader of MHP, Bahçeli, compared the agreement between the HDP and the Turkish government during the Kurdish-Turkish peace process to the Treaty of Sèvres, saying that it "will lead to the collapse of the Turkish Republic."[47]

For these reasons, we can say that since 2011, but especially since the end of the peace process in 2015, the Turkish leadership's narrative has

---

[45] "Ankara bombing: Erdogan seeks to widen terrorism definition," BBC News Europe, March 14, 2016, accessed September 30, 2017, http://www.bbc.com/news/world-europe-35807987.

[46] *Financial Times,* "Erdogan launches crackdown after failed Turkish coup," July 16, 2016, accessed September 30, 2017, https://next.ft.com/content/ba2f3a5a-4b3f-11e6-8172-e39ecd3b86fc.

[47] *Ebru News,* "MHP leader says Kurdish peace process will 'ruin' Turkey," March 3, 2015, accessed September 30, 2017, http://news.ebru.tv/en/mhp-leader-says-kurdish-peace-process-will-ruin-turkey.

identified the Kurdish issue more and more as a terrorist threat, reviving the old concept of an internal enemy against the Turkish nation and Turkish identity. This shows once again a low level of ontological security.

Regarding the second element of Steele's indicators, the discourse of the international community, one can also see how Turkey started to manifest a low ontological security. The president and government reacted with angry declarations when some external power, in particular the EU, criticized Turkey regarding its democratic retrogression and the treatment of Kurds in recent years. Such insecurity also manifests in Turkey's tense reactions to historical mistakes or possible crimes that Turkey may have committed in the past.

One particular example that shows the pride of Turkey and its consequent feeling of external intrusion is the Armenian, Assyrian, and Greek genocides during the First World War (considered by Turkey to be mass killings, not genocides). Zarakol argues that precisely over concerns related to ontological security, states adopt strategies of denial of genocides.[48] Recently, Germany joined the 29 states around the world, in particular in Europe, that officially recognize the genocide (Turkey and Azerbaijan are the only states that directly and officially deny it).[49] As it has done every time a state recognizes the Armenian genocide, Erdogan threatened Germany and the EU with serious economic, political, and security consequences, including the withdrawal of its ambassadors. Turks who have acknowledged the genocide, like the writer Orhan Pamuk, have faced criminal charges for "insulting Turkishness."[50] These behaviors and narratives again demonstrate a low level of ontological security, an inability of the state to deal with its own past. Turkey cannot accept that its founding fathers may have made mistakes, much less committed atrocities, even though the international community and most genocide scholars and historians say they did. Nevertheless, to admit past errors is the only path to reconciliation with one's past; this applies to both individuals and entire countries: no country in the world can claim to have been born with only good thoughts and righteous actions (consider slavery in the USA).

---

[48] Ayşe Zarakol, "Ontological (In)security and state denial of historical crimes: Turkey and Japan," *International Relations,* vol. 24, n. 1 (2010): pp. 3–23.

[49] *The Economist,* "Name and shame. Deciding what to call a century-old Turkish atrocity," June 2, 2016, accessed September 30, 2017, http://www.economist.com/news/europe/21699952-deciding-what-call-century-old-turkish-atrocity-name-and-shame.

[50] http://www.vox.com/2015/4/22/8465257/armenian-genocide.

But besides past issues, current issues also make Turkish identity feel threatened by the actions and narratives of the international community. For example, the Turkish government was angered when its closest Western ally, the USA, started to support the YPG, the Kurdish faction in the Syrian war against ISIS. The Turkish narrative became very tense even on small issues, such as its protest of US forces wearing the YPG patch while training YPG forces.[51] The conflictual relationship with the USA worsened when Erdogan accused Fethullah Gulen, exiled in the USA, of being responsible for the attempted coup in July 2016, calling for the USA to arrest and extradite him: "Dear Mr. President: I told you this before. Either arrest Fethullah Gulen or return him to Turkey. You didn't listen. I call on you again following the coup attempt. Extradite this man in Pennsylvania to Turkey. If we are strategic partners or model partners, do what is necessary."[52]

In conclusion, it may be asserted that the ontological security of Turkey since the democratization period grew at the beginning but later declined, in particular since 2013, and with it the securitization of the Kurdish issue increased. This suggests that there is an important relationship between this interacting variable and the final outcome.

INDONESIA: ONTOLOGICAL SECURITY AND AUTONOMIZATION OF ACEH

Indonesia differs historically and geographically from Turkey. Indonesia is not the heir to a dismembered empire but a former Dutch colony. It is an archipelago of 17,000 islands that cannot be conquered completely or dismembered. Furthermore, Indonesian identity is pluralistic and diverse; is not caught between two competing realities (like West and East for Turkey) but relies on Asian values of harmony and balance and Islamic ethical values of trust in the future and in "others." Furthermore, the secularization process was not imposed from outside as it was in Turkey. Paradoxically, secularization did not hinder values of Indonesian faith and

---

[51] *Business Insider*, "Turkey slams 'unacceptable' photos of US troops wearing Kurdish patches while they fight ISIS," May 27, 2016, accessed September 30, 2017, http://www.businessinsider.com/us-soldiers-ypg-patches-syria-2016-5.

[52] *New York Times*, "Live More Coverage: Coup Attempt in Turkey," July 16, 2016, accessed July 16, 2016, http://www.nytimes.com/live/turkey-coup-erdogan/erdogan-calls-on-u-s-to-arrest-or-extradite-fethullah-gulen/.

spirituality but instead came from a tradition of religious pluralism and even religious syncretism. With this history and identity, in general, Indonesia experienced a higher level of ontological security compared to Turkey. Nonetheless, the internal divisions of ethnic groups have always represented a possible threat to Indonesia's national self-identity. During the period of dictatorship, like every authoritarian and military regime that does not feel legitimate or supported by its population, President Suharto often felt threatened and created enemies to justify to the population his authoritarian rule.[53]

Even if the traditional and historical ontological security of the country may have been at a higher level than in Turkey, during its history the Indonesian state at times experienced anxieties, fears, and almost a sense of paranoia. As explained in Chap. 6 about geopolitics, the possible fears over Indonesia did not come from external enemies but instead mostly from internal ones. Such fear of internal security threats had a great impact on the repression of ethnic minorities—besides the repression of the communist threat with hundreds of thousands of killings during the 1960s—specifically the Acehnese minority because Aceh had a long history of rejecting foreign rule at any cost. However, while one can consider the communist threat an threat to Indonesian state identity, ethnic concerns threatened mostly territorial unity and sovereignty. This is another important difference between Indonesia and Turkey, though this study will not examine it in depth (because it does not look at inclusion from the perspective of the ethnic minority): the history of the separatist movement, the causes of its rebellion, and how this affected the feeling of national or ontological security of the country.

As discussed in Chap. 4, Acehnese rebellion arose from a particular history as an independent kingdom from the fifteenth century and a progressive alienation of the population in reaction to Indonesian policies. These policies created extensive human rights abuses and the waste of resources and wealth by the central government.[54] This made the Acehnese rebellion more a question of sovereignty than a question of identity,[55] while the

[53] Elizabeth Drexler, *Aceh, Indonesia: Securing the Insecure State* (Philadelphia: Pennsylvania University Press, 2008).

[54] Larry Niksch, "Indonesian separatist movement in Aceh," in E. McFlynn, *Economics and Geopolitics of Indonesia* (New York: Nova Science Publishers, 2002). Larry Niksch, "Indonesian Separatist Movement in Aceh," *CRS Report for Congress*, January 12, 2001.

[55] Edward Aspinall, *Islam and nation: separatist rebellion in Aceh, Indonesia* (Palo Alto: Stanford University Press, 2009).

Kurdish one was related to territory but also to the recognition of Kurdish identity and even national participation in the political sphere. Therefore, the threat to the ontological security of the two countries can be considered different: "Turkishness" was felt to be under threat by Kurdish separatism, while "Indonesianness" was not; the threat there was to national sovereignty and territorial integrity. This can also be seen in the different natures of the repressions in Turkey and Indonesia: apart from the common direct violence in the military repression, the long-term "structural violence" for Aceh was based more on economic marginalization. In the Kurdish case it was more a cultural and symbolic violence.[56] For these reasons one may assert that historically Indonesia enjoyed stronger ontological security, above all in connection with its history, geography, and identity, but also with the type of ethnic rebellion that was more a territorial than an identity one.

For example, during the 1958 rebellion in the "Outer Islands," in particular Sumatra and Maluku with the "revolutionary governments" established by certain rebel colonels, the country's ontological security did not feel threatened, but the physical and national security, territorial integrity, and sovereignty of the Indonesian state were clearly threatened. For this reason, the state reacted with repressions.[57] However, in the 1960s the "safety and order" motto of the New Order regime of Suharto made security a fundamental element of the Indonesian state based on the control of "subversive forces," which at the time were mostly communist forces, and some ethnic minorities were connected to them. This created in some parts of the Indonesian state a sort of "political paranoia" over internal enemies, similar to the state of Turkey, which could have threatened Indonesian identity based on democracy and national independence from foreign influence.[58] During these times, therefore, one could consider Indonesia's ontological security as being at a low level. As a consequence, the state resorted to securitization policies, in particular with the killings of hundreds of thousands of people during the period 1965–1966, targeting alleged communists but also ethnic Chinese, whom the state associ-

---

[56] Sumanto Al Qurtuby, "Interethnic Violence, Separatism and Political Reconciliation in Turkey and Indonesia," *India Quarterly* 71(2) (6/2015): p. 141.

[57] Ted Piccone, *Five Rising Democracies and the Fate of the International Liberal Order* (Washington, DC: Brookings Institution Press, 2016): p. 212.

[58] Tim Lindsey, "The Criminal State: Premanisme and the New Indonesia," In *Indonesia Today. Challenges of History*, G. Lloyd and S. Smith, eds. (Singapore: Institute of Southeast Asian Studies, 2001), pp. 283–297.

ated with the same threat. During decolonization and the subsequent annexation of East Timor in 1976 (as well as the start of the GAM fight in Aceh), the Indonesian state again seemed to experience a threat to its national territory, similarly to the Outer Islands rebellion of the 1950s. Once again, however, the threat was not so much to its national identity or ontological security.

With the democratization process starting in 1998, the ontological security of Indonesia did not seem to decline much, at least initially, even though the Indonesian state could have feared losing part of its national sovereignty with the risk of fragmentation into independence movements in different islands. Likewise, the delicacy of the transition could have jeopardized the stability of the country and its identity given the fact that the transition could have led to amending or rewriting the constitution. In addition, before the democratic transition, the Asian financial crisis in 1997 could have made the state feel a low level of ontological security, given the problems of living in globalized times with external threats impacting the economies of nation-states. Therefore, the securitization of minorities, with the escalation of violence under the presidencies of Wahid and Megawati, could have been put in place not only to fight ethnic separatism but also to redress the ontological (in)security of the democratic transition and globalized times. However, ontological insecurity did not seem to appear under the Megawati presidency, even though it was affected by the Bali bombing and the US Global War on Terror after 9/11.

This surprising resilience of ontological security during Indonesia's democratization happened, according to some scholars, because the risks of ethnic centrifugal force and the threat to Indonesian identity stemming from the democratic transition and globalization were counteracted by traditional local authorities who played an important role in maintaining a sense of security of the country's self-identity. Bubandt in particular argues that in Indonesia, the ontological insecurity created by globalizing forces, as well as by the fight against secessions and terror, interacted with a "vernacular," local, grassroots sense of "onto-political" security.[59] Administrative decentralization, according to the scholar, opened up new possibilities for traditional and local identities that provided some sense of self-security based on spirituality and customs, besides the rational national

---

[59] Nils Ole Bubandt, "Vernacular security: governmentality, traditionality and ontological (in)security in Indonesia," *Danish Institute for International Studies*, Working Paper no 24, 2004.

approach to security. For this reason, instead of weakening the sense of the nation-state, decentralization reinforced the sense of security among former bureaucrats who had "traditional legitimacy" (for example, with sultanate titles). As Bubandt says, "Against the rationalism of 'securitization,' these neotraditional bureaucrats built an alternative political imaginary in which what they saw as a truly democratic tradition ensured 'ontological security.'"[60]

Besides this argument, though (for which other evidence is presented in the previous chapter regarding decentralization during democratization), one could argue that the ontological security of Indonesia did not decline during the first phase of democratization, in part owing to the other factors, both domestic and international, analyzed in this study. First, the gradual transition maintained the old elites in areas of power (Chap. 5). Second, the international and geopolitical situation was stable, much more so than in Turkey (Chap. 6). Third, as previously discussed, Indonesia has historically experienced a higher level of ontological security in its institutions (Chap. 7). Finally, with the democratization process there was little disruption of older routines and identity (in contrast to Turkey with the reinsertion of Islamic identity with AKP regime) as the old routines of a pluralistic identity were maintained and even reinforced with the democratization process. Also, the "Aceh openings" of peace negotiations did not seem to create peace anxieties as they did in the Kurdish case. Aceh did not have a national party threatening Indonesian identity, as in the HDP case. Therefore, we can argue that the ontological security of Indonesia, unlike Turkey's, remained robust also during the time of democratization. This in turn contributed to opening the door to the decentralization process, and specifically the autonomization of Aceh.

Narratives of Indonesian Presidents in Democratic Transition

How, specifically, did the first presidents of the Indonesian democratic transition express the feeling of the country's ontological security toward ethnic minorities and in particular Aceh? As recounted in Chap. 4, during the first phase of democratic transition, Indonesia had two presidents: Habibie, from May 1998 to October 1999, and Wahid, from October 1999 to July 2001. Their narratives revealed little fear and anxiety in con-

[60] Ibid., p. 2.

nection with the ontological security of the Indonesian state as they did during Suharto's time, even if the second president escalated the violence against Acehnese separatism.

Habibie was a supporter of human rights and democracy. As some scholars argue, Indonesia was lucky to have him to manage the country in transition, a trained engineer with managerial capacity but without political ambitions, with a leadership style based on a relaxation process and approximation approach.[61] Habibie was a technocrat, an intellectual and devoted Muslim, educated in Germany, where he had a career as engineer. He was a disciple of Suharto, but Suharto (together with many other Javanese people) considered him a traitor when he supported the referendum in East Timor that granted independence to one province of Indonesia that moreover had a Roman Catholic majority. In some of his speeches we can see his approach of pluralism and lack of fear of dismemberment or ontological insecurity. At the opening of an Asian-German Editors Forum in February of 1999, he said that "Indonesia is like one huge piece of sponge which absorbs every new cultural strain and in the process strengthens itself.…We will not declare Indonesia a Muslim state even though 95 per cent of the Indonesians are Muslims," confirming that Indonesia will always follow its secularism and state ideology of Pancasila.[62] He also said at the same time that "burning churches is unnatural to them"[63] (Indonesians), explaining that these acts were done by criminals and troublemakers not because of some type of sectarian conflicts fueled by hatred and fears.

Wahid, the first president of Indonesia elected by the parliament, was, by contrast, a Muslim religious, long-time president of the religious association Nahdlatul Ulama, who had created a new party after the Reformasi (in addition to the three parties that existed during the Suharto regime). He had won just a few votes more than Megawati. His presidency was affected by party and elite competition, who, among other objections, did not want a party full of Nahdlatul Ulama people ruling the country. Unlike Habibie, he was not a very competent manager of the centrifugal forces and fear of national disintegration he found himself up against, which

---

[61] Dewi Fortuna Anwar and Bridget Welsh, eds. *Democracy Take-Off: The B. J. Habibie Period* (Jakarta: Sinar Harapan, 2013).

[62] Zainon Ahmad, "Habibie—the 'unpresidential' master of Indonesian politics," *New Sunday Times*, 21 February 1999, accessed September 30, 2017, https://www.library.ohiou.edu/indopubs/1999/02/21/0018.html.

[63] Ibid.

added to the growing opposition to him.[64] His speeches toward the end of his presidency showed a defiant attitude on the risk of "national disintegration," which was the narrative of fear (justified by the rise of collective violence in the country) of some political elites: "I know Indonesia. I know what they want. The public as well as the armed forces are behind me."[65] But actually the risk of instability led the military to remove him just a year after he took office, when he finally decided to declare a state of emergency in July 2001, replacing him with the first woman president, Megawati.

During the presidency of Megawati in 2003–2004, the Aceh conflict passed through its most brutal period, showing concern with not only national sovereignty but also foreign interference: Megawati tried to connect the Aceh rebellion to international terrorism.[66] Her early narrative expressed more trust and a desire to accommodate than the previous president, though she remained firm on national unity: "Concerning the intention of some citizens to separate from Indonesia, in my opinion there is no country in the world that would tolerate disintegration…I believe that we can provide more room for people to regulate themselves especially during the implementation of regional autonomy."[67] But one year after President Megawati was elected, she had to respond to the Bali bombing in October 2002, which forced her policies to evolve. As the 1960s fear of communism encouraged Indonesia to follow US Cold War policies, now the fear of Islamic extremism has aligned Indonesia with the US Global War on Terror, an alignment that in part affected the ontological security of Indonesian state and altered its internal security policies. According to some scholars, US global politics, which always considered Indonesia the key actor in Southeast Asian security, played a major role in this shift.[68] Because fundamentalist Islam planted no roots in Indonesia, like communism instead had in the 1960s, the Bali bombing was used as an occasion for the resecuritization of ethnic minorities, as in the New Order during

[64] "Gus Dur Told to Avoid State of Emergency," *The Jakarta Post*, June 27, 2016, accessed September 30, 2017, http://blog.indahnesia.com/entry/200106280002/gus_dur_told_to_avoid_state_of_emergency.php.
[65] Ibid.
[66] Dewi Fortuna Anwar and Bridget Welsh, *Democracy Take-Off*, 2013, p. 214.
[67] "Megawati Pledges National Unity," *The Jakarta Post*, June 1, 2001, accessed September 30, 2017, https://www.library.ohiou.edu/indopubs/2001/06/01/0046.html.
[68] Paul Dibb, "Indonesia: The Key to Southeast Asia's Security," *International Affairs*, 77(4) 2001: 829–842.

Suharto. Following the Bali bombing, the government started to define GAM as a terrorist group in order to make it an "existential threat" to the state that had to be repressed. As a strong believer in a unified state, Megawati feared that the terrorist attacks might contribute to the chaos of ethnic independence movements. For this reason, she increased the securitization of ethnic minorities with a new hard line against sectarian violence, in particular in Sulawesi, Maluku, Papua, and, especially, Aceh. She famously made a speech in Aceh on July 30, 1999, before being elected, declaring "for the people of Aceh, believe me, I will not let a single drop of blood be spilled in Aceh."[69] However, she was the president who escalated the securitization of Acehnese, sending 40,000 troops to Aceh, in the framework of the martial law that was imposed between 2002 and 2003.

When a military officer, Susilo Bambang Yudoyono, a retired army general, ascended to power in 2004, Indonesia's ontological security seemed to improve once again. First of all, military elites again acquired some form of power, though no longer in a position of a "dual function" (Chap. 5). The ruling general gave the population the ontological security of a gradual and stable transition. Second, the decentralization process started to bear fruit. Special regional autonomies acceded to minority demands that certain of their needs be satisfied. Finally, the fear of terrorism that started in late 2002 and the reaction of the Megawati presidency diminished in intensity. This contributed to making the peace process with Aceh successful in finding a final positive solution following the tsunami disaster. Even though Yudoyono, when Minister for Political, Social and Security in the Megawati presidency, had said that "armed revolt can never be resolved through dialogue,"[70] following the tsunami he declared: "The time for peace—real peace, permanent peace—is now."[71]

We may conclude that in Indonesia, as in Turkey, the state's ontological security varied during its history and corresponded with periodic intensification of securitizing policies. However, with democratization, ontologi-

[69] Megawati speech in Aceh, from *Atjehcyber.net*, July 30, 1999 (published in 2013) accessed September 30, 2017, http://www.atjehcyber.net/2012/08/janji-cut-nyak-megawati-di-tanah-serambi.html#ixzz4CLrvDR7A.
[70] Richel Langit-Dursin, "Acehnese Want Justice, Not Bullets," Asia Times, August 31, 2001, accessed September 30, 2017, http://www.atimes.com/se-asia/CH31Ae01.html.
[71] "Yudhoyono calls for peace with Aceh rebels," *United Press International*, February 16, 2005, accessed September 30, 2017, http://www.upi.com/Yudhoyono-calls-for-peace-with-Aceh-rebels/18781108542339/.

cal security did not decline very much, apart from the period between the Bali bombing and the end of Megawati's presidency. This pushed the government to strengthen the process of peace negotiations and a final autonomization that failed to materialize in Turkey.

Conclusions

The goal of this chapter was not to prove or disprove the ontological security thesis. It is a relatively new theoretical approach to applying emotions and psychological issues to a state, which in part explains why scholars have not yet effectively quantified its meaning or operationalized the variable in a clear way. Nonetheless, the chapter advanced a plausible argument regarding ontological security in Turkey and Indonesia. It found sufficient evidence to suggest that ontological security is a driving factor in the treatment of ethnic minorities in both countries, but specifically in Turkey, where the Kurdish issue was also an identity issue, not only one of territory, security, or sovereignty. It is also important to stress that ontological security is different from the other variables discussed in this study because it is a socio-psycho-ideational explanation, not a rationalist-materialist-structuralist one like the others. In addition, ontological security cannot be considered an independent variable like the others but more an interacting one that recursively affects the factors of elites and international structure and is affected by them and by the country's institutions and history.

At least three elements impact the ontological security of a country: geography, history, and identity. Regarding geography, if the country is in a stable region, ontological security will be higher. Also, the geographic contours of a country could have an impact: flat countries are more vulnerable to invasion than mountainous ones, and islands are harder to invade the mainland. Island countries should be more concerned about losing peripheral islands, but they cannot be conquered completely, which makes the ontological security of the country stronger; this applies in particular to Turkey, which is more vulnerable geopolitically speaking, situated as it is between opposing countries and "worlds," and in particular following the chaos of Syria and Iraq. But ontological security is shaped by history as much as by geography. Turkey has been historically fearful because of how it emerged from an empire dismembered by foreign powers, while Indonesia gained independence as a whole. Also, the type of identity can create a higher or lower ontological security. A loose island country such as Indonesia, even though it is a unified state like Turkey, is founded on the basis of a pluralistic identity. It has never had a sense of ethnic homogeneity and closed identity, out of which the fear of losing identity might arise.

In conclusion, we may assert here that Turkey's sense of self-identity, which is based on the Kemalist secular nationalist philosophy but also on military strength, had been more or less stable for seven decades, since its founding at least until the 1990s and perhaps into the 2000s, when the first moderate Islamist party was elected and real democratization started. The democratization that led to the inclusion of Islamic identity and a first attempt to include Kurdish identity (at least with cultural rights if not self-rule and local autonomy) required a transformation of Turkish identity and its adaptation to a new reality. On the one hand, this gave the Turkish state (increasingly represented by the AKP regime) greater ontological security, but it also could have represented a challenge to the country's self-identity by introducing new anxieties. Economic growth and the new approach to foreign policy (Turkey had been quite isolated until then, but with the new century it took a new assertive diplomatic approach based on the so called zero-problem with neighbors) allowed its ontological security to remain more or less stable and even increase. Later, though, as the regional situation started to change, the events of the Arab Spring and regional turmoil introduced new tensions to the sense of Turkish self-identity, causing the old ontological insecurity to reemerge.

Based on the Pancasila nationalist philosophy and military strength, Indonesia also had a stable sense of self for five decades, from decolonization until the end of the dictatorship. When democratization started, however, there was a new need for the inclusion of ethnic minorities. This resulted in administrative decentralization and some form of local autonomy, though not cultural rights at the national level. This process of decentralization occurred in rather fluid and changing international (from the end of the Cold War to the Asian economic crisis) and domestic environments (from decentralization to the referendum on East Timor independence). Initially, these could have created some insecurity in Indonesia's self-identity, but in fact its level of ontological security did not diminish very much. Its sense of self-identity, and thus its ontological security, remained strong.

Hence, we could say that with the beginning of democratization in the twentieth century, the level of ontological security of the two countries moved in the same direction at first but then diverged: after a few years

Turkey went back to its traditional ontological insecurity, especially as a result of the Middle Eastern chaos and the threat of transborder terrorism. By contrast, Indonesia propelled its ontological security to higher traditional levels thanks to decentralization, regional stability, and an ethnic minority whose threat was more territorial than it was related to identity. These different levels of ontological security therefore had an impact in the opposite treatments of the ethnic minorities analyzed in this study.

References

Ahmad, Zainon. 1999. Habibie—The 'Unpresidential' Master of Indonesian Politics. *New Sunday Times*, February 21.

Akturk, Sener. 2016. The PKK and PYD's Kurdish Soviet Experiment in Syria and Turkey. *Daily Sabah*, January 27. http://www.dailysabah.com/op-ed/2016/01/27/the-pkk-and-pyds-kurdish-soviet-experiment-in-syria-and-turkey#. Accessed 30 Sept 2017.

Al Qurtuby, Sumanto. 2015. Interethnic Violence, Separatism and Political Reconciliation in Turkey and Indonesia. *India Quarterly* 71 (2): 126–145.

Anwar, Dewi Fortuna, and Bridget Welsh. 2013. *Democracy Take-Off: The B. J. Habibie Period*. Jakarta: Sinar Harapan.

Aspinall, Edward. 2009. *Islam and Nation: Separatist Rebellion in Aceh, Indonesia*. Palo Alto: Stanford University Press.

BBC News. 2016. Ankara Bombing: Erdogan Seeks to Widen Terrorism Definition, March 14. http://www.bbc.com/news/world-europe-35807987. Accessed 30 Sept 2017.

Bubandt, Nils Ole. 2004. Vernacular Security: Governmentality, Traditionality and Ontological (In)security in Indonesia. *Danish Institute for International Studies*, Working Paper No. 24.

Business Insider. 2016. Turkey Slams 'Unacceptable' Photos of US Troops Wearing Kurdish Patches While They Fight ISIS, May 27. http://www.businessinsider.com/us-soldiers-ypg-patches-syria-2016-5. Accessed 30 Sept 2017.

Çelik, Ayşe Betül. 2015. The Kurdish Issue and Levels of Ontological Security. In *Conflict Resolution and Ontological Security*, ed. Bahar Rumelili, New Security Studies, PRIO. Abingdon: Routledge.

Daloglu, Tulin. 2013. Erdogan's Many Positions on the Kurdish Issue. *Al Monitor*, April 23. http://www.al-monitor.com/pulse/originals/2013/04/erdogan-kurdish-issue-flip-flop-turkey-peace.html. Accessed 30 Sept 2017.

Demira, Ipek, and Welat Zeydanlioğlub. 2010. On the Representation of 'Others' at Europe's Borders: The Case of Iraqi Kurds. *Journal of Contemporary European Studies* 18 (1): 7–23.

Dibb, Paul. 2001. Indonesia: The Key to Southeast Asia's Security. *International Affairs* 77 (4): 829–842.
Drexler, Elizabeth. 2008. *Aceh, Indonesia: Securing the Insecure State.* Philadelphia: Pennsylvania University Press.
Ebru News. 2015. MHP Leader Says Kurdish Peace Process Will 'Ruin' Turkey, March 3. http://news.ebru.tv/en/mhp-leader-says-kurdish-peace-process-will-ruin-turkey. Accessed 5 July 2016.
Financial Times. 2016. Erdogan Launches Crackdown After Failed Turkish Coup, July 16. https://next.ft.com/content/ba2f3a5a-4b3f-11e6-8172-e39ecd-3b86fc. Accessed 30 Sept 2017.
Giddens, Anthony. 1991. *Modernity and Self-Identity: Self and Society in the Late Modern Age.* Palo Alto: Stanford University Press.
Guida, Michelangelo. 2008. The Sèvres Syndrome and "Komplo" Theories in the Islamist and Secular Press. *Turkish Studies* 9 (1): 37–52.
Gursel, Kadri. 2016. Ouster of Kurdish MPs Threatens to Fuel Separatism in Turkey. *Turkey Pulse, Al Monitor, The Pulse of the Middle East*, May 23.
Hurriyet Daily News. 2016. There's No Kurdish Issue in Turkey, Just Terrorism: Erdogan, January 6. http://www.hurriyetdailynews.com/theres-no-kurdish-issue-in-turkey-just-terrorism-erdogan.aspx?pageID=238&nID=93511&NewsCatID=338. Accessed 30 Sept 2017.
Jung, Dietrich. 2003. The Sèvres Syndrome, Turkish Foreign Policy and Its Historical Legacies. *American Diplomacy*, August. http://www.unc.edu/depts/diplomat/archives_roll/2003_07-09/jung_sevres/jung_sevres.html. Accessed 30 Sept 2017.
Kentel, Ferhat. 2011. Nationalist Reconstructions in the Light of Disappearing Borders. In *Nationalisms and Politics in Turkey: Political Islam, Kemalism, and the Kurdish Issue*, ed. Marlies Casier and Joost Jongerden. New York: Routledge.
Kinnvall, Catarina. 2004. Globalization and Religious Nationalism: Self, Identity and the Search for Ontological Security. *Political Psychology* 25 (5): 741–767.
Kinzer, Stephen. 2008. *Crescent and Star: Turkey Between Two Worlds.* New York: Farrar, Straus and Giroux.
Kurdistan Tatort (Author) and Janet Biehl (Translator). 2013. *Democratic Autonomy in North Kurdistan: The Council Movement, Gender Liberation, and Ecology—in Practice: A Reconnaissance into Southeastern Turkey.* Porsgrunn: New Compass Press.
Kymlicka, Will. 2004. Justice and Security in the Accommodation of Minority Nationalism. In *The Politics of Belonging: Nationalism, Liberalism, and Pluralism*, ed. Alain Dieckhoff. Lanham: Lexington Books.
Langit-Dursin, Richel. 2001. Acehnese Want Justice, Not Bullets. *Asia Times*, August 31. http://www.atimes.com/se-asia/CH31Ae01.html. Accessed 13 Oct 2016.

Lindsey, Tim. 2001. The Criminal State: Premanisme and the New Indonesia. In *Indonesia Today. Challenges of History*, ed. G. Lloyd and S. Smith. Singapore: Institute of Southeast Asian Studies.

Megawati Speech in Aceh. *Atjehcyber.net*. July 30, 1999 (Published in 2013). http://www.atjehcyber.net/2012/08/janji-cut-nyak-megawati-di-tanah-serambi.html#ixzz4CLrvDR7A. Accessed 13 Oct 2016.

Mitzen, Jennifer. 2006. Ontological Security. In *World Politics: State Identity and the Security Dilemma*, European Journal of International Relations, 12 (3).

New York Times. 2016. Live More Coverage: Coup Attempt in Turkey, July 16. http://www.nytimes.com/live/turkey-coup-erdogan/erdogan-calls-on-u-s-to-arrest-or-extradite-fethullah-gulen/. Accessed 16 July 2016.

Niksch, Larry. 2001. Indonesian Separatist Movement in Aceh. *CRS Report for Congress*, January 12.

———. 2002. Indonesian Separatist Movement in Aceh. In *Economics and Geopolitics of Indonesia*, ed. E. McFlynn. New York: Nova Science Publishers.

Nykanen, Johanna. 2013. Identity, Narrative and Frames: Assessing Turkey's Kurdish Initiatives. *Insight Turkey* 15 (2), Spring: 85–101.

Piccone, Ted. 2016. *Five Rising Democracies and the Fate of the International Liberal Order*. Washington, DC: Brooking Institution Press.

Rumelili, Bahar. 2014. Peace Anxieties: Ontological Security and Conflict Resolution. Seminar at Koç University, May 2. https://www.youtube.com/watch?v=wkQUbYN7BH4. Accessed 30 Sept 2017.

———. 2015. *Conflict Resolution and Ontological Security: Peace Anxieties*. New York: Routledge.

Steele, Brent J. 2008. *Ontological Security in International Relations: Self-Identity and the IR State*. Abingdon: Routledge.

The Economist. 2016. Name and Shame. Deciding What to Call a Century-Old Turkish Atrocity, June 2. http://www.economist.com/news/europe/21699952-deciding-what-call-century-old-turkish-atrocity-name-and-shame. Accessed 30 Sept 2017.

The Jakarta Post. 2001. Megawati Pledges National Unity, June 1. https://www.library.ohiou.edu/indopubs/2001/06/01/0046.html. Accessed 30 Sept 2017.

———. 2016. Gus Dur Told to Avoid State of Emergency, June 27. http://blog.indahnesia.com/entry/200106280002/gus_dur_told_to_avoid_state_of_emergency.php. Accessed 30 Sept 2017.

United Press International. 2005. Yudhoyono Calls for Peace with Aceh Rebels, February 16. Accessed 30 Sept 2017.

Unver, Akin. 2015. *Turkey's Kurdish Question: Discourse and Politics Since 1990*. London: Routledge.

Weiner, Myron. 2001. The Macedonian Syndrome: An Historical Model of International Relations and Political Development. *New Balkan Politics-Journal of Politics* 2: 665–683.

Yegen, Mesut. 1999. The Kurdish Question in Turkish State Discourse. *Journal of Contemporary History* 34 (4): 555–568.

———. 2007. Turkish Nationalism and the Kurdish Question. *Ethnic and Racial Studies* 30 (1): 119–151.

Yetiv, Steve. 2013. *National Security Through a Cockeyed Lens: How Cognitive Bias Impacts U.S. Foreign Policy*. Baltimore: John Hopkins University Press.

Zarakol, Ayşe. 2010. Ontological (In)security and State Denial of Historical Crimes: Turkey and Japan. *International Relations* 24 (1): 3–23.

CHAPTER 9

Conclusions

SUMMARY OF FINDINGS

Let us briefly review the findings for each of the four approaches analyzed in this study to assess the impact of the different variables and to understand whether any of these variables are either necessary or sufficient. First, we can fairly say that none of them is necessary *and* sufficient, as none of them alone can cause the outcome of the dependent variable studied here: they are not uniquely sufficient to cause either securitization or autonomization. Nevertheless, one of them seems necessary, the interacting one: in both Indonesia and Turkey, low levels of ontological security correspond strongly to securitization, while high levels are associated strongly with autonomization. The other independent variables seem neither exclusively sufficient nor exclusively necessary, as we can have either securitization or autonomization without any one of them—elites who rationally seek political gains; international factors such as diasporas, intergovernmental organizations impact, or nearby civil strife; and historical institutions that reproduce an exclusive conception of the political community.

Which of the four approaches seems therefore more persuasive? In a sense, we can say that the study finds evidence for all four approaches, even if with different impact in different periods. Thus, we can fairly state that these different factors have a synergistic, complex, and dynamic interaction that impacts securitization and autonomization. In particular, we found that the historical institutionalist variables and the ontological security variables are more background variables (changing slower with respect to the other two), while the international environment and the elite power variables are more contingent variables (changing faster with respect to the other two) that can drive the timing of securitization or autonomization. Therefore, the four approaches of the independent variables are arguably complementary. However, the ontological security variable can be understood as an interacting variable, one that impacts but also is impacted by the other independent variables, in particular by the ways elites compete for power.

In fact, elites' competition and ontological security interact in a surprising way: when ontological security is low, the fear of the minority becomes a political tool that elites may use in competition for power—for example, elites can compete for the claim to be the protectors of the state or repressors of minorities. But the opposite path can be true, too: elites can create fear of minorities to legitimate their policies, in turn exacerbating ontological insecurity. Elites may use the strategy of "othering" to achieve their goals. This can be seen today not only in the case studies researched here but also in mature democracies: in Europe or North America many politicians appeal to the people in a populist and demagogic way, creating a fear of new immigrants or religious minorities and so reducing the country's ontological security, as part of party competition and power struggle.

Therefore, ontological security can go in two directions: when it is high, it pushes the state toward autonomization, and when it is low toward securitization, but elites can also create a lower level of ontological security as part of their struggle for power, in a self-reinforcing dynamic. The interaction of ontological security with this other variable is not a linear process. It is characterized by feedbacks that may amplify securitization: cultural fear may legitimize state securitization, while elites' power struggles can manufacture cultural fear. The theoretical model of this study therefore is not a simple "additive relation" between independent variables, as the variables of elites and ontological security can work together in a reinforcing dynamic, shaping the model in a more nuanced way.

Let us conduct a small excursus now specifically on the impact of the different variables. In the case of Turkey, in particular for the first variable, the study found that the reduction in the authority and power of military elites represents an important explanation of policy shifts, as well as the fact that the state remained a centralized state after moderate Islamists took power. The new Islamist elites needed the support of the Kurdish minority for its plan for power and Islamist reintegration and so started out with engagement and accommodation. When the elites failed to win this support, they opted for securitization. Having a very centralized state, the costs of repression in Turkey were still lower than the costs of toleration, which is why it was rational to restart securitization.

For the second variable composed of geopolitical issues, the international community and diaspora, the study finds that the presence of regional wars and transborder Kurd kinship, the reduced European pressure because of the Cyprus veto and refugee crisis, and the lack of an active diaspora in the solution of the conflict pushed the state toward the final securitization of the Kurdish minority.

For the third variable, a history of nationalist and exclusive institutions created a path dependency for Turkey that did not allow for much accommodation of minorities. In Turkey, because the nation preceded state formation, citizenship laws emphasize group rights and a nationalist-assimilationist model. For this reason, Turkey is an ethnic democracy that associates rights with ethnic groups, predominantly the Turkish ethnicity. Even when Turkey, with the new Islamist elites in power during the last democratization, engaged in some form of accommodation for Kurds, it refused to discuss the possibility of having another official language in the country or another language taught in the public schools or any type of territorial decentralization. The absence of these accommodations reflects Turkey's history as an ethnically defined nation prior to the establishment of modern state institutions. To allow such accommodation would require a reconceptualization of the nature of the nation.

Finally, for the fourth variable, Turkey had a historically low level of ontological security. This stems from the historical implosion of the Ottoman Empire; a delicate geopolitical position between Europe, Russia, and the Middle East; a complicated and complex identity with a Western model to follow and an Eastern identity to avoid; and finally values of unity and homogeneity that traditionally excluded tolerance of diversity. The inclusion of the Islamist identity in mainstream politics and the start of the peace process did not seem to reduce very much the country's ontological security as expected, but the turmoil in the wake of the Arab Spring in neighboring countries did contribute to reducing it.

Regarding the Indonesian case, in terms of the first variable, the study found that the power shift from military nationalist elites to the new elites was more gradual. Notably, Indonesia did not have an Islamist party that came to power as occurred in Turkey. In addition, the secular nationalist elites did not need Acehnese support for their national power, so initially they continued their policies of repression and securitization, in large part out of fear of disintegration. But when decentralization occurred, the costs of repression increased with respect to the cost of toleration, which is why it was rational to accommodate and autonomize the minority.

As for the second variable, regarding the geopolitical situation, the study found that the lack of regional spillover and the example of repression in East Timor producing independence favored policies of autonomy. With respect to the international community and the diaspora, the study found that the active role of NGOs as well as the diaspora in Aceh (but not the involvement of foreign governments or international organizations) played a positive role in the resolution of the conflict and the autonomization of the region.

With respect to the third variable, the inclusive type of historical institutions in Indonesia opened the door to the inclusion of minorities and autonomization of Aceh in the long run, allowing for decentralization when democratization arrived. In Indonesia, state formation preceded nation formation, and the citizenship adopted a communitarian-liberal model of accommodation. Because of this history, Indonesia is not an ethnic democracy based on a singular ethnic group as Turkey is. This conceptualization of the nation was more favorable to policies of autonomization.

Finally, in terms of the fourth variable, Indonesia experienced a high level of ontological security since it is an archipelago that is difficult to conquer and has a history of trade and exchange, a pluralistic identity, and Asian values of tolerance and harmony in diversity. Although the processes of democratization and decentralization happening in a rather fluid and changing international and internal environments could have created some insecurity in the self-identity of Indonesia, in fact these did not reduce the country's level of ontological security.

In conclusion, we can say that in the Turkish case, the international factors of instability and minority kinship in the Middle Eastern region, supported by structural historical preconditions of exclusive nationalist institutions and low ontological security, itself reduced by the specific circumstances (in particular the regional situation), made it rational during the democratization period for elites to lean in the direction of resolving the minority conflict, with a preliminary attempt at autonomization but a final policy of securitization.

Regarding the Indonesian case, the relatively isolated environment and the interests of the international community, the structural preconditions of inclusive-decentralized nationalist institutions, the high ontological security, and the specific circumstances (in particular the tsunami disaster) caused the elites during the democratization process to ultimately favor autonomization for Aceh.

As we can see, the various factors interact in a synergistic, complex, and dynamic interrelation that suggests that all the variables affect the final outcomes. No variable is either exclusively sufficient or exclusively necessary, as either securitization or autonomization is possible without any one of them. Nevertheless, one of the factors seems necessary: in both Indonesia and Turkey, low levels of ontological security correspond strongly with securitization across time, while high levels are strongly associated with autonomization.

Therefore, we can conclude that prescriptive elements or policy suggestions to fledgling democracies facing the challenge of inclusion of minorities, in particular if there is an open armed conflict with a self-determination movement of a minority, should favor the intervention of external mediators, processes of decentralization, and a gradual transition of power among elites, in hopes of creating inclusive historical institutions, a peaceful and secure regional situation, and a trustful country history that make for high levels of ontological security.

Some Meta Questions

The first meta question that comes out of the research starts from the fact that the two cases studied here are both newly democratized states. One possible question to ask is this: What is it about transitional or emerging democracies that make them more susceptible to securitization and autonomization? Is there something about transitional democracies that make them vulnerable to one or the other?

One explanation could be that electoral competition creates incentives for short-term policies and gains. As the book *Electing to Fight*[1] shows, when a new democracy starts an electoral competition, the different parties tend to have conflicting relationships. This in turn could facilitate an environment of securitization but would not explain autonomization. Another factor could be that democratizing states need to come to terms with the level of inclusiveness in the society. As Fukuyama writes, "Identities can also be altered to fit the realities of power politics or established around expansive ideas like that of democracy itself that minimize

[1] Edward D. Mansfield and Jack L. Snyder, *Electing to fight: why emerging democracies go to war* (Cambridge: MIT Press, 2005).

exclusion of minorities from the national community."[2] Besides the intrinsic value of inclusiveness, there is also a pragmatic reason for the inclusion of minorities in new democracies: in democracy, without the support of the different parts of society, ethnic minorities included, new parties cannot build coalitions that win elections. This clearly has been one of the reasons for the process of temporary autonomization for the Kurds. At the same time, if the support of the ethnic minorities is lost, the government and its elites may resort to violence and repression to maintain order in a relatively fragile emerging democracy. And this has also been one of the reasons for the process of securitization after the peace process with the Kurds failed to produce electoral benefits for the AKP.

Nevertheless, as we said at the beginning of this book, autonomization and securitization are extreme points on the continuum between multiculturalism and assimilation. These can be defined as the two principal policies in mature democracies today that deal with immigrant minorities. Thus, abstracting from this point, the second meta question to ask is this: Why are assimilation and multiculturalism insufficient to resolve conflicts with ethnic minorities in mature democracies today? The tentative answer is that both fail to produce sufficient inclusion and incorporation. Both can be considered a failure of the inclusion of minorities as they do not really integrate minorities in the polity and the society, either suppressing their identity or allowing them to keep it but without integrating them into the broader society.

Today, we see these examples in Europe. The assimilationist approach in France and the multiculturalist approach in the UK failed to build genuine integration of migrants with autochthonous identities. On the one hand is the forcing of a common identity (assimilation), and on the other hand is classification in cultural boxes (multiculturalism). Both failed to recognize diversity and at the same time grant equal rights for full citizenship. An ideal policy would take the good sides of each system: the maintenance of cultural identities of multiculturalism and the equality in a society of citizens of the assimilationist model. In reality, on the European continent, we are looking nowadays at embryonic developments of different types of policies, sometimes with the securitization of new migrants, with their constant control and even repression (like a mutation of failed assimilation) and sometimes with their autonomization, with their

---

[2] Francis Fukuyama, *Political Order and Political Decay: From the Industrial Revolution to the Globalization of Democracy*, p. 8, Farrar, Straus and Giroux, Kindle Edition, 2014.

attempted repatriation (like a mutation of failed multiculturalism). However, neither one seems a very wise and efficient solution for the future, as we can see in France, Hungary, and other Central European states, which are moving toward the securitization model, or Italy, Spain, and other Southern European countries, which are moving in the direction of extreme autonomization in the sense of repatriation of migrants.

Devolution or decentralization has been a process in several European states, not only states with ethnic minorities: for example, Italy and Spain have autonomous regions and communities, but they are not specifically related to ethnic minorities concentrated in these areas. The fact is that a real process of autonomization for ethnic minorities seems difficult in mature democracies because of the historical spread of ethnic minorities throughout the country, rather than their settlement in specific regions. Furthermore, the urbanization of communities and the large settlement of ethnic minorities in cities make autonomization impractical because it is impossible to separate out the different communities within the metropolitan area. One cannot envision a Kurdish autonomous area in Istanbul, for example, any more than one can foresee a Turkish autonomous area in Berlin.

But besides history, geography also matters: the placement of Aceh at the tip of an island made autonomization a feasible strategy. Not many countries are like that. But there are mature democracies that do have conflicts with ethnic minorities concentrated in specific regions and have resolved those conflicts by either autonomization or securitization. The third question therefore is which mature democracies have succeeded in finding a solution to the autonomization of ethnic minorities, as Indonesia did with Aceh, and which ones have failed in moving toward securitization of minorities, as Turkey did?

Regarding the first case, we need to look in particular at the UK with Northern Ireland. Northern Ireland started as a political and nationalist conflict, but it also had ethnic and religious dimensions. It was primarily a sovereignty and territorial issue, much like the case with the Acehnese, and actually ended in a similar way with an autonomous region inside the UK starting in 1998, after around 30 years of war. In fact, one could argue that the establishment of the Republic of Ireland as the Free Irish State in 1922 is also an important historical example of autonomization. By contrast, the physical barriers in Belfast manifest the securitization of Catholics in Northern Ireland during the "troubles."

Regarding the second case, Sri Lanka with the Tamil minority seems a similar example to Turkey. Even if the minority conflict was a civil war between the national government and the Liberation Tigers of Tamil Eelam that had total control over an entire region, and even if the Tamil language is one of two national languages, the securitization of Tamils has been evident during the history of the conflict and with the end of it after 26 years. The national government crushed the Tamils with a final offensive in the northern part of the island in 2009, and as a result no autonomous region was created for the Tamil people. Study of these cases could bring new insights into the causal analysis studied here, besides the general view that when a minority is concentrated in a specific region and does not threaten national politics, governments tend to accept some form of autonomization. In the opposite case, securitization is preferred by the state to deal with and resolve the ethnic minority struggle.

Finally, we must mention that the narrative of the War on Terror legitimated and has often facilitated securitization of autochthonous or migrant minorities in recent years, first of all in fledgling democracies, from the Philippines to Thailand, from Pakistan to Myanmar. The terrorist attacks in Europe, supposedly by ISIS even though many times the terrorists have just been lone wolves, actually also give governments of mature democracies new ways to securitize minorities, in particular the Muslim minority. From the current securitization of Muslims in the UK and France[3] to the USA, with its recent ban on citizens from Muslim Middle Eastern countries, this is often the discourse before the securitization of immigrant minorities, not the threat of minorities in itself. Thus, the final question would be this: Is combating terrorism in reality a smokescreen for the securitization of minorities, either ethnic or religious? To answer this question would be to enter another world, one of national security policies more than democratization theories. But one thing we can say is that to mix the securitization need with a terrorist threat is a process requiring a sizeable investment in the national narrative: an important factor in this process of identification of minorities with terrorism is the depiction of the threat through media, which delegitimizes the minority with the terrorist discourse. Therefore, a deeper critical study of the rhetoric of securitization would be required: "speech acts" construct securitization in terms of terrorism rather than in terms of minorities, which can be an excuse to simply disguise more social control and power.

---

[3] Jocelyne Cesari, *Securitisation of Islam in Europe*, CEPS CHALLENGE Programme, EU, Research paper n. 15, April 2009.

Rival Explanations and Next Steps

In conclusion, where might this research take us? What rival explanations can be studied, what are the next steps to take, and what other examples in the world might this research help us to understand?

Regarding the variables and explanations, besides the four hypotheses tested, we must acknowledge the existence of at least four other rival explanations. First of all, the actions of individual leaders, not necessarily based on rational choice or ontological security but perhaps on personal characteristics or biases, might matter. Therefore, a future agency-oriented perspective on the treatment of ethnic minorities in these countries might be a useful approach to expanding the research. Second, the political culture and ideology of both the incumbent government and the minority armed group might be important too in the final outcome. The fact that the Kurdish minority struggle had for a long time a Marxist approach to the independence movement may have played a role in a country like Turkey, where Western capitalism and Islam were both arrayed against such socialist philosophies. For this reason, we may suggest that future research should look also at the role of political culture and ideology in the resolution of minority conflicts and in the consequent inclusion or exclusion of ethnic minorities. Third, socioeconomic elements may play an important role in securitization versus autonomization. We could study, for example, the degree to which the socioeconomic class of a minority and the wealth of a region affect the dynamics between the minority and the state. We could ask, for example, to what degree the lower economic stratum of the Kurds in Turkey, versus the more favorable status of Acehnese in Indonesia, may have influenced the different outcomes. Or to what degree might the wealth of the territory in Aceh, with its natural resources, and the poverty of the Kurdistan region have played a role. In theory, as stated earlier, the outcome should have been the opposite of what it was: securitization should have favored the richer area of Aceh and not the poorest one of Kurdistan, but a deeper study should be done to present evidence for such a hypothesis. Fourth, as stated early on, the most evident geographic and demographic elements—the fact that one minority, the Kurds, makes up around 20 percent of the state's population and is located in a large area of the country adjacent to neighboring states with Kurds, while the other, the Acehnese, make up just 1.4 percent of the national population and are located at the tip of one of the many islands—may have had a great impact on the final exclusion/inclusion of these minorities.

Another possibility for future expansion of this research would be to study how the state might use the treatment of ethnic minorities for foreign policy purposes. For example, we could argue that Turkey used the Kurdish question previously in a positive way, to improve its position with respect to its application to join the EU, and then, in a negative way, to legitimize intervention in Syria. In service to the aspiration of being a strong regional power, Turkey might need to legitimize its interventions in Syria and Iraq, so the securitization of the Kurdish issue could become a tool of foreign policy. In such a case, the terrorist narrative may serve not only for internal repression but also for external interventions (as we saw already with other great power militaries intervention abroad, like the USA, Russia, or Israel). Nevertheless, it is more difficult to explain a domestic policy action with foreign policy goals when the minority has no kinship and subsequent spillover effects in neighboring countries, as in the Indonesian case.

Other possible avenues of research could also develop a better theoretical understanding of different kinds of securitization and autonomization, given the fact that the types of repression or accommodation of ethnic minorities may take different paths with the continuum from assimilation to multiculturalism. A nuance to study would also be the variable impact of the majority of voters on the rational choice of elites. In the Turkish case, one could research how the majority of Turks, not only Kurds, voted with respect to the AKP following Turkish engagement with the Kurdish minority, whether they supported it or not. In the Indonesian case, again by contrast, this specificity would probably be less important, as the majority of Indonesian voters did not feel very affected by the negotiations with the Aceh region, suggesting voter preferences favored autonomization rather than securitization.

This study may help us also to analyze other case studies. As explained in Chap. 3 on methodology, the choice of these two countries is based on commonalities that serve as control variables; nevertheless, other countries could be included in a comparison. First would be earlier cases like, as stated earlier, Northern Ireland and Sri Lanka. Looking at other Muslim-majority countries that are currently democratizing, we could ask: Would we draw different conclusions if we had different cases? The particular models studied here are obviously contextual models, appropriate in particular areas, so what would be the outcomes if the conditions in which those models worked were no longer in place? This could be an important extension of the research, first of all for countries like Senegal and Kirgizstan, which have a strong ethnic minority with a history of conflict and a recent democratization process. Also Bangladesh, Pakistan, and Malaysia, even if with more limited success in democratization, could serve as case studies to expand the analysis.

This study controlled for the religious variable to open to door to the possibility of expanding the research to non-Muslim-majority countries that have a multicultural/pluralistic society trying to build a democratic polity. Newly independent states like Montenegro and South Sudan, for example, have very heterogeneous societies at the ethnic level but are religiously homogeneous, with the majority being Christians. These countries could be studied to see how they deal with ethnic minorities, whether in a multicultural or assimilationist way. A concluding important question would be: Would we see these tensions in other democratizing states that are not Muslim-majority countries? What would be the result of these tensions? Researchers may wish to look into this in the future as the idea of this study was to control for the religious variable in order to make the model extendible to non-Muslim countries.

Furthermore, we stated at the beginning of the book that the importance of this research lay at the intersection of three main current theoretical debates in international relations theory and comparative politics: democratization, national security, and radicalization. Therefore, this work also had three indirect objectives that are open to further analysis: to prove the extent to which Muslim countries with ethnic minorities can make their democratization more efficient and sustainable (this has been done showing the processes of autonomization in both countries); to suggest how this improvement is done in a way that guarantees stability and security for the country (with the Acehnese negotiations, and also during the peace process with the PKK, the stability and security of the countries became evident); and to show how this might avoid social radicalization, often connected to the disenfranchisement or repression of minorities (again the autonomization of Aceh was able to reduce and even eliminate radicalization as the GAM became a political party, while the PKK is still considered a terrorist group).

To conclude the study, we may assert that the level of inclusiveness remains *a*, or probably *the*, fundamental criterion for the substantiveness, meaningfulness, and sustainability of a democracy. Actually, the most important implication of this research is that Turkey's democratization process with the new AKP regime ultimately failed and, probably especially, because of its inability to completely include the Kurdish minority in the Turkish state, society, and polity. On the other hand, the Indonesian democratization process ultimately succeeded also, and probably especially, because of that country's final ability to include all minorities, above all the Acehnese, in the state, society, and polity.

But the results of this study also imply that we should be worried today about the democratic decline we are seeing not only in fledgling but also in mature democracies, that both arises from and contributes to the lack of inclusion of minorities in a reinforcing cycle of exclusion and political regression away from democracy. Elements of polarization, populism, the impoverishment of the middle class and economic inequality, globalization with its complex interactions and domestic effects, institutional weaknesses of states, and the ontological insecurity of nations resulting from the increasingly complex and chaotic nature of the world create challenges for societies to maintain the social contract at the base of a democratic state. In addition, the lack of visionary leadership makes the agency of leaders another crucial factor in the retrocession of democracies. In postmodern liberal democracies, leaders no longer guide the masses; they mirror them. This is creating more and more problems for the inclusion of minorities, in particular immigrants, who leaders and citizens alike often scapegoat for internal problems related to economic or political crises.

Although this study is about emerging democracies, it is evident that there is a growing backlash against minorities in mature democracies as well, including Western liberal democracies, as recent events show. All countries are passing through the current complex transitional phase of a cultural reaction against multiculturalism that could reverse the democratic future to a past of racism, nationalism, and securitization of minorities. Populist movements in Europe, from France to Austria, from Hungary to Poland, are increasingly proposing the securitization of minorities. Even in the USA, there could be problems of securitization, as evidenced by the Trump Administration's proposal to deport millions of undocumented immigrants, besides the ban on immigrants from Muslim countries.

The nation-state as an institution is less than 400 years old, and, as with all its predecessors (city-states, kingdoms, and secular or religious empires), it will not last forever. New supranational states are seeing the light of day, first of all the EU, but also organizations like ASEAN, OAS, or Shangai Cooperation Organization. The monoethnic identities of the traditional European model are being challenged by different nation-state models with a more pluralistic identity, from Asia (India) to Africa (several states in Central Africa), from the Middle East (Afghanistan) to

North America (Canada). Although the future is unpredictable, if globalization and migration are unstoppable phenomena and democracy must be inclusive to evolve, then multinational, supranational, or other forms of pluralistic states shall see the light of day as new forms of polities and social contracts, to continue to bend the arc of history toward human inclusion, liberation, and justice.

REFERENCES

Cesari, Jocelyn. 2009. *Securitisation of Islam in Europe*. EU: CEPS Challenge Programme, Research Paper no. 15.

Fukuyama, Francis. 2014. *Political Order and Political Decay: From the Industrial Revolution to the Globalization of Democracy*. New York: Farrar, Straus and Giroux, Kindle Edition.

Mansfield, Edward D., and Jack L. Snyder. 2005. *Electing to Fight: Why Emerging Democracies Go to War*. Cambridge: MIT Press.

Index[1]

A

ASEAN Association of Southeast Asian Nations, see
Assimilationism, 8–12, 8n19, 14, 34, 39, 50, 82, 82n11, 84, 190, 191, 191n23, 194, 197, 240, 244, 245
Association of Southeast Asian Nations (ASEAN), 17, 67, 170, 171, 246
Authoritarianization, v, 3, 14, 24, 38, 90–92, 94, 124, 131, 132, 140, 156, 187n11, 214, 219, 222
Autonomization, vi, 3, 9–12, 14, 17, 26, 29, 31–41, 44, 45, 50, 52, 59–61, 66, 70–72, 75, 79–114, 121, 122, 128–146, 151–154, 166–169, 171, 172, 174, 175, 182, 183, 185–187, 195–198, 201, 204, 221, 229, 235, 236, 238–245

C

Consociational democracy, 11, 28, 39
Critical theories, vi, 10, 17, 25, 32, 41–52, 74

D

Democracy, v–vii, 1–5, 1n1, 7, 7n15, 11, 13, 17, 21–31, 33, 34, 38, 39, 60–62, 64, 64n22, 79, 123, 124, 153, 182, 184, 186, 187n11, 214, 236, 239–242, 246
Democratization, vi, vii, 2–7, 2n5, 11–17, 23, 25–28, 30, 31, 34, 40–44, 50, 52, 61, 64–67, 70, 74, 79–114, 121, 124–129, 135, 139–141, 145, 152, 154, 159, 166, 169–171, 173, 174, 182, 183, 185, 186, 189, 195–198, 209, 212, 216, 221, 224, 225, 228, 230, 237–239, 242, 245, 246
Democratizing Muslim majority states, vi

---

[1] Note: Page numbers followed by 'n' refer to notes.

© The Author(s) 2018
M. Geri, *Ethnic Minorities in Democratizing Muslim Countries*, Minorities in West Asia and North Africa, https://doi.org/10.1007/978-3-319-75574-8

E

Elites' power interest, vi, 17, 41–44, 71, 121–146
Ethnic minorities, v, vi, 1–7, 11–13, 16, 17, 26–28, 31, 38, 46, 50, 61, 62, 65, 66, 70, 71, 81, 83, 86, 106, 121, 125, 132, 136, 139, 143, 145, 152, 153, 155, 166, 167, 169, 174, 175, 181–198, 201, 204–206, 213n33, 222, 223, 225, 227–231, 240–245
European Union (EU), 17, 34, 47, 67, 71, 72, 81, 86, 95, 96, 98, 100, 101, 112, 132, 134, 135, 137, 152–154, 158–166, 163n33, 163n34, 170–172, 175, 190, 205, 212, 213, 220, 244, 246

H

Historical-institutionalist theory, vi, 17, 41, 49

I

Inclusiveness, v, vii, 1, 4, 5, 7, 12, 21, 22, 24, 25, 28–31, 43, 45, 49, 50, 52, 66, 73, 85, 95, 121, 125, 182, 184, 192, 194, 198, 206, 212, 238–240, 245, 247
Indonesia, vi, 1, 29, 61, 79–114, 121, 139–145, 153, 182, 202, 235
Institutions and history of the state, vi, 16
International factors, vi, 3, 16, 17, 44–47, 71, 96, 114, 151–176, 197, 198, 201, 235, 238

M

Minority rights, 10, 11, 25, 28, 29, 38, 47, 67, 74, 79, 82, 87
Multiculturalism, 8n20, 9, 10, 12, 14, 25, 39, 50, 185, 240, 241, 244–246

N

National security, 4, 6, 34, 94, 100, 112, 134, 140, 153, 174, 202, 206, 207, 223, 242, 245

O

Old or new minorities, v, 2
Ontological security, vi, vii, 12, 15–17, 51–52, 74, 94, 104, 114, 137, 152, 189, 198, 201–231, 235–239, 243

P

Peace processes, 10–12, 14, 15, 72, 81, 87, 88, 95, 96, 98, 113, 136–138, 138n41, 159, 168, 170, 171, 206, 213–216, 218, 219, 228, 237, 240, 245
Policies of autonomy, 10–12, 14, 38, 73, 125, 141, 144, 151, 152, 169, 170, 175, 238

R

Radicalization, 1, 4, 6, 7, 9, 88, 158, 166, 185, 196, 245
Rational choice theory, vi, 17, 41–44, 71, 121, 123, 124, 140

S

Scapegoats, v, 246
Securitization, vi, 3, 9–12, 14–17, 27, 31–37, 41, 44, 45, 50, 59–61, 66, 70, 71, 73–75, 79–114, 121, 122, 125, 127–146, 151–153, 157, 158, 162, 168, 174, 175, 182, 183, 185, 187, 188, 195, 197, 198, 201–206, 209–216, 219, 221, 223–225, 228, 235–244, 246

Self-determination, vii, 4–6, 10, 13, 65, 70, 72, 101, 167, 239

T

Turkey, vi, 1, 33, 61, 79–114, 121, 151, 155–166, 182, 202, 235